Sheila
150 Hal
Deer Par

ABOUT THE AUTHORS

THOMAS H. ELIOT of Washington University has been chairman of the political science department there since 1952, and holds the Charles Nagel Professorship of Constitutional Law and Political Science. He has been lecturer on government at Harvard and M.I.T. and visiting research professor at Princeton. Earlier, his twelve years in public life included service as a Representative in Congress and as general counsel of the Social Security Board.

WILLIAM N. CHAMBERS is Professor of Political Science at Washington University, where he received his Ph.D. after graduating from Harvard. He is co-author of *The American Social System* and author of the political biography, *Old Bullion Benton: Senator from the New West.*

ROBERT H. SALISBURY is Assistant Professor of Political Science, Washington University. A graduate of Washington and Lee University, he completed his graduate study at the University of Illinois. He is a contributing author of *Functions and Policies of American Government.*

DAVID FELLMAN
Professor of Political Science, University of Wisconsin
ADVISORY EDITOR TO DODD, MEAD & COMPANY

AMERICAN GOVERNMENT: READINGS AND PROBLEMS FOR ANALYSIS

Thomas H. Eliot

William N. Chambers

Robert H. Salisbury

AMERICAN GOVERNMENT: READINGS AND PROBLEMS

for Analysis

Dodd, Mead & Company
NEW YORK • TORONTO
1959

© 1959 BY THOMAS H. ELIOT, WILLIAM N. CHAMBERS,
AND ROBERT H. SALISBURY
NO PART OF THIS BOOK MAY BE REPRODUCED IN ANY FORM
WITHOUT PERMISSION IN WRITING FROM THE PUBLISHER
LIBRARY OF CONGRESS CATALOG CARD NUMBER: 59–8035
PRINTED IN THE UNITED STATES OF AMERICA

ACKNOWLEDGMENTS

We are, of course, greatly indebted to many people who have assisted us in the preparation of this book. Our first debt is to the several hundred students at Washington University who, since 1953, have worked with the problems, or the predecessors of the problems, which make up this book. At the beginning, these students were exposed to inevitable ambiguities and imperfections in the problems as originally drafted. Their responses—vocal, critical, and in the main enthusiastic—helped us to perfect the problems.

Their instructors, too, including all our colleagues in the Department of Political Science, have earned our thanks for their perceptive comments and suggestions. The criticisms of two graduate assistants, Donald Flesche and Robert L. Rothweiler, have been discerning and constructive. Victor K. Heyman participated actively and helpfully in formulating some early problems for trial, and similar assistance was given us by two other former graduate students, Lee Roy Hatfield and Cleon O. Swayzee III.

Our appreciation to numerous authors and publishers for permission to reprint selections from their works is hereby warmly expressed. To our own publishers and to their advisory editor in political science, Professor David Fellman of the University of Wisconsin, we are in debt for a happy combination of co-operation and stringent criticism.

The clerical and stenographic work entailed in this project included the production of small mountains of mimeographed material over several years, in addition to the preparation of the final manuscript. We thank the Social Science Institute of Washington University for useful typing services. For much laborious mimeographing, cheerfully performed, we express special appreciation to Miss Earline Ingram. And it has been our great good fortune to have with us as Miss Ingram's successor Mrs. Dorothy B. Conard, whose dexterity and zeal command our respect and gratitude.

We have refrained from encumbering this book with extended reading references. As every teacher knows, and as every student should know, standard texts in American government and politics include useful and extensive bibliographies, and this book is designed to be used in combination with such texts.

THOMAS H. ELIOT
WILLIAM N. CHAMBERS
ROBERT H. SALISBURY

Washington University
St. Louis, Missouri
September, 1958

CONTENTS

THE USES OF THIS BOOK ... 1

PART I. SOME BASIC CONCEPTS
1. Facts and Values in Political Analysis ... 7
2. Politics, Democracy, and Government Decisions ... 14
3. Government, Social Control, and Individual Freedom ... 27

PART II. ROOTS OF THE REPUBLIC
4. The Declaration of Independence and the Constitution ... 37
5. Social Foundations of Constitutions ... 45
6. The Motives of the Framers of the Constitution ... 58

PART III. THE SEPARATION OF POWERS
7. Checks and Balances: Formal and Nonformal ... 67
8. Separation of Powers and Delegation of Powers ... 78
9. Judicial Review and the Legislative Process ... 82

PART IV. THE FEDERAL SYSTEM
10. The Nature of Federalism ... 89
11. Intergovernmental Relations ... 92
12. States' Rights: Slogan or Reality? ... 102

PART V. "LIBERTY AND JUSTICE FOR ALL"

13. Freedom of Speech — 107
14. Due Process of Law: Procedural Safeguards — 115
15. Due Process: Protection against Arbitrary Legislative Action — 125
16. Equal Protection of the Laws — 133

PART VI. THE POLITICAL ARENA: PARTIES, INTEREST GROUPS, ELECTIONS

17. Distortion of the Representative System — 137
18. Political Action by an Interest Group — 146
19. More "Responsibility" in Political Parties? — 151
20. Availability and Presidential Nominations — 156
21. Presidential Nominating Procedures — 162
22. An Informal Experiment in Voting Prediction — 167
23. Propaganda Strategy in a Congressional Campaign — 179

PART VII. THE LEGISLATIVE POWER

24. The Legislator's Choice — 187
25. Strategic Pressure Points in the Legislative Process — 194
26. The Seniority Rule — 199
27. Congressional Investigations — 204

PART VIII. THE EXECUTIVE POWER

28. The Institutionalization of the Presidency — 213
29. The Role of the President in Legislation — 222
30. Independent Regulatory Commissions and Interest Groups — 229
31. Quasi-Legislative and Quasi-Judicial Functions — 235

PART IX. THE JUDICIAL POWER

32. The Task of the Judge — 241
33. The Supreme Court, the Senate, and Democracy — 244
34. The Judicial Power as a Check on the Executive — 254

PART X. THE GOVERNMENTAL PROCESS: MAKING POLICY DECISIONS

35. Democracy and the Making of Foreign Policy   *263*
36. President and Congress in Foreign Relations   *267*
37. Co-ordinating Action in an International Crisis   *277*
38. Governmental Policies Concerning Labor   *279*
39. Agriculture   *282*
40. National Resources Policy   *291*

AMERICAN GOVERNMENT:
READINGS AND PROBLEMS
FOR ANALYSIS

The Uses of This Book

I

The problems in this book are the product of several years of exchange between teachers and students. They are the winnowing of innumerable problems, which the authors have prepared and tested in their classes and discussion sections in American government and politics at Washington University. They are designed to help in achieving two goals in the introductory course —the goal of stimulating students who are simply "taking the course for credit," and the goal of challenging those who are already concerned with the subject. Among the latter group, in political science, there are usually students who believe that a high school course has given them a thorough understanding of the American political system. These may particularly benefit from the problems, for despite excellent schooling they are likely to find that they still have much to learn—and this is the beginning of wisdom.

The introductory course may have several objectives. For one thing, it may be a preparation for citizenship or political participation. Adequately to play a part in public affairs, young men and women must have some knowledge of how those affairs are organized and run, some acquaintance with the dynamic operation of government and politics.

To others, the harvest which the introductory government and politics course can produce may appear more modest. It may be limited to assuming that in a democracy there is an obligation at least to vote, and vote intelligently. Woodrow Wilson as President sometimes troubled his lustier followers by speaking, like the political science professor he had been, of "the thinking people of America," and of "all thoughtful Americans." Like his former academic colleagues, he was committed to the notion of an electorate at once well informed and capable of analyzing the great issues of the time. And today, despite the despairing strictures of Mr. Walter Lippmann and the apparent success of new public relations techniques in politics, we are still committed to the democratic ideal of a knowledgeable, thoughtful electorate. Thus though teachers or students may lack eagerness for the political battle, both have at least the objective of creating or becoming intelligent voters. To achieve this, again, there must be information or data. And to serve well, such data must be not only recorded and memorized, but analyzed.

Indeed, the *use* of data in many fields is central to a third major objective of introductory political science—the objective of a liberal education. The freshman comes to the campus to "grow in wisdom." Wisdom is not merely the assimilation of assorted facts: profitable as this may prove in television contests, it is the least part of wisdom. The greater, vital part is the gradual growth of an ability to make reflective decisions. This is wisdom, or if you will, judgment, and this should be the hallmark of the educated man. The teacher of political science must strive to develop such judgment in his students, even in those who have little interest in the subject matter of the course.

There is a fourth aim that cannot be overlooked in the introductory course in American government. Colleges and universities are the seedbeds of scholarship, and among college freshmen there will be a significant few who are potential scholars, the possible political scientists of the future. These few may be deflected from the scholarly path if their first taste of political science is flat and unappetizing—if, indeed, they are forced to endure only factual exposition or stale indoctrination. The nature of a large and youthful class precludes, to be sure, the advanced application of scientific methods to the study of politics. But for those who wish to see, it is possible to open some vistas and make familiar some of the fundamentals of the scientific approach. Such vistas are offered, for example, in Problems 5 and 22 of this book.

II

The question, then, is how to organize a course which can aim at these four objectives, and what materials to use. Commonly the materials are a fat textbook and a shorter compilation of selected readings. These may serve well, but perhaps not well enough, for they leave one great gap for the student, and create one major difficulty for the teacher.

The gap is the absence of active student participation, of personal experience in the application of general principles to concrete cases. A student, for instance, may be letter-perfect in reciting a definition of "federalism," but can he be sure that he knows what the term means until he has tried to apply that definition? In Problem 10 in this book, he is asked to do just that. He is likely to emerge with a realization that the words of the definition have a practical meaning, and with a sense of accomplishment at this discovery. He has connected the abstract with the tangible, the concept with the data. So with problems dealing with such other concepts as constitution, politics, majority rule, civil liberties, due process of law, or judicial review.

The difficulty for the teacher is felt especially in the smaller classes or sections where the subject for discussion is either a portion of the text or one of the selected readings. It is hard to focus such a discussion, and unless it is focused it is likely to be a waste of time. Different questions, only vaguely related, are raised by different students; unimportant aspects of the reading are chewed over at length; the hour passes in desultory and profitless conversation. An instructor can avoid this difficulty by simply lecturing, but this sacrifices the values of student participation. Or he can surmount it by careful preparation and rigorous insistence that the discussion be centered on the points he wishes to have discussed. But he can overcome the difficulty much more easily and with less resistance from his students if the assigned reading is specifically pointed to a particular question or questions. Students can then think out possible answers to such questions in advance of class, and on the basis of such focused and common reflection and preparation, discussion can proceed at once freely and relevantly, and with excitement.

Thus the purposes of this book are to aid the teacher and especially to fill the gap for the student. It is a flexible book. It can be used in various ways. It may be treated simply as a volume of readings, or, conceivably, all the problems could be assigned for discussion, one or more a week. Experience in many classes, however, leads to the suggestion that each instructor select among the problems, in accordance with his interests and the needs of his students. Several of the problems are good for two hours of useful discussion, rather than one; some seem especially fit for oral discussion (with students preparing outlines in advance), while others lend themselves better to full written essays. In a one-semester course, a typical program might include one problem from each Part, eight or nine for discussion and one or two for written essays; but the instructor can pick and choose as he sees fit. The arrangement of the book follows the general pattern of most textbooks, but there is nothing hard and fast about it. For instance, Problem 2, dealing with the concepts of politics, democracy, and representation, can be used appropriately in Part VI of the book as well as in Part I. And one or more of the problems in the sections on the legislative and judicial branches might serve equally well in the section on the separation of powers.

Eager to drive quickly into the conventional, "factual" part of the course, some teachers may prefer to skip Part I altogether. Others, anxious to introduce their students to the difficult business of dealing with concepts, could spend four sessions on that Part alone. Students who have used the problems in Part I have responded to them with a kind of surprised (and perhaps surprising) exhilaration. The very first problem, for example, requires them to wrestle with a subject that few of them have ever thought about before, the difference between descriptive statements and value judgments. While some instructors may lack time or inclination for this exercise, others may find it particularly important and useful as a preliminary to the study of politics, because political analysis is so often encumbered by a mass of preconceived value judgments or prejudices. Furthermore, the role of value judgments in political analysis is integral to some of the later problems.

III

Two questions may arise that should be dealt with here. The first is: What are the correct answers to the problems? These are not mathematical problems, and for most of them there is no single "correct answer"; but all of them can elicit a thorough, thoughtful response, which shows a comprehension of the issues and an ability to relate facts and concepts, and arrive at defensible formulations.

The second question may be expressed as a criticism: Why are the factual situations so often set forth in fictional rather than actual "case histories"? The answer is that most real "cases," properly recounted, inevitably involve so many factors that they are ill adapted for use in an introductory course. As a teaching mechanism, fiction serves a very useful purpose, for it can enable one to eliminate those elements which unduly complicate the problem or are irrelevant to the central point. Thus the fixing of a focus is facilitated. As a matter of fact a good deal of the fictional material is based on real events. The case history of the Campanella bill in Problem 2, for instance, parallels recent history in a large American city, and the source of the short and light-hearted story in Problem 18 was an actual humorous veto message written by a famous governor.

This response to the two questions can be given with some assurance because of the reaction to the problems in many classes. The students found the fictitious situations recognizable and understandable. The frequent use of role-playing imparted a satisfying sense of involvement in the political or governmental process. The emphasis on analysis and processes allowed the class to escape the futility of uninformed and fruitless argument about whether this policy is better than that.

Another question may be raised—the use of a problems book in courses with large numbers of students, where discussion sections are not scheduled. Here again, the book may be used simply as a book of readings. More extensively, many of the problems may be dealt with in brief, positive outlines, which students may prepare and submit for grading and comment, and some of the problems can be assigned for fuller essays, possibly in place of an hour quiz. Finally, in large lecture sections oral statements and discussion by a few selected students may be useful, with different students assigned as discussants in different hours to maximize the number who will finally participate.

The task imposed by the American government and politics course is not easily accomplished. This book has been prepared in constant awareness of the fourfold nature of that task. Though it is intended to brighten the hours of the student and lighten the load of the teacher, it is not aimed at softening the job of learning, but rather at making learning a happier and more satisfying occupation. It is devised in the conviction that intellectual effort, analytical thinking, and the maturing of judgment are highly worthwhile.

PART I

SOME BASIC CONCEPTS

PROBLEM 1

Facts and Values in Political Analysis

Anyone undertaking the study of a subject which calls itself a "science" ought to have some idea of what he is letting himself in for. Political science, as it deals with the study of American government and politics, involves the investigation of a wide range of facts, or description, explanation, and sometimes prediction. But it is likely also to involve our opinions, prejudices, preferences, or "values"—we may, for example, favor or oppose the president in office, or a certain foreign policy, or "welfare state" measures. Thus, it is wise for the student to seek a certain degree of self-understanding or awareness as to the way in which he approaches the field of political science.

Self-understanding may begin with contemplation of the *position of the observer, the student of politics*. For the purposes of an inquiry by a human investigator, particular facts (data) are chosen or "taken" from a vast range of possible particular facts. Because the data of political science lack the precision of the data of physics or chemistry, and because the student of politics is human and fallible, he is subject to many pitfalls in choosing facts for study. Four general cautions may be noted.

1. The student should begin by considering what he knows,

what he does not know, and how much of what he thinks he knows may consist actually of misconceptions or misunderstandings. Many people think they "know," for example, that to be democratic a political system *must* include a written constitution; separation of powers between legislative, executive, and judicial branches; and a federal division of powers between national and state governments. In short, it must conform to the pattern of our American democracy. Yet, this is not true. The student of comparative politics knows that these things do *not necessarily* go together, and can cite as evidence the cases of Great Britain, France, and Italy, or the Soviet Union and Yugoslavia. The first three are all democracies, yet Britain has no written constitution, and none of them includes separation of powers as we understand it, or federalism, in their governmental structure. The last two both encompass, formally at least, federal systems, but neither of them is a democracy. Again, some prominent journalists and news commentators thought they "knew" that an unusually high proportion of Republican votes among women as compared to men was decisive in Eisenhower's election in 1952, but the most reliable survey data indicate that this was not the case. It is well to become fully aware of the possibility that one's preconceived notions may be quite incorrect, and learn to test them against evidence.

A peculiar kind of misconception or misunderstanding is oversimplification, or what has been called "the heresy of simplicism." To the uninitiated, for example, the problem of corruption in government or politics may seem very simple indeed—it's all due to bad men in office, and if we just voted the bad men out, corruption would disappear. The informed observer knows that this question is immensely complex, however. He is aware, for example, of the great pressures that operate on government officials, and that the source of corruption is frequently someone outside government rather than the man in government, and he is conscious of the degree to which activities that may be thought acceptable in business, such as lavish entertainment, are considered unacceptable when a government official is concerned. Many students bring such oversimplified notions to their study of government and politics, whether they involve corruption, or judicial review, or the way pressure groups work, or the role of patronage in political parties. Once again, students should seek to become aware of such oversimplifications in their thinking, seek to grasp the facts in something like their actual complexity.

2. The student should become aware of the distinction between what may be called *descriptive statements* on the one hand and *value judgments* on the other hand. We must interpret "descriptive statement" broadly here. It may be a statement of a particular fact, such as, "In 1956 Eisenhower received approximately 57 per cent of the popular vote for president." It may be a more general statement, such as, "Younger people tend to vote Democratic in higher proportions than older people do." Or it may be a forecast or prediction, such as, "If a serious depression occurs, then the party in power will suffer at the next election." Of course a descriptive statement may be true or false. An important characteristic of descriptive statements is that they can be tested by reference to observation, evidence, or data. Although predictions are not subject to testing at the moment they are made, they are subject to testing by observation at a later date. For example, the statement, "On the side of the moon that cannot be seen from the earth there is a mountain higher than Everest," is *descriptive,* even though we cannot test it now—and we may be able to test it soon. What we have called "value judgments," on the other hand, are not efforts simply at description. Rather, they are expressions of one's feelings about a matter, expressions of preference, of liking or disliking, expressions of what one thinks is "good" or "bad," or "right" or "wrong," or "desirable" or "undesirable," of what "should" or "should not" be. However strongly one may defend such value judgments, they cannot, *as such,* be tested by observation, by reference to facts, evidence, or data. Often, of course, value judgments are expressed in a way to make them look, at first glance, like descriptive statements. To say, "The Eisenhower administration has taken the wrong road by carrying on the New Dealish and Fair Dealish ideas of Roosevelt and Truman" is to make a value judgment. Its "rightness" or "wrongness" cannot be demonstrated simply by reference to facts, however strongly one may "believe" or "disbelieve" in the sentiment expressed.

All of us subscribe to certain value judgments. Our personal backgrounds (family, economic, social class, community or neighborhood, religious, ethnic or racial, and educational), our particular experiences and situation in life, and our general personality tendencies predispose all of us toward particular attitudes, value judgments, or opinions about politics. Usually such attitudes are unexamined, in that we have not consciously inquired into them or analyzed the grounds on which they rest. Sometimes such value judgments become so "hardened," so overlaid with emotion, that they take the form of prejudice. Some people are prejudiced against Negroes, Catholics, or Jews, or all (or nearly all) Democrats or Republicans, and they find it impossible to believe that a person falling into such a category can ever be anything other than "bad." Again, some people may be deeply prejudiced against government welfare programs as noxious "socialism," or against American involvement in world politics as "globaloney." To the extent that an individual holds on, emotionally, to such prejudiced views or value judgments and refuses to weigh the facts and arguments pro-and-con, his whole view of politics may be distorted.

Thus, our *value* judgments or prejudices may significantly affect our efforts to understand politics. First, they may influence our selection of facts for study, leading us to overlook data that may be unpalatable to our value preferences. For example, Republicans, bent on "proving" that the Truman administration was "soft on Communism," might ignore the *fact* that the Truman administration took many steps to combat Communism. Second, our value predispositions may lead us to confuse what-we-wish-were-the-case with what-is-the-case. For example, Democrats may *want* their party to win the next presidential election so badly that they come to believe that the Democrats *will* win. Third, our value judgments may influence the way in which we interpret data. For example, one observer may state the facts about the legislative process in Congress and conclude that they present a picture of "inefficiency" and "chaos," while another may state the same facts and declare that they represent a "practical" adaptation to the social and political realities of American life. The student should become aware of these "factual statement"–"value judgment" pitfalls and the problem of prejudices. He should try to achieve some self-consciousness concerning his own value predispositions and how they may affect him in his role as an observer of politics. In ordinary, daily writing and conversation, factual statements and value judgments tend to come all mixed together. In scientific inquiry, a primary step is to get your facts straight, *and to learn to separate descriptive statements from value judgments.*

All this does not, however, mean that a student of politics is precluded from having any opinions or value judgments about politics. He inevitably will, and the point is only that he should become conscious of this and strive to keep the distinction clear between *what he prefers* on the one hand and *what is the case* (or what is likely to be the case in the future) on the other. A number of the problems in this book require the student to take a value position, but in such problems the emphasis is on considering the *grounds* on which the value judgment rests.

3. Words are tricky, and a statement may be vague or ambiguous (susceptible of being understood in two or more meanings), instead of clear and precise. Where such ambiguity occurs, it is often very difficult to distinguish whether a statement was meant as a descriptive statement or as a value judgment. If it was meant as a descriptive statement, there may be difficulty, because its meaning is unclear, in testing it to see if it is true or false. For example, the statement, "Political parties play a tremendous role in American elections, national, state, and local," is both vague and ambiguous. Is the word "tremendous" meant to indicate a fact, or to express a value judgment? If the former, what does "tremendous" mean in operation, that is, what particular facts would we look for to determine whether parties do or do not play a "tremendous" role? Students should be careful to spot and question ambiguities in what they read or hear, and to avoid ambiguities in their own discussion or writing.

4. Finally, the student should be aware of how little his own limited personal experience can tell him about the over-all pattern of American government and politics. We are all, in a sense, "cave-dwellers." As Plato suggested, we all live in the "caves" of our limited experiences, in our own limited environments, and we cannot at firsthand see the world whole. Thus what a person may find in his own "cave," from his own limited observation, may *not* be the case generally. For instance, it may be true that all the college graduates *you* happen to know are Republicans; but this does not mean that there is a *general* truth, that all college graduates are Republicans. Firsthand observation is essential to under-

standing, but we should not take uncritically the "findings" of our own limited experience and impressions.

These four cautions should be kept in mind throughout one's study of political science. The more a student learns about the substance of political science, the more he should understand about the difficulties involved in the position of an observer.

Consider carefully the points made in the above discussion, and then:

A. Write out three important *descriptive statements* about American government or politics that you believe to be *true*, and three *statements of value* about American government or politics to which you personally subscribe.

B. Think over as fully and clearly as possible the *grounds* on which you would defend both your *descriptive statements* and your *value judgments*.

C. Think over carefully the following seven statements, and for each indicate: (a) whether you would classify it as an effort to make a *descriptive statement* (whether true or false), or as a *value judgment;* (b) if it is a descriptive statement, whether you think it is *true,* or *false,* and *why* you think so; and (c) if it is a value judgment, whether you *agree,* or *disagree,* and *why* you do so.

    1. The men who framed the Constitution of the United States in 1787 were primarily concerned with broadening political democracy for American citizens.

    2. Though it contains an amending clause and has been amended when circumstances required it in the past, the Constitution of the United States does not now need amending in any important way.

    3. Although business proprietors and managers compose only a small part of the total population, there are more businessmen among the members of Congress than there are persons from any other occupation.

    4. The national government has no business enforcing integration of whites and Negroes in the schools in communities where a majority of the people are opposed to such integration.

5. In a democracy, the will of a majority should take precedence over the wishes of a minority.
6. Despite the civic activities of many women, men generally vote in higher proportions in American elections than women do.
7. Despite talk of international co-operation and mutual security, American aid to foreign nations has really become, in fact, just a giveaway program.

D. In class discussion, try to determine how many of the statements you subscribed to in Questions A and C above may really be misconceptions of what is actually the case (facts), and how many statements you took to be descriptive statements turn out on analysis to be partially or wholly value judgments.

E. Try to think through the factors in your own background or position as an observer that may have led you to such misconceptions or to such confusions of descriptive statements with value judgments.

PROBLEM 2

Politics, Democracy, and Government Decisions

Though we in the United States generally take pride in the belief that we have a democratic political system, we are likely to admit to a good deal of confusion as to just what we mean by "politics" and by "democracy." At best these are difficult ideas, or concepts. Often, indeed, we think of democracy as "good," and politics as "bad"; but any serious student of the matter must perceive that democracy is impossible without something called politics.

Before you go any further, write down briefly, but as clearly and comprehensively as you can, what you think these terms "politics" and "democracy" mean. Retain what you have written for future reference.

Keeping in mind your definitions of "politics" and "democracy," read and analyze the following case study of politics in operation. This case history, though it is derived from the actual facts or data of a recent political conflict in an American city, *involves general concepts, questions, and principles which could relate as well to politics in a state, or to politics in the United States as a whole.* It is an attempt to present some of the problems of politics and democracy in microcosm.

The Campanella Bill—A Political Case History

The city of Zenith, in the state of Winnemac, is a typical American city of about 500,000 population. Its people are predominantly white and Protestant, though the Roman Catholic church is important, its parishioners comprising about 35 per cent of the population. In the northeastern corner of Zenith, a district known as the "Hill" is occupied by a closely knit group of Italo-Americans, who still speak Italian frequently, and who adhere to many "old world" or Italian customs. This ethnic minority, about 7 per cent of the total population of Zenith, usually supports in a relatively united way the dominant Italo-American leader of the moment, who is often referred to as the "King of the Hill." Thus the Italo-Americans tend to act as a cohesive, though not formally organized, interest group in Zenith politics. For the past twenty years Giuseppe "Buster" Campanella, Alderman for the Eighteenth Ward, a Democrat, has been the recognized spokesman of the Italo-Americans, and has attained a position of considerable power or influence in the city as a whole. He attended Zenith City College and law school, and is widely respected as an intelligent, successful lawyer and capable political leader. In Zenith, there is substantial competition between the Republican and Democratic parties, but in recent years the Democrats have been dominant.

At the 1955 election for mayor, the Democratic candidate was Rufus Barker, a professor of civil engineering at Jefferson University in Zenith. In his strenuous campaign for mayor, Professor Barker was supported by many business, labor, and professional groups, by both Protestants and Catholics, and by Zenith's crusading morning newspaper, the *Sentinel-Telegraph*. This, coupled with his great personal appeal as a candidate, along with his program to "make Zenith a better city to live in," gave him victory by an overwhelming majority. The keynote of his campaign was: "Progress or Decay? Zenith Must Decide!"

In office, Mayor Barker moved promptly to put his program for "Progress" into effect. Among many other things, he worked with the Zenith Chamber of Commerce to bring new industry to Zenith. At the same time he launched a city-wide survey of local zoning patterns by the City Planning Commission and a Citizens' Committee for Land Use, to which he appointed representatives of important groups throughout the community. The result of this survey was a comprehensive zoning proposal, aimed at planned use of the city's land areas for industrial, commercial, residential, recreational, and other purposes, to promote economic "Progress" and new industrial development and at the same time provide neighborhood environments that would help "make Zenith a better city to live in." The Mayor recommended to the Board of Aldermen a comprehensive zoning ordinance based on the survey proposal.

The members of the Board of Aldermen, where the Democrats had a fourteen-to-eight majority, were elected one from each of the twenty-two wards in the city. Mayor Barker's zoning proposal was immediately denounced by some aldermen who thought that people in the wards they represented would be injured by the new zoning plan. With the support of community leaders and the local newspapers, the Mayor was able to insist on acceptance of his plan, and the Board of Aldermen decided by a thirteen-to-nine vote to adopt it. Six Republicans and three Democrats voted against it. In the following months, however, when individual aldermen submitted bills of specific interest to special groups or neighborhoods in their particular wards—proposals, for example, to enact "spot zoning" ordinances to open certain lots in areas previously classified as residential, so retail stores could be built— the Board of Aldermen often carried bills over Mayor Barker's objections, and even overrode his vetoes. Usually such measures were carried by the long-established practice of *"aldermanic courtesy."* Under this practice, members of the Board would regularly "go along" with nearly any request by a particular alderman for the passage of an ordinance of special interest to people in his particular ward. The Mayor vehemently condemned the practice of aldermanic courtesy, and charged that it was "a device to serve the narrow interests of local groups in the wards at the expense of general, community-wide purposes." On the other hand, several aldermen stoutly defended aldermanic courtesy as "grassroots democracy in action," declaring that the people of their neighborhoods, and the aldermen as their representatives, knew what was best for their neighborhoods, and that they had a right to expect their "democratically elected representatives" to be responsive to their needs.

Toward the end of his first four-year term in 1959, Mayor Barker announced that he would be a candidate for re-election. In a campaign similar to that which first put him in office, he called this time for support to enable him to carry his program to completion. He specifically and frequently condemned the practice of aldermanic courtesy, and suggested that aldermen ought to be elected from the city at large, instead of from particular wards. Numerous opponents of city-wide election of aldermen, however, charged that this would make it possible for "a few downtown big business leaders and the Squash Club big shots to control the city government," at the expense of "the welfare of the plain people in the poorer neighborhoods," whose interests could be given fair consideration only by aldermen who were in close contact with their constituents on a neighborhood or ward basis. In fact, the Mayor's ties with large business groups had become increasingly close during his first term. In addition, many party and civic leaders now felt that Mayor Barker was becoming too well impressed with himself and his position in Zenith—"He thinks he's the cheese, the big-I-am, and he gets more arrogant and domineering every day," one prominent Democrat declared privately. Nonetheless, the Mayor won re-election, though by a slightly decreased vote.

Shortly after the beginning of Mayor Barker's second term, the aldermen and the Mayor faced an important decision on a zoning issue. It involved a twenty-acre tract of nearly vacant land in the Millbank Valley, adjacent to the Italo-American occupied Hill, and within the boundaries of "King" Campanella's Eighteenth Ward. The land, owned by the Penn-Matthewson Lumber Company, was zoned as an industrial area, and a special provision prohibited residental construction on the land. The report of the City Planning Commission, the Citizens' Committee for Land Use, and Mayor Barker's comprehensive zoning ordinance passed in 1956 by the Board of Aldermen continued it as an area classified for industrial development only. The main line of the Winnemac-Atlantic railroad ran about half a mile from the tract, and the railroad had expressed its willingness to build a spur to serve any industry that might be built on the tract. As alderman from the Eighteenth Ward, the "King of the Hill" now offered a bill to rezone the area as residential, and thereby open it to the construction of multiple-family dwellings. He had introduced his bill, Alderman Campanella said, in response to the requests of several people in his ward, some of whom approached him informally to point out what they called "the need for more living room near their families" for the expanding Italo-American population. Many families were doubling up in the existing homes in the overcrowded Hill district. The local leader of the demand to have the area rezoned was a Catholic priest, the Rev. Patrick McCarthy, who was a respected and influential figure among Catholics and non-Catholics throughout Zenith, and who was popular among his present parishioners in the Hill district. Under Father McCarthy's quiet but effective leadership, a petition to open and limit the tract to residential use was signed by 634 citizens in the Eighteenth Ward and delivered to Alderman Campanella. In addition, a syndicate of real estate men and contractors supported Campanella's motion; these men, some of whom lived on the Hill and others elsewhere in Zenith, hoped to build two-family frame dwellings and one large apartment in the area. Finally, the Campanella bill was supported by the clothing workers' union, one of the labor groups most active politically in Zenith, which happened to include among its membership many people who lived in the Hill district. The proposal was opposed by the City Planning Commission, the Citizens' Committee for Land Use, the Zenith Chamber of Commerce, some of Zenith's labor unions, and other civic groups who maintained that the area was an ideal site for the location of new industries. It was also opposed by two business firms who had a direct interest in the area—the Penn-Matthewson Company, who maintained that the land they owned had a value of $400,000 as an industrial area, but would be valued at only $150,000 if it were classified as residential, and by the Thyssen Die-Casting Company, which had already drawn up plans to build on the tract a new plant employing about 500 men.

The Mayor promptly took sides in this conflict. He opposed Campanella's bill as another attack by special, local groups on his efforts for "Progress" against "Decay," for which the people of Zenith had voted twice by electing him mayor. He also argued that Zenith needed industrial sites and industrial development more than it needed residential construction, and that the Millbank Valley area was better suited to industrial than to residential development. In this stand Mayor Barker was vigorously supported by the crusading *Sentinel-Telegraph*, which printed the results of a carefully conducted public opinion survey indicating that 38 per cent of Zenith's citizens *supported* the Mayor's stand, while 13 per cent *opposed* it, and 49 per cent had no opinion.

Meanwhile, Campanella had been busy in the Board of Aldermen, where the initial decision would be made. He spoke privately to James Michael Rooney, who as majority floor leader in the Board of Aldermen had virtual control over deciding when bills would be brought before the Board for consideration and action. During long years of service on the Board together, Campanella and Rooney had become close personal friends, and Campanella now told Rooney, "Jim, this bill means a lot to me." When the Board took up the bill, the "King of the Hill" reminded his fellow aldermen that he had represented the Eighteenth Ward for twenty years, declared again that his rezoning bill was "of vital concern to the people in my neighborhood," and asked that it be passed. In reply Alderman Benton Reeves, of the "silk stocking" Twentieth Ward, a Democrat who was sometimes called the "Millionaire Liberal," denounced the bill as "the selfish, bastard progeny of the illicit, undemocratic practice of aldermanic courtesy," as "the spawn of a dark *liaison* between Giuseppe 'Buster' Campanella and his political friends and playmates on the Board." When Reeves had finished, Campanella angrily retorted that the opposition to his bill was "another example of the power of big-business groups and the Squash Club aristocrats in Zenith." These men, and the Mayor as their spokesman in this case, he complained, were "putting the interests of *money* ahead of the interests of *men*—in this case the interests of profitable industrial expansion ahead of the welfare of the common people I represent in my ward, who ought to have homes." He reiterated that he had been "the democratically chosen spokesman of my people on the Hill" for twenty years, and that he and his "people" knew what was "best for their welfare—and *that* is democracy." The Board then passed the bill without further discussion, thirteen to eight; five of the eight Republicans and three of the fourteen Democrats voted against it, with one Democratic member absent. Many factors affected this decision in the Board, including (1) loyalty to the practice of aldermanic courtesy, (2) friendship toward Campanella or antagonism toward Mayor Barker, (3) a feeling among some aldermen that similar situations might arise in their own wards when they would be expected to "get results" for local groups, (4) deference to the substantial Catholic support for the bill resulting from Father McCarthy's influence, and (5) the influence in several wards of the militant clothing workers' union, which supported the bill in the interest of their members in the Hill area.

The Zenith city charter gave the Mayor power to "veto" bills from the Board of Aldermen, by returning bills to the Board without his signature. In such cases, bills did not become law unless the Board of Aldermen repassed them by a simple majority. The Campanella bill was promptly vetoed by Mayor Barker. He returned it with a stinging veto message, in which he reviewed the issues of the conflict, and called upon "all truly democratic, all genuinely Zenith-minded aldermen" to sustain his veto, which would require a majority of the whole Board, or twelve votes. In an interview with a *Sentinel-Telegraph* reporter, Campanella said, "I have always felt that my first duty was to the Eighteenth Ward and the people there," and declared hotly that Mayor Barker's veto was a "fresh example of his arrogant, domineering, and big-business-minded attitude." The *Sentinel-Telegraph's* survey showed that the Hill dwellers supported the "King" overwhelmingly.

With only one day available before the Board of Aldermen considered Mayor Barker's veto, Alderman Reeves set to work to try to get it sustained, so that the ultimate decision would be against rezoning. He talked to as many members of the Board as he could, insisting that a "clear majority of the people of Zenith" had shown that they supported the Mayor's program of planned land use for "Progress"; as evidence, he cited the election and re-election of Mayor Barker, and the fact that the *Sentinel-Telegraph* poll showed widespread popular support specifically for the Mayor's stand against the Campanella bill. He proclaimed that "loyalty to the ideas of democratic government and community welfare" required that the aldermen vote to sustain the veto. Getting wind of this, Alderman Campanella also talked with members of the Board, urging them in the name of aldermanic courtesy and of democracy as he understood it as a spokesman for his constituents in his ward to override the veto.

Now, study, analyze, reflect on, and compare carefully the following statements. Note that Statements A and B offer different conceptions of what *politics* is, while Statements C and D offer different ideas of what *democracy* is, or ought to be.

STATEMENT A
Politics as People

As Calvin Coolidge once remarked, "Politics is people: it is personal, it is individual, and nothing more." By this statement he meant to stress that politics consisted of individuals working with, or opposing, other individuals, and that elements of friendship or personal antagonism were basic to politics. He also suggested that at bottom all politics could be understood in terms of individual action, and that basically politics was "nothing more" than this. This is a view quite commonly held among working politicians, who see politics as a kind of individualistic, "who's who," or "who is doing what with or to whom," game.

STATEMENT B
Politics and Interest Groups

Politics is concerned with the workings of all groups, but we can simplify our effort . . . by limiting ourselves to a particular type, the *interest group*. This is any group that, as a *result of sharing certain attitudes, makes claims on other groups in order to realize aims arising from these attitudes*. These interest groups are of many types. Some interest groups are formal *associations* or *organizations*. But not all interest groups are so organized. There may be, for example, in a particular place and at a particular time an "old people's" interest; that is, a group sharing certain attitudes and making claims on others that is nevertheless not formally organized into a particular association . . .

Politics is largely a conflict among competing groups with conflicting ideas. . . . In political arguments it is inevitable that we talk about special interests versus the general welfare. But in political analysis it is better to talk about *this* group's idea of the general welfare as compared with *that* group's idea. As political partisans we are all committed to particular ideas and values, but as social scientists we cannot pretend to set up a clearly defined general interest. . . .

The relation of groups to other forces is a two-way one; it is *mutually* interactive. Thus . . . government affects interest groups; at the same time groups help create and shape . . . government. Indeed, the process is more than a two-way one; it is multidirectional and many-sided. What we have is a gigantic web of interactions, flowing from interests, associations, governments, beliefs, techniques, and many other elements. A movement anywhere in this web will set the whole elastic network in motion. . . .[1]

STATEMENT C

A Model of Democratic Government

Most writers on democracy, whatever else they may insist must be present in order for a government to be called a "democracy," are . . . committed to the view that it must exhibit the following minimum characteristics: (1) Those who hold office in it must stand ready, *in some sense,* to do whatever the people want them to do, and to refrain from doing anything the people oppose; (2) each member of the "community" for which it acts should have, *in some sense,* as good a chance as his fellows to participate in the community's decision-making—not better and not worse; and (3) it must operate in terms of an understanding that when the enfranchised members of the community disagree as to what ought to be done, the last word lies, *in some sense,* with the larger number and never the smaller—i.e., the *majority* of the electorate and not the minority should carry the day. . . .

Let us . . . present in summary form a list of the leading characteristics of [a] model of democracy. . . .

1. *Popular sovereignty.* The whole power of government resides in the whole people—that is, in *all* the members of the community, and not in any special ruling class or in any single individual.

2. *Political equality.* Each member of the community has the same formal right as all the other members to participate in the community's total decision-making process.

---
[1] James M. Burns and Jack W. Peltason, *Government by the People,* Third Edition (Englewood Cliffs, New Jersey: Prentice-Hall, 1957), 240–241, 250–251. Emphasis in original.

3. *Popular consultation.*
   (a) The community's laws are made by a representative assembly.
   (b) The electoral arrangements for selecting members of the representative assembly are such that the assembly will be as subordinate to the people as the latter wish it to be.
   (c) Failing (b), the members of the assembly make decisions as the *whole people* would make them if the latter were present and voting.
   (d) The assembly supervises, holds accountable, and has full control over all other public officials.
   (e) There are arrangements for communicating to the people full factual knowledge and understanding of all public problems they wish to do something about.
   (f) The citizens participate in the *development* of proposals for public policy as well as give or withhold consent to such proposals.
4. *Majority rule.*
   (a) No decision as to public policy or procedure is deemed valid if *opposed by more than half of the members of the community*.
   (b) A majority of the representative assembly has the same power over the assembly's decisions as a majority of the town meeting has over the latter's decisions.
   (c) Majorities forebear from tyranny and minorities from irredentism and civil war because of a sense of *obligation* to do so on the part of *all* the members of the community (and of their elected representatives) based on the feeling of each that he needs to keep all the others loyal to the community if he is to realize his own values.
   (d) Decisions are made after a process of creative discussion in which all the members of the community are trying to find out what is *best for the community.*[2]

---

[2] Austin Ranney and Willmoore Kendall, *Democracy and the American Party System* (New York: Harcourt, Brace and Company, 1956), 23, 54–55. Emphasis added in some instances.

STATEMENT D

An Alternative Model for Democracy

A system of democratic theology has grown up; and the temptation to take it seriously and apply it literally can be held responsible for many [misunderstandings] . . . The first and broadest [argument of those who believe in this unrealistic and misleading theology] is that in a democracy "the people rule. . . ." The keystone of this doctrine is the assumption that there exists in every political society a "will of the people" which declares itself at elections and operates through the instrumentality of elected officials; and it is thought to be the object of democracy to see that this "popular will" gets itself translated into governmental [decisions], and that governmental action is determined by nothing else. . . . One of the principal grounds of [criticism of] democratic institutions is that they do not achieve this aim—that instead of ensuring that governmental action shall be guided solely by *the popular will*, they permit it to take its direction from *the will of small groups or special interests*. . . .

[But, in fact as opposed to unrealistic theology], the larger number of members of any political society have no opinion, and hence no will, on nearly all the matters on which government acts. The only opinion, the only will which exists is the opinion, the will, of special groups. . . . The [actual] task of government, and hence of democracy as a form of government, is not to express an imaginary popular will, but to *effect adjustments among the various special wills and purposes* [of particular interest groups] which at any given time are pressing for realization. . . .

This is the task of governmental decisions ranging in importance from where to locate a new street or sewage-disposal plant to whether or not to go to war. Government, from this point of view, is primarily an arbitrator, and since practically every arbitration must result in giving to one side more of what it thinks it ought to have than the other side is willing to admit, every governmental [decision] can be viewed as favoring in some degree some particular and partial "will," or special interest. It is therefore meaningless to criticize government, whether democratic or not, merely because it allows special interests to attain some measure of what they think themselves entitled to. . . .

Where a society in its normal condition embraces a wide variety of competing interests of approximately equal strength, which are pressing restlessly and aggressively against one another . . . a type of government is required through which *the conflict of interests can result in compromises*, and in compromises, furthermore, whose necessity is brought directly home to the warring [interest groups] themselves. . . .

This may be something quite different from *pure* democracy, or government by mass-meeting, which is almost as archaic a governmental type as pure monarchy.[3]

Now, consider carefully for class discussion or for a written exercise:

1. If *you* were the alderman who was absent on the first vote on the Campanella rezoning bill, how would *you* vote—to sustain the Mayor's veto, or to override it and thus make Campanella's bill law? What factors would you have to take into account in making your decision? Justify your decision in terms of (a) your general *conception of democracy*, as you originally stated it and as you may want to revise it as a result of your study of this problem and Statements A-D, as they might relate to the Campanella bill case; *and* (b) your *conception of politics*, and the particular factors described here as these would relate to the necessities of practical political action that you would have to face as an alderman, in the Board and in your ward.

Next, undertake the following lines of analysis. Two warnings: remember that you are called upon to relate *all four* of the general statements of democracy and politics to the Campanella bill case, and remember that there is no "set answer."

2. Suppose, *first*, that the Board OVERRIDES the Mayor's veto, and thus Campanella's bill becomes law:
   (a) How does the history of the Campanella bill, thus completed, "fit" or fail to "fit" the conception of politics contained in Statement A, and alternatively in Statement B?

---

[3] John Dickinson, "Democratic Realities and Democratic Dogma," *American Political Science Review*, 24 (1930), 288, 291–293. Emphasis added.

(b) To what extent is the history of the Campanella bill, thus completed, in accord with or not in accord with the conception of democracy contained in Statement C, and alternatively in Statement D?

3. Suppose, *second,* that the Board SUSTAINS the Mayor's veto, and the Campanella bill thus does not become law. If this happened, what changes, if any, would you make in your analysis of how the complete history of the Campanella bill would "fit" or fail to "fit" the conceptions of politics and of democracy contained in Statements A, B, C, and D?

4. Think through carefully what you have learned from the case history of the Campanella bill, and from your reading of Statements A-D as you have related them to this case history. How would *you now* define *your own* conceptions of "politics" and of "democracy"?

PROBLEM 3

Government, Social Control, and Individual Freedom

Every individual person, in every social system, finds that his conduct or behavior is subject to some degree of regulation or *control* by other people. At the same time, he may find that he has varying degrees of *freedom*, that is to say, areas within which he may make personal *choices* or personal *decisions* as to what he will do.

Let us consider some familiar examples. The young man or young woman in a family may find that he is subject to parental control as to whether or not he may have the car, or when he or she must be home after an evening date. On the other hand, he or she may be given more or less freedom to choose the person he dates, or to decide on what college to attend. At college, the student is subject to innumerable regulations or controls at registration, in the dormitory, on the campus, in arranging parking space for a car, or in his studies; but as compared with high school he may be given a wide area within which he may choose or decide how to spend his time or what courses to take. After graduation, the young man or young woman may enjoy a broad freedom to decide on what job he will seek, but once he or she goes to work the individual finds himself required to abide by various regulations or controls established and enforced by the management of the firm or institution which employs him. Still, the individual may find considerable freedom of choice both on the job and in the way he orders his life outside of working hours.

In every durable human group and in every society or social system we find this mixture of *social control* and of *individual freedom* or opportunity to make personal choices or personal decisions. If we understand social *control* to mean *the regulation of the behavior of an individual by a group,* whether that group be a small, face-to-face group like a family or an entire society of 170,-000,000 people like the United States, we may see also that in modern societies *government* acts as a major agency of social control. This is true whether the society is the United States or the Union of Soviet Socialist Republics. Yet governments may differ greatly, as the USA and the USSR differ, in the scope of social control they exercise and thus in the amount of individual freedom they allow.

Read and analyze carefully the following selection. You will observe that in this discussion social control and government are not treated as abstract, bloodless, impersonal social and legal entities. Rather, they are understood in terms of the actual behavior of persons who operate the agencies of social control or government and the effect of their activities on the day-to-day behavior of ordinary individuals.

> An American college girl some years ago wrote of her dating difficulties. A girl's choice among boys was "limited," she complained, by the group of girls she went with—"every boy that she dates is discussed and criticized by the other members of the group. This rigid control often keeps a girl from dating at all. If a girl is a member of a group in which the other girls are rated higher on the dating scale than she, she is often unable to get dates with boys who are considered to be desirable by her friends. In that event she has to decide whether to date the boys that she can and choose girl friends who approve, or she must resign herself to not dating."
>
> This experience suggests certain elements that are common to a wide variety of other social situations. These range from family, school, and church life, to the total structure of a society. . . .
>
> Our distressed young lady found herself belonging to a particular *group,* and thereby found herself subject to certain *controls* which this group exercised over her behavior. Finally she

found that she had a limited range within which she could make certain (personal) *choices* or *decisions*, an area of freedom set by the group's controls. It is these aspects of our young lady's dating difficulties that make her situation in some sense typical. . . .

Social Control in a Soviet Factory

The limits on her contact with boys described by our disappointed dater are minor compared to the regulation of nearly every aspect of their lives experienced by Ivan and Ivanovna, the Russian equivalent of John and Jane Doe.

A major goal of the Union of Soviet Socialist Republics today is industrialization, the further expansion of factory production. . . . In pursuing this goal, the Soviet Union depends largely on a new, a specially trained technical and managerial intelligentsia. This class has been a major by-product of the driving industrialization of the several Five Year Plans. Let us consider, then, the situation in which a member of the class is likely to find himself.

For our Ivan, we will take the manager or director of a middle-sized factory, which is of course owned by the government. Formally, the factory director is the "boss" over production in his factory, and his actual power is extensive. Under him Ivan has a ramifying group of subordinates, from his chief engineer and various assistant directors, through section foremen who are listed as the "lowest commander(s) of production," to the so-called "brigade leaders" among the bench workers, and the workers themselves. In short, within his factory the factory manager stands at the peak of an elaborate bureaucracy—increasingly the typical pattern of organization in all phases of Soviet life. . . .

But this new Soviet "boss" is by no means free to make whatever decisions for his factory he likes. He too is subject to an elaborate pattern of controls, which largely determine every action of his working life. . . .

The instruments by which Soviet society and Soviet factories are governed come in triplicate. They are the government administration, the Communist Party, and the security police.

First, the immediate impact of government administration. . . . The factory bureaucracy over which our Ivan presides is a part of the larger bureaucracy of the government. . . . Through the government administration the Five Year Plans and lesser plans of economic development are established, with their production quotas to be fulfilled and their allocations of raw materials and supplies. As a subordinate member in the larger bureaucracy, the factory director is subject to authority from above, to a barrage of demands, direct orders, questions, inspections, and criticisms, all buttressed by punishments and rewards. These devices of control are exercised by higher administrators. . . .

Behind every important agency of administration in the Soviet Union stands some unit of the Communist Party. This group holds preponderant effective power. Through the 1920's and 1930's the Communist Party was increasingly organized as a bureaucracy, with directives flowing down along its chain-of-command while information moves up. Today the *apparatchiki* (officials, "apparatus-wielders") of the disciplined ruling party operate at every level of Soviet society, seeing to it that the Communist Party policy or "line" is understood and carried out in every area of life. Party organization parallels government organization from top to bottom, and serves as it were as the "muscle" of government organization. This brings the Communist Party into a factory director's life as an additional instrument of control, aimed primarily at realizing the value of efficiency and secondarily at ensuring loyalty. Every important step our Ivan takes is subject to supervision by party groups and *apparatchiki* in the factory, district, and ministry. . . .

Maintaining a constant watch over every important aspect of Soviet life are the Soviet security agencies and secret police. While the Communist Party supplies the "muscle" of state administration, the [secret police] supply its "public eyes" and "muscle men." The [security police] has its own armed forces, which guard factories as well as frontiers, its own "court" system headed by a "Special Board," which can order severe sentences, and its own labor camps and other penal installations. In every important Soviet factory there is a "Special Section" under [a security] official, who is independent of the factory director and his organization. . . . Through the penetrating eye of constant surveillance and the strong arm of threatened or actual punishment, the [secret police] add two more links in the pattern of controls in which our Ivan finds himself enmeshed. . . .

To maintain their continuing control over factory directors, the top Russian authorities utilize two major means. These are, first, compulsion, restraints, and coercion; and second, incentives, inducements, consent, the prospect of rewards. These means are the standard components of social power. The compulsion controls that operate on our Ivan include the direct pressures of bureaucracy, party, and police; demotion or firing, or the threat of demotion or firing; denunciation and public or semipublic disgrace; arrest for alleged "economic crimes" (or failures), and possible "liquidation" or imprisonment, or threats of arrest, execution, or imprisonment. Incentive controls include high salaries; attractive bonuses for exceeding production quotas; special perquisites, like automobiles, superior housing including country retreats or *dachas,* and servants; high public prestige and honors; real through limited power; a feeling of pride or satisfaction in building, producing, or achieving, as an end in itself or for the Soviet motherland; and the chance for promotion to higher positions that bring still greater income, prestige, power, and other rewards. With this mixture of reward and restraint, the pattern of Soviet control over its factory directors is complete. . . .

Establishing Controls in the Mining Camps

Let us now consider a situation where at first there might seem to be no control at all—the mining camps on gold-bearing rivers in central California, during the great gold rush of 1848–1853.

During this period, some 300,000 men swarmed over vast areas of previously unsettled land. The lure of gold to be washed or "panned" out of stream-beds swept the nation, as immigrants sang:

> Oh! California, that's the land for me!
> I'm bound for the Sacramento
> With the washbowl on my knee.

Prospectors lived in makeshift, often temporary "camps" or "diggings" or "districts." Later some of the camps grew to large towns, but at the beginning they were limited to a canyon or a river bar. Miles from established civilian and military officials and courts, these camps were isolated from any external authority, as far as their daily lives went. Prospectors, generally strong and rough men bent on getting rich quick, were free to come and go as they liked, singly or in groups. With everyone seeking wealth and anyone likely to find it, a broad equality prevailed. No man had the standing to make him master over another.

In such wild, permissive, and isolated situations, one might expect a condition of disorder or anarchy. Actually, this was not the case. In many of the early mining camps, despite their here-today-gone-tomorrow character, a high degree of order existed; crimes of any sort including theft were rare and were summarily punished when they occurred, and miners found it possible to leave large quantities of gold in their tents unprotected, with little danger that it would be stolen. In short, even in these situations an important degree of control operated. . . .

The controlling agencies generally took one of three forms. The first was the "miners' court," or rule by the whole group in a particular camp in general meeting. . . . The second form of control was that of the select and permanent committee or council, in which the group as a whole gave nearly absolute authority to a small, elected committee. At Rough and Ready Camp in 1850, for example, a mass meeting of most of the several hundred prospectors chose a council of three equal members and left the management of the camp entirely in their hands, subject only to the check of an occasional general meeting. The third form of control was the *alcalde* system. In this system a single, multipowered, elected supreme official or *alcalde* was given nearly supreme legislative-executive-judicial authority by the group, subject only to recall by the whole group. The name and general idea came from Spanish-Mexican culture, in which *alcaldes* had long been fixtures. . . .

Of the several forms of organization, the "miners' court" was generally the earliest and probably the most widespread. An account of the organization of one such court, at Gold Hill Camp, Nevada County, California, in 1850, will illustrate the way in which a situation of practical anarchy was speedily converted into one of effective, though informal, little-structured, irregular control.

First prospected by a small group, the camp within a week had a population of twenty. At first there was no one in charge, no organization, "and every man's conduct conformed to his own ideas of right and justice"—in short, each man's reading of the customs and values he had brought with him. By the end of the first week, however, one miner argued that his rights had been infringed on by another; he and his friends circulated among the enlarging population of the camp, which had now passed fifty, urging a general meeting; unless some rules were adopted, they maintained, disorder would result. A meeting assembled, one miner called the assembly to order and proposed a permanent chairman, who was promptly elected, and the whole group proceeded to decide upon boundaries for the camp, adopt regulations concerning the size and handling of claims, and agreed to reassemble at the chairman's call. Subsequent meetings settled by general vote later disputes over claims, and decided punishments for thefts and other offenses. Crude, simple, but effective, this mass agency of group control operated until the organization of state government in California brought state civil and criminal law to the community. Each miner acted as a "public prosecutor" in bringing cases to the meetings. Punishments were immediately executed by special committees appointed by the chairman.

Here again, in the mining camps of California a century ago, we find some kind of group controls operating. Far from established governments, laws, courts, and police, far from family systems or church systems or class systems or other traditional systems of regulation, in a wild, permissive, or broadly free situation, we find men rejecting anarchy to establish new, often temporary, generally irregular, but working systems of group control. To be sure, this control was relatively narrow in its direction. Compared to the controls operating in the Soviet Union, for example, it left a wide range of [personal] *choice* or *decision* to the individual. But it was control nonetheless. . . .

American Government and Social Control

"We can't make you do it," says the seasoned sergeant to the raw Army recruit, "but we can sure make you wish you had." Generally the soldier knows that it is better for him to obey the orders he receives without demur than to suffer the deprivations of a stretch on kitchen police, the denial of a week-end pass, or even some time in the guardhouse. Here we have an example of social control over the individual person by *government,* through *coercion.*

This, however, is only one kind of relationship between government and individuals. In the armed forces and in many other areas of government activity, milder means are used to secure compliance. An example is the demonstration-farm program launched by the Tennessee Valley Authority in 1935. Many of the 225,000 farms in the Tennessee River watershed were in trouble. The productivity of the land was low, the soil was washing away and gullies were appearing where crops had grown. The electricity production of TVA could make phosphate fertilizers available in abundance, and TVA experts were ready to teach improved technology and new farming methods. The problem, however, was to get the active co-operation of a million or more farmers. The government's goal was not realized by telling people what to do and how to do it, "for their own good."

"We did not want a method of restoring soil whereby the farmer would be ordered; he would learn *by doing,* on his own place; his neighbors would learn by watching him and adopting what 'worked out.' Nor did we want a mere false front, using the outward form of voluntary and educational methods to disguise actual coercion. . . ."

Thousands of local farmers who were willing to experiment were selected by their own fellow farmers to set up "whole farm demonstrations," utilizing the new fertilizer and technology. As the productivity of the demonstration farms rose, the tendency among other farmers to persist in old, wasteful ways and to feel suspicious of the "gov'ment" experts gave way to a spreading willingness to try new methods. Here we have an example of social control over the individual person by *government,* through *consent.*

We have already seen other examples of control by coercion and by consent, operating together. In the Soviet Union the established regime maintains its control over the factory manager (as well as others) by coercive measures like demotion, firing, denunciation, arrest, imprisonment, and execution, and by measures which promote consent, like high salaries, bonuses, special privileges, prestige, honors, the grant of power, and promotions. In any political or governmental situation, we are likely to find a mixture of coercion and consent. The mixture may vary, however, with the use of (or readiness to use) coercion running higher in one social system than in another. This is certainly one of the basic differences between Soviet society (and government) and American society (and government).

Still, social control by government in American society is constant and significant. Every individual meets it in countless ways. . . . One scholar was able to list forty-five particular ways in which the government touched the life of a college student from the moment of his waking in the morning to the moment he entered his nine o'clock class. . . .[1]

Now review in your text and in your class notes materials relating to the nature of government and to the relationship between government and individual freedom or liberty.

For class discussion, or as a written exercise:

1. Make an orderly list, *first,* of all the ways you can think of in which social control by government (whether national, state, or local) affects your daily life; and, *second,* a list of some of the main ways in which the operation of American government (as compared, for example, with government in the USSR) leaves open areas of individual freedom or personal choice and decision.

2. Arrange informal interviews with at least three persons of postcollege age. Their contacts with social control by government will probably be more extensive than yours. Ask them, *first,* to tell

---

[1] Stuart A. Queen, William N. Chambers, and Charles M. Winston, *The American Social System: Social Control, Personal Choice, and Public Decision* (Boston: Houghton Mifflin Company, 1956), 3–10, 264–266.

you all the ways they can think of in which government affects their daily and working lives, that is, all the ways they can think of in which they come into contact with or are subject to control or regulation by government agencies, whether national, state, or local. For working adults, such contacts with government may range from birth certificates to business regulation to taxes, from defense contracts to social security to automobile traffic controls. *Second*, ask the three people whom you interview what they consider to be the most important areas of individual freedom, choice, or decision which the American system of government leaves open to them, as compared, for example, with the situation in which a Russian factory manager finds himself in relation to *his* government. Get as much information or as many data as you can, and after you have completed your interviews summarize your data in two orderly lists, as in Part 1 above, dealing with the area of social control and the area of individual freedom. If possible, arrange one of your interviews with an active business proprietor or manager.

3. On the basis of your findings in Parts 1 and 2, above, compare the situations of the individual in the Soviet factory, in the California mining camp, and under the American government today, in terms of the most important similarities and differences these situations exhibit in the impact of social controls, and in the areas left open for individual choice or decision.

PART II

ROOTS OF THE REPUBLIC

PROBLEM 4

The Declaration of Independence and the Constitution

Read and analyze carefully the following interpretation by the historian Carl Becker of trends involved in the American Revolution, and their effect on the Declaration of Independence:

The American Revolution was . . . primarily a struggle between the Colonies and Great Britain over the question of self-government. . . . But there was also another phase of the Revolution, and that was the struggle within the Colonies themselves between the little commercial and landowning aristocracies that had hitherto governed the Colonies and the "people," the unfranchised "humble folk," who now were coming to demand a measure of political equality.

This struggle runs throughout the period of the controversy with Great Britain from 1765 to 1776; and while it was somewhat diminished during the period of the [Revolutionary] war itself, it broke out again with renewed force after the war was over. In fact, the American Revolution was not only a movement for national independence from Great Britain; it was also a movement for the democratization of American society and politics—a movement which has continued from that day to this and which is the central theme of our history. [In most American colonies conditions] were such as to place a determining influence in the hands of a small coterie of wealthy families—the so-called "best families" of the province. These best families . . . made a very distinctive and powerful upper class—a well-intrenched aristocracy which was the real governing force in each colony. . . . Sharply distinguished from these "gentlefolk," in dress and manners as well as in social and political influence, was the great mass of the population—artisans and laborers, tenant and small freehold farmers. . . .

The conflict between the interests and ideals of these two classes . . . was already beginning when the controversy between the British government and the Colonies began; and from the first the two issues became more or less identified. . . . The radicals wanted to democratize . . . social and political institutions . . . while the old leaders wanted to maintain their supremacy. . . .

As the Revolution ceased to be a mere contest [for independence] and took on the character of a contest for the rights of man, . . . American patriots came to think of themselves as hazarding their lives and their fortunes for the sake of a new social order, the ideal society founded upon the enduring principles of liberty, equality, and fraternity. There is a striking similarity between the ideals and the language of the American patriots and the radical leaders of the French Revolution. . . .

It is thus clear that the American Revolution was a twofold movement: it was a movement for the separation from Great Britain; it was also a movement for the abolition of class privilege, for the democratization of American politics and society, in some measure for the inauguration of an ideal state. The Declaration of Independence reflects and expresses this twofold character of the Revolution. On the one hand it is a declaration of the reasons which justified the separation from Great Britain; on the other hand it is a charter of democracy. . . .

The first years of independence were taken up with attempts to solve the many problems of peaceful reconstruction under a federal government which was one of the weakest ever devised by the hand of man . . . the movement for strengthening the Articles of Confederation resulted in the Constitutional Convention of 1787 which formulated the present Constitution. . . . It was essentially over the questions giving rise to the formation of a new Constitution, and over the question of the new Constitution itself and of its approval or rejection, that the people gradually divided into two chief political parties. . . . They differed in their respective attitudes toward popular government, its sources of strength and of weakness, and the limitations which should be placed upon it. The . . . [opponents of the new Constitution] were what would be today called a radical party, the Federalists [proponents of the Constitution] a conservative party. Hamilton had little faith in the virtue or the wisdom of "the people," and none at all in their capacity for efficient government. According to him only the people with property had a sufficient interest in good government to be intrusted with political power. . . . The mass of the people, if they were given power, having nothing to lose, would be keen for depriving others of that which they had themselves never been sufficiently industrious or intelligent to acquire. . . .

Many Federalist were not so frank as Hamilton in expressing their views, but they all shared his anti-democratic philosophy. The experience of the Revolutionary War and the years immediately following had made many men more conservative than they had once been. . . .

The Federalists therefore voted for the Federal Constitution and were in favor of enlarging the functions of the federal government, not only because a strong federal government would serve the economic interests of the industrial and moneyed classes, but also because it would be less amenable to popular control than state governments had been, and would serve as a "needed" check upon such radical political tendencies as might find expression in certain parts of the country. The "dangerous" ideas of Thomas Jefferson might gain complete ascendancy in Virginia, but as long as the Federal Constitution held, the state of Virginia would never be able to carry out a program that involved anything so revolutionary or Jacobinical as "impairing the obligation of a contract.". . .

[Meanwhile] . . . Jefferson, the author of the Declaration of

Independence, still held to the doctrine that "all men are created equal," and never lost his faith in those ideals of popular government and republican virtue . . . which furnished the driving force of the American and French revolutions. . . .[1]

Now read and analyze the following somewhat different interpretation, based on the analysis of the political scientist Louis Hartz, dealing with the American Revolution and what has been often called the "conservative reaction" of the framing of the Federal Constitution in 1787:

> Once the American Revolution was thought of as a purely "political revolution," involving independence from Great Britain. It could thus be distinguished from the Puritan Revolution in England in the Seventeenth Century, or the French Revolution of the Eighteenth Century, where the whole structure of the old social order was attacked.
>
> More recently, however, historians have sought to classify the American Revolution as a "social" or "democratic" revolution also. They have pointed to the attack on the principle of monarchy, to the abolition of such "feudal" practices as quitrents, primogeniture, and entail in the South, and to the disestablishment of the Anglican church and the separation of church and state. Thus the American Revolution is equated, at least in part, with the great European democratic revolutions, as an attack on outmoded feudal and aristocratic institutions, to clear the way for a new democracy, and the American Revolution and the Declaration of Independence are seen as great "liberal," even "radical" milestones. By contrast, the adoption of the Federal Constitution in 1787 is painted as a "conservative reaction," quite out of keeping with the revolutionary democratic ferment of the previous decade.
>
> This social revolution theory, however, and any attempt to equate the American Revolution with the great European revolutions, distorts the whole picture. Social changes there were in the America of the 1770s. But they were not on a par with the

---

[1] Carl Becker, *Our Great Experiment in Democracy: A History of the United States* (New York: Harper and Brothers, 1927), 34–40, 47–48, 50–51, 108–114.

revolutions which took place in Europe. These really did involve attempts to destroy an old feudal order and to establish a new "bourgeois" order; and these efforts were followed in turn by genuinely conservative or aristocratic reactions, the return of the Stuart monarchs or the restoration of the Bourbon kings and the old order or *ancien regime* which they symbolized. In America, however, matters were different. Feudalism never found real foothold on this side of the Atlantic; property ownership, particularly in small, freehold farms, was widespread; and there never was a true American aristocracy (at least of any size or importance) in the old European, feudal sense. To use the European term "aristocracy" for American planters or "bourgeois" merchants who happened to be well-to-do, and paint them as locked in basic conflict with a submerged "people," is grossly misleading. By contrast with Europe, with a centuries-old feudal tradition, American society was always in fact, and even more in belief, ideology, or thought, free or liberal, broadly equalitarian, and middle class in outlook. The peculiar fact of American life, as the French observer Tocqueville put it in 1835, was that Americans "arrived at a state of democracy without having to endure a democratic revolution; and that they [were] born equal, instead of becoming so." Practices such as primogeniture were abolished with surprising ease and little conflict, simply because they were relics or shadows, rather than integral parts of a going feudalism. Even the Virginia "aristocrats" of 1785 succumbed with scarcely a blow, evoking as Jefferson said more "pity than anger" from the people. Similarly, the American "radicalism" of the Revolutionary period and the 1780s was tame as compared to European radicalism, because it had no entrenched feudal aristocracy to fight. Even at the outmost limits of American "radicalism," Daniel Shays and Shays's Rebellion were unable to generate anything like the "leveling" or socialist vision of the radicals of the Puritan and French revolutions, of a Wynstanley or a Babeuf; and Shays like other American "radicals" represented a fundamentally middle-class, property-holding or bourgeois outlook. Where there is no significant feudal order or *ancien regime* to fight back, where property ownership is widespread, and where "radicals" like "conservatives" are fundamentally middle class in their ideas, it simply confuses matters to speak of a "social revolution" or a "revolutionary" democratic movement.

It follows that where there is no going old order or aristocracy to fight back, there can be no full-blooded conservative reaction on the model of the Stuart or Bourbon restorations. It is thus misleading again to paint in bold, black-and-white strokes the framing of the Constitution of 1787 as a thoroughgoing "conservative reaction," though this is just what many of our recent historians have done. If it was a "reaction" at all, it was a reaction of moderate liberalism, quite middle-class in outlook, rather than an "aristocratic reaction" or a basically "conservative reaction." It was something more fundamental to American society than Washington's modesty or self-abnegation that preserved us from monarchy or dictatorship, something more concrete in the American social order than lucky Providence that rescued us from aristocratic rule at the hands of the Constitution-framers and the Federalist party. It was, as Madison pointed out, the fact that the country would not stand for autocratic rule that saved us from monarchy or dictatorship. It was, as John Dickinson explained, the fact that there was no genuine American aristocracy and that an aristocracy cannot be manufactured overnight that saved us from aristocratic rule.[2]

Read the Declaration of Independence, and analyze it carefully to pick out the main ideas therein concerning the foundations, basic purposes, and basic structure of government. Give particular attention to the ideas contained in the following paragraph:

We hold these truths to be self-evident, that all men are created equal, that they are endowed by their creator with certain unalienable rights; that among these are life, liberty and the pursuit of happiness; that to secure these rights governments are instituted among men, deriving their just powers from the consent of the governed; that whenever any form of government becomes destructive of these ends, it is the right of the people to alter or abolish it, and to institute new government, laying its foundation on such principles and organizing its powers in

---

[2] Adapted from Louis Hartz, *The Liberal Tradition in America: An Interpretation of American Political Thought Since the Revolution* (New York: Harcourt, Brace and Company, 1955), *passim*, Chapter III.

such form, as to them shall seem most likely to effect their safety and happiness.[3]

Read the Constitution of the United States, as originally written and ratified in 1787–1789, and analyze it carefully to pick out the main ideas concerning the foundations, basic purposes, and basic structure of government which it contains.

Review in your text and in your lecture notes materials relating to the proclamation of the Declaration of Independence and to the formulation and ratification of the Constitution.

Assume that you are an impartial, well-informed observer of American politics in 1789. A European friend who sympathized with the ideas of the "radicals" in the American Revolution and with the ideas expressed in the Declaration writes you that he has heard that the new Constitution does not fully embody these ideas, and indeed represents a "conservative reaction" against what he thinks of as the "democratic" or "radical" aspects of the American Revolution, which he sees as underlying the Declaration of Independence. He asks you if this is the case, and if so, to what extent the Constitution itself is "reactionary," fails to embody the ideas of the Declaration of Independence, and instead gives effect to other ideas, and specifically in what ways. He also asks you for an explanation of how this situation came about, as you understand it. You review all you know about the political conflicts that were involved in and led up to the Revolution and the Declaration on the one hand and the framing of the new Constitution on the other, and you also review both documents carefully. You then answer the questions your European friend has addressed to you.

Bearing in mind the somewhat different interpretations of Becker and Hartz, work out carefully the answer you would give to your European friend, with particular attention to:

1. The main ideas concerning the fundamentals of government set forth in the Declaration of Independence.

---

[3] For a good discussion of the ideas in the Declaration, see Carl Becker, *The Declaration of Independence: A Study in the History of Political Ideas* (New York: Harper and Brothers, 1953).

2. The extent to which the Constitution
    a. reflects or applies these ideas,
    b. does not reflect or apply these ideas,
    c. contains other or contrary ideas.
3. Possible main explanations for the similarities and differences between the Declaration and the Constitution in relation to the above.

PROBLEM 5

Social Foundations of Constitutions

A constitution, to be effective and durable in a free society, cannot be merely a document handed down from on high by a group of wise men. It must, rather, grow out of, reflect, and in its general nature and specific provisions "fit" the society, the social and political situation, and the climate of political ideas in which it is to operate. This general statement is illustrated by the establishment of the Constitution of the United States in 1787–1791 and by the framing of the Constitution of the Confederate States of America in 1861.

Study in your text and in your lecture notes materials relating to the background and formation of the Constitution of the United States and its early amendment, in the period 1787–1791. Then read carefully the following two statements concerning the developments that led to the establishment of a new Confederacy or nation in the South and the framing of a constitution for this Confederacy.

STATEMENT A

The Clash of Interests: Background for the Confederacy

From *Charles A. and Mary R. Beard*[1]

Amid the clashes, personalities, and rhetorical flourishes of the political campaigns [of the decades preceding the secession of the southern states, certain primary issues] remained fairly constant as sources of . . . differences. [These included:]

Low tariffs in the interests of planters and farmers vs. high tariffs for the protection of American "infant industries."

Federal aid to internal improvements—highways, canals, and railways vs. state aid, or none at all, to such enterprises.

Free land vs. sale for revenue purposes.

Freedom vs. slavery in the territories. . . .

Not long after Southern [leaders] . . . had agreed to the tariff of 1816, they began to change their minds and oppose the very idea of protection for American industries. Within a few years they formulated a well-rounded argument against it and began to denounce it as a form of robbery under government auspices. Special duties on imported manufactures, they claimed, are contrary to the interests of all agricultural states, North and South; such protection raises the prices of goods which planters and farmers must buy; it is, in effect, a tax on them for the benefit of manufacturers; planters and farmers can prosper best by selling their produce abroad and buying their manufactures from the industrial nations of the Old World with their cheaper labor. . . .

While Jeffersonians . . . were still nominally in power, Congress raised the duties on imports twice—in 1824 and in 1828. The second act, decried as "the tariff of abominations," though modified later in details, produced a revolt in South Carolina. In 1832 the state legislature called a convention, and that assembly, duly elected, condemned the protective tariff as contrary to the Constitution of the United States and hence null and void. . . .

Infuriated by the threat of South Carolina, President Jackson issued a proclamation denouncing its action from start to finish. He branded nullification as a violation of the letter and spirit of the Constitution. He exalted the Union as supreme and perpetual and spurned the thesis that it was a mere league of sovereign states from which they could withdraw at will. . . . Yet Jack-

---

[1] Charles A. Beard and Mary R. Beard, *A Basic History of the United States* (New York: New Home Library, 1944), 252–266. Abridged and edited.

son also strove for peace. He advised Congress to alter the tariff that had made the trouble. . . . Under the leadership of Henry Clay a compromise was reached in 1833. . . .

It was only a truce. Fired by their victory in 1840, the Whigs broke the compromise of 1833 and raised the protective duties on imported manufactures. They made it clear that Clay's "American System" of protection for manufacturing industries was to be a fixed part of their domestic policy. The battle line was thus firmly drawn and Democrats [under predominantly southern influence] accepted the challenge. In their platform of 1856 they endorsed the idea of progressive free trade throughout the world. . . .

Over internal improvements . . . [another] leading question of the time . . . the ranks of both parties were badly broken. Yet, in general, Democratic presidents were inclined to the [southern] view that Congress had no constitutional power to build great national roads and should not engage in the business anyway. . . .

As railroads were extended from the East into the Mississippi Valley and gave easier access to the Western territories [another] . . . political issue became more acute—the disposition of the unoccupied land in the national domain. . . . A clamor went up for a sharp reduction in the price of government land, and finally for a law giving it away to settlers in lots of one hundred and sixty acres. For [southern] leaders . . . this proposal made trouble. . . . Planters in the South could reason that free land would mean a more rapid growth of the Northwest, more free states, and the supremacy of free states over slave states in Congress and the Union. . . .

The division . . . over federal land policies deepened as the agitation over the slavery question grew more intense and reached a climax in 1859. Free land for the poor was eloquently and steadfastly championed in Congress. . . . [But] entangled with the free homestead problem was the question of slavery or freedom in the territories. . . . By act of Congress, at the time of the Missouri Compromise in 1820, the major portion of the Louisiana Territory had been dedicated to freedom and the smaller portion tacitly left open for slavery. After a great region had been wrested from Mexico by war [1846–

1848] the issue was revived and brought on a spirited contest in Congress and outside.

Once more an adjustment resulted—the Compromise of 1850—in which both sides sought peace. . . . The slave trade, not slavery itself, was abolished in the District of Columbia. That was a concession to freedom if a slight one. It was more than offset, however, by a new and drastic law making it easier for masters to secure the return of slaves who had run away to the North. Under its terms a master merely had to claim a Negro as his slave before the proper federal agent. . . . As to the *new territories,* the Compromise of 1850 provided that they could come into the Union in the future with or without slavery as their constitutions might provide at the time of their admission. . . .

[T]he issue of slavery in the new territories might have been allowed to languish. But . . . the old Missouri Compromise on slavery was abrogated in 1854 by an act of Congress for the organization of the Kansas and Nebraska territories.

These districts were in that part of the Louisiana Purchase where slavery had been abolished by the agreement of 1820. Nevertheless, the new law of 1854 provided that the people of the two territories, or territories formed out of them, might come into the Union with or without slavery as their constitutions prescribed at the time—in short might have slavery if they wanted. . . . In this way the vast interior of the continent, dedicated to freedom in 1820, was thrown open to slavery under the doctrine of what was called "squatter sovereignty." A question long regarded as closed became again the subject of a nationwide clash. . . .

All the . . . primary issues . . . were debated in the form of constitutional interpretations. Whatever the Whigs demanded, some Democratic orator was almost certain to declare unconstitutional. At length, in the [predominantly southern] Democratic view, a protective tariff was unconstitutional. . . . So were internal improvements and subsidies for shipping, as well as the exclusion of slavery from the territories. . . .

In the course of the constitutional debates . . . two well-rounded [doctrines] . . . as to the very nature of the Constitution were formulated. These [doctrines] . . . were given definite shape during a great debate in the Senate in 1830 between Robert Y. Hayne, of South Carolina, and Daniel Webster, of Massachusetts. The Union established by the Constitution, Hayne asserted, is merely a *compact* between *sovereign states;* it is simply a *league of independent states;* and states may at their pleasure lawfully withdraw from the Union. On the other side, Webster protested that the Constitution is ordained and established by the people of the United States; the Union is perpetual; its laws are binding on the states; and states cannot lawfully leave the Union. . . .

At the height of their power, in 1857, the Democrats had a majority in the Senate and House of Representatives. The presidency was in their hands. And a majority of the Supreme Court had come from their ranks. On such good grounds they [and their southern supporters] could exult.

Yet over the bright horizon a tornado was brewing. . . . Public protest was mounting, and an opposition party was preparing to drive slavery out of the territories. . . .

In many ways, apart from its merits or demerits, slavery was involved in Democratic measures, actions, and successes. Slaves furnished the labor for the plantations of the agricultural South; and planters were powerful in the councils of the Democratic party. . . . If slavery was to be preserved and the planting interests promoted by federal laws, it was necessary for Southern planters to have more slave states to maintain a balance of power in the Senate against the growing number of free states in the North. . . .

[But by the 1850's, dissatisfied with the pro-southern, pro-slavery policies of the Democrats], many citizens in the North demanded a new party squarely committed to shutting slavery out of the territories; that is, to preventing its expansion. At a public meeting in Wisconsin, called shortly after Congress repealed the Missouri Compromise, a committee . . . was appointed to start the organization of this party. . . . [The newly-organized] Republicans nominated as their candidate for President in 1856 John C. Fremont . . . and adopted as their campaign motto, "Free labor, free speech, free men, free Kansas, and Fremont!" They were defeated in the election but the size of their vote . . . encouraged them to expect victory in the next presidential contest. . . .

[T]he Republicans in 1860 drafted a platform that made a wider appeal to voters. They renewed their pledge to shut slavery out of the territories but they inserted two new planks. One of these endorsed the device of a protective tariff to encourage the development of "the industrial interests of the whole country." . . . Another new plank advocated a homestead law giving a farm of moderate size to anybody who was inclined to go out and till it. . . . In other words, Republicans in 1860 "had three strings to their bow"—opposition to slavery in the territories, protection for American industries, and free homesteads for people discontented with their lot in the East. News of Lincoln's election in November 1860 was taken as a signal for secession in South Carolina. . . . Early the next year other Southern states followed this example: Florida, Georgia, Alabama, Mississippi, Louisiana, and Texas.

In February delegates from six of the states met at Montgomery, Alabama, [and] formed a new union called the Confederate States of America. . . . A few weeks later a . . . constitution was framed for the Confederacy, [and] was ratified by the seceded states. . . .

STATEMENT B

The American Political Faith: Background for the Confederacy

From Ralph Henry Gabriel [2]

This is not the place to recount again the familiar story of [the North-South] sectional rivalry. For the present purposes only a few points need be recalled. The central issue was security. Two economic systems took form in the United States in the first half of the nineteenth century. One was staple crop agriculture founded on slavery. The other was industrial capitalism based on the wage system. . . .

---

[2] Ralph Henry Gabriel, *The Course of American Democratic Thought*, Second Edition (New York: The Ronald Press Company, 1956), 116–124, 127. Abridged and edited.

In time the two economic systems collided. . . . Slavery was more than the solution of the economic problem of finding a supply of laborers. . . . It was a social discipline. . . . Because the Negro population was large and because in many places it outnumbered that of the whites, social discipline seemed to be the first need of the people. Without it the white man feared either that his civilization would fall into slow decay or that it would be consumed in the holocaust of a race war. . . . When the constitutional weapon of nullification was denied the South, its leaders increased their efforts to strengthen their section by carving out a slave empire within the national domain.

A sense of insecurity goaded the South to what were finally desperate efforts to increase its political power by westward expansion. By 1850, however, the leaders of the section recognized that the contest was unequal. Talk of secession grew ominous in the courthouse yards of the Cotton Kingdom. The appearance of the idea of secession signified that in the South the sentiment of loyalty to the national group was undergoing erosion. It was being worn away by the growing conviction that the Northern majority was a threat to Southern civilization. . . . When an appreciable number of Southerners became convinced that their families and their civilization were no longer safe within the political framework of the United States, they began to dream of a *new nation* which with their own hands they could shape into a shield and buckler. Few men can exist without some loyalties. If loyalty is withdrawn from one object or cause, it is transferred to another. Such a transfer occurred among the Confederates in 1860–1861. Armed invasion, validating old apprehensions, made the Confederacy a spiritual as well as political reality. . . .

Numberless partisans on either side accepted without question, as they had for decades, the first doctrine of the democratic faith, that of the fundamental law. . . .

Partisans on both sides, moreover, looked upon the war as a battle for the doctrine of the free individual, a war for liberty. Here, however, the details of the patterns diverged.

Abolitionists had for years affirmed that human slavery was an offense against the fundamental moral law. It was a denial, they asserted, of the right of every unoffending individual to be free. . . .

But Southern Americans believed also in the doctrine of the free individual. That the doctrine did not extend to the colored men and women who were held as bond servants was not the result of the volition of the master. The inferior status of the Negro was written, said the Southern philosophers, in the fundamental law of nature and of God. By this law the races are unequal. Alexander H. Stephens reflected a universal Southern sentiment when he spoke of the "great barrier . . . which the Creator has placed between this, our inferior class, and ourselves."

From this premise followed inevitably the arguments and the institutions of the South. Slavery was an adjustment to a fact of nature; it was an institution constructed in obedience to a law of God. In spite of its manifest evils it was not founded upon mere exploitation. Slavery laid burdens upon the master as well as conferring benefits upon him. It provided for the security of the laboring masses. At its best it expressed the principle of stewardship. . . .

When Southern leaders beheld the triumph at the polls of [the Republican] party . . . they brought about the secession of the plantation states. They declared that their fundamental rights as free men had been invaded. . . . "Whatever may be said of the loyalty or disloyalty of any, in the late most lamentable conflict of arms," remarked Stephens sadly after the guns had been silenced, "I think I may venture safely to say, that there was, on the part of the great mass of people . . . of the entire South, *no disloyalty to the principles of the Constitution of the United States. . . . With us it was simply a question as to where our allegiance was due in the maintenance of these principles*—which authority was paramount in the last resort—State or Federal.". . .

As President of the new Southern nation, Jefferson Davis never ceased to insist that the Confederates were the true disciples of the American [political tradition or] faith against a tyrannical Northern majority. "Our present political position has been achieved in a manner unprecedented in the history of nations," he said in his inaugural as President of the Provisional Government. "It illustrates the American idea that governments rest on the consent of the governed, and that it is the right of the people to alter or abolish them at will whenever they become destructive of the ends for which they were established. The declared purpose of the *compact* of the Union from which we have withdrawn was to 'establish justice, insure domestic tranquility, provide for the common defence, promote the general welfare, and secure the blessings of liberty to ourselves and our posterity'; and when in the judgment of the sovereign states composing this Confederacy, it has been perverted from the purposes for which it was ordained, and ceased to answer the ends for which it was established, a peaceful appeal to the ballot box declared that, so far as they are concerned, the Government created by that compact should cease to exist. In this they merely asserted the right which the Declaration of Independence of July 4, 1776, defined as [sic] *'inalienable'!"*. . .

Both North and South, then, made war to defend the tenets of *an established American faith.* . . . Each party to the conflict justified its position by reference to an eternal and absolute law which transcends the laws of men. The . . . faith, which had aided in postponing the sectional conflict, manifested, then, after Sumter fell, a new utility. To both the Blue and the Gray it provided those *ideals* for which men are willing to die. It laid the *spiritual foundation* for a prolonged and desperate war. . . . Both North and South believed that theirs was the true witness. At the level of ideas and of ideals the separation of the sections was similar to a religious schism. *Each side felt that it alone was faithful to the old truths and to the ancient faith.* . . .

Before 1861 the American faith had provided those common agreements which made democratic debate possible when the Constitution became an object of controversy. From 1861 to 1865 this same cluster of social beliefs, *variously interpreted,* provided the [basic ideas or ideology] . . . of both antagonists in a mighty war. . . .

Compare carefully the immediate background, framing, and establishment of the Constitution of the United States with the background and framing of the Constitution of the Confederate States of America. Note that the Beards on the one hand and Gabriel on the other stress different aspects of the events that led to the Confederate Constitution and determined its character. The

Beards emphasize the role of concrete particular interests peculiar to the South, with reference to such issues as tariffs, "internal improvements," slavery in general, and slave-versus-free settlement of the new western territories. By contrast, Gabriel stresses the role of ideas or ideology, of broad political faiths, and political loyalties.

Bearing in mind both of these interpretations, consider the Confederate Constitution, framed at Montgomery, Alabama, early in 1861. This constitution was *identical (word for word) in form and substance with the Constitution of the United States,* as adopted at Philadelphia in 1787 plus Amendments I through XII, *except for certain significant changes and additions.* The most important of these are given below.

PREAMBLE

We, the people of the Confederate States, each State acting in its sovereign and independent character, in order to form a permanent federal government, establish justice, insure domestic tranquility, and secure the blessings of liberty to ourselves and our posterity—invoking the favor and guidance of Almighty God—do ordain and establish this Constitution for the Confederate States of America. . . .

Article I, *Section 8.* The Congress shall have power—

(1) To lay and collect taxes, duties, imposts, and excises, for revenue necessary to pay the debts, provide for the common defence, and carry on the Government of the Confederate States; but no bounties shall be granted from the treasury; nor shall any duties or taxes on importations from foreign nations be laid to promote or foster any branch of industry; and all duties, imposts, and excises shall be uniform throughout the Confederate States. . . .

(2) To regulate commerce with foreign nations, and among the several states, and with the Indian tribes; but neither this, nor any other clause contained in the Constitution shall be construed to delegate the power to Congress to appropriate money for any internal improvement intended to facilitate commerce; except for the purpose of furnishing lights, beacons, and

buoys, and other aids to navigation upon the coasts, and the improvement of harbors, and the removing of obstructions in river navigation, in all which cases, such duties shall be laid on the navigation facilitated thereby, as may be necessary to pay the costs and expenses thereof. . . .

Article I, *Section 9.* . . .

(4) No bill of attainder, or *ex post facto* law, or law denying or impairing the right of property in negro slaves shall be passed. . . .

Article II, *Section 1.*

(1) The Executive power shall be vested in a President of the Confederate States of America. He and the Vice-President shall hold their offices for the term of six years; but the President shall not be re-eligible. . . .

Article IV, *Section 2.*

(1) The citizens of each State shall be entitled to all the privileges and immunities of citizens of the several States, and shall have the right of transit and sojourn in any State of this Confederacy, with their slaves and other property; and the right to property in said slaves shall not be thereby impaired. . . .

Article IV, *Section 3.* . . .

(3) The Confederate States may acquire new territory; and Congress shall have power to legislate and provide governments for the inhabitants of all territory belonging to the Confederate States, lying without the limits of the several States, and may permit them, at such times, and in such manner as it may by law provide, to form States to be admitted into the Confederacy. In all such territory, the institution of negro slavery, as it now exists in the Confederate States, shall be recognized and protected by Congress and by the territorial government; and the inhabitants of the several Confederate States and Territories shall have the right to take to such territory any slaves lawfully held by them in any of the States or Territories of the Confederate states. . . .

Keeping in mind the background of the formation of the Constitution of the United States and of the formation of the Confederate Constitution, and the interpretations of the Beards and of Gabriel, ponder the following general principles concerning constitutions. Applied to the historical backgrounds of the two constitutions, these principles should help you to understand or explain the reasons for their similarities, and their differences.

PRINCIPLES CONCERNING CONSTITUTIONS

1. If it is to be durable and workable in a free society, a constitution must reflect the shared historical experiences, or basic political ideas, ideology, or faith that prevail in the society for which the constitution is adopted.

2. If it is to be durable and workable in a free society, a constitution must provide satisfaction for the major purposes, interests, or demands of powerful groups in the society for which it is adopted.

Review in your text and in your class notes materials concerning constitutions, and in particular concerning the background, framing, and adoption of the Constitution of the United States and the first ten amendments.

As a written exercise or for class discussion:

1. Prepare an orderly summary by subject matter, e.g., slavery, internal improvements, and so on, of the most important ways in which the Confederate Constitution DIFFERED from the Constitution of the United States. Grouping these differences by subject matter, cite the specific Articles, Sections, and Clauses of the Confederate Constitution in which these differences may be seen.

2. Making full use of your knowledge of the historical antecedents of the two constitutions, and applying the *Principles Concerning Constitutions* presented on this page, EXPLAIN the reasons for the differences you have listed. Your explanation should be in terms both of the general principles and of particular facts as they relate to general principles.

3. Making full use again of your knowledge of the historical background, and applying the *Principles Concerning Constitutions,* consider and EXPLAIN as completely as you can why the framers of the Confederate Constitution at Montgomery, given the particular political situation of the moment, did not prepare a wholly new "plan of government" for the new Confederacy. Again, give attention both to the general principles and to relevant particular facts.

REMEMBER that in Questions 2 and 3 your job is NOT to tell the story of secession or to explain the Civil War as such. It IS, rather, to explain the differences and similarities between the United States and Confederate constitutions, utilizing all you have learned from your reading, lectures, and the problem, including the Beard and Gabriel selections.

PROBLEM 6

The Motives of the Framers of the Constitution

Majority rule, strictly speaking, means that decisions are made by *50 per cent plus 1* of those who vote, whether as voters in a general election or as representatives in an assembly. "Government by the people," it has been suggested, is a meaningless phrase if in fact a majority of the people are prevented from having their way. A few safeguards for minority rights (such as the First Amendment, forbidding the enactment of laws that suppress free speech) may be consistent with the democratic principle; but—so the argument runs—a system in which a minority can block action desired by most of the people is not *wholly* democratic. To this argument the answer has sometimes been made that a wholly democratic system cannot last. If a majority imposes its will on a bitterly hostile minority, it is said that there will be civil strife, and in suppressing rebellion, tyrannical measures may be necessary. Accordingly, some who sincerely believe in democracy insist that the members of a minority must be guaranteed not only freedom to criticize, but also some power to prevent the majority from taking "oppressive" action against them.

The framers of the Constitution, by and large, feared and opposed straight majority rule, and especially feared the action of "fleeting" or "temporary" majorities. They believed that men often join together to promote their own selfish interests through political action, and that if such men, so joined, obtained majorities in all the organs of government, they probably would exercise their power to do immediate harm to the minority, and perhaps lasting harm to the nation. Thus, should the poor farmers, the "debtor class," gain a majority, they might promptly enact laws wiping out all debts, and thus ruin the creditors, the minority.

During the great debate that followed the signing of the Constitution and preceded its ratification by state conventions, an article published in the New York *Packet* of December 14, 1787, included the following paragraphs:

> [T]he fundamental maxim of republican government . . . requires that the sense of the majority [of the people] should prevail. . . .
>
> *To give a minority a negative* upon the majority (which is always the case where more than a majority is requisite to a decision), is, in its tendency, to subject the sense of the greater number to that of the lesser. . . . The necessity of unanimity in public bodies, or of something approaching towards it, has been founded upon a supposition that it would contribute to security. But its real operation *is to embarrass the administration, to destroy the energy of the government, and to substitute the pleasure, caprice, or artifices of an insignificant, turbulent, or corrupt junto, to the regular deliberations and decisions of a . . . majority.* In those emergencies of a nation, in which the goodness or badness, the weakness or strength of its government, is of the greatest importance, there is commonly a necessity for action. The public business must, in some way or other, go forward. If a pertinacious minority can control the opinion of [prevent decisions by] a majority, respecting the best mode of conducting it, the majority, in order that something may be done, must conform to the views of the minority; and thus the sense of the smaller number will overrule that of the greater, and give a tone to the national proceedings. Hence, tedious delays; continual negotiation and intrigue; contemptible compromises of the public good. And yet, in such a system, . . . upon some occasions things will not admit of accommodation [compromise]; and then the measures of government must be injuriously suspended, or fatally defeated. It is often, by the impracticability of obtaining the concurrence of the necessary number of votes, kept in a state of inaction. Its situation must always savor of weakness, sometimes border upon anarchy.

It is not difficult to discover, that a principle of this kind [allowing a minority to prevent action] gives greater scope to . . . domestic faction,* than that which permits the sense of the majority to decide; though the contrary of this has been presumed. The mistake has proceeded from not attending with due care to the mischiefs that may be occasioned by obstructing the progress of government at certain critical seasons. When the concurrence of a large number is required by the Constitution to the doing of any national act, we are apt to rest satisfied that all is safe, because nothing improper will be likely *to be done;* but we forget how much good may be prevented, and how much ill may be produced, by the power of hindering the doing what may be necessary, and of keeping affairs in the same unfavorable posture in which they may happen to stand at particular periods. . . .

At the time that this article appeared, the proposed Constitution was being widely criticized as an "undemocratic" document which in numerous respects denied majority rule in an effort to protect the interests of the "aristocratic" owners of large amounts of property. This criticism was perhaps well founded, at least to the extent that it accurately identified the interests of the framers. Some historians have implied that the framers of the Constitution were *solely motivated* by the desire to safeguard the material, social, and political advantage of the well-to-do property-owning class. Other historians suggest that other and nobler motives at least helped to shape the framers' thinking.

The first school of thought is represented by the following, from Charles A. Beard:

> The movement for the Constitution of the United States was originated and carried through principally by four groups of [personal property] interests which had been adversely affected under the Articles of Confederation: money, public securities, manufactures, and trade and shipping.
>
> The first firm steps toward the formation of the Constitution were taken by a small and active group of men immediately interested through their personal possessions in the outcome of their labors.

---

* Self-seeking group.

No popular vote was taken directly or indirectly on the proposition to call the Convention which drafted the Constitution.

A large propertyless mass was, under the prevailing suffrage qualifications, excluded at the outset from participation (through representatives) in the work of framing the Constitution.

The members of the Philadelphia Convention which drafted the Constitution were, with a few exceptions, immediately, directly, and personally interested in, and derived economic adtages from, the establishment of the new system.

The Constitution was essentially an economic document based upon the concept that the fundamental private rights of property are anterior [prior, precedent] to government and morally beyond the reach of popular majorities.

The major portion of the members of the Convention are on record as recognizing the claim of property to a special and defensive position in the Constitution. . . .

The Constitution was . . . the work of a consolidated group whose interests knew no state boundaries and were truly national in their scope.[1]

The second school of thought is represented by the following, from Richard Hofstadter:

The Fathers [of the Constitution] were intellectual heirs of seventeenth-century English republicanism with its opposition to arbitrary rule and faith in popular sovereignty. If they feared the advance of democracy, they also had misgivings about turning to the extreme right. Having recently experienced a bitter revolutionary struggle with an external power beyond their control, they were in no mood to follow Hobbes to his conclusion that any kind of government must be accepted in order to avert the anarchy and terror of a state of nature. They were uneasily aware that both military dictatorship and a return to monarchy were being seriously discussed in some quarters—the former chiefly among unpaid and discontented army officers, the latter in rich and fashionable Northern circles. John Jay, familiar with sentiment among New York's mercantile aristocracy,

---

[1] From Charles A. Beard, *An Economic Interpretation of the Constitution of the United States* (New York: The Macmillan Company, 1913), 324-325.

wrote to Washington, June 27, 1786, that he feared that "the better kind of people (by which I mean the people who are orderly and industrious, who are content with their situations, and not uneasy in their circumstances) will be led, by the insecurity of property, the loss of confidence in their rulers, and the want of public faith and rectitude, to consider the charms of liberty as imaginary and delusive." Such men, he thought, might be prepared for "almost any change that may promise them quiet and security." Washington, who had already repudiated a suggestion that he become a military dictator, agreed, remarking that "we are apt to run from one extreme to the other."

Unwilling to turn their backs upon republicanism, the Fathers also wished to avoid violating the prejudices of the people. "Notwithstanding the oppression and injustice experienced among us from democracy," said George Mason, "the genius of the people is in favor of it, and the genius of the people must be consulted." Mason admitted "that we had been too democratic," but feared that "we should incautiously run into the opposite extreme." James Madison, who has quite rightfully been called the philosopher of the Constitution, told the delegates: "It seems indispensable that the mass of citizens should not be without a voice in making the laws which they are to obey, and in choosing the magistrates who are to administer them." James Wilson, the outstanding jurist of the age, later appointed to the Supreme Court by Washington, said again and again that the ultimate power of government must of necessity reside in the people. This the Fathers commonly accepted, for if government did not proceed from the people, from what other source could it legitimately come? To adopt any other premise not only would be inconsistent with everything that they had said against British rule in the past but would open the gates to an extreme concentration of power in the future. . . .

What the Fathers wanted was known as "balanced government," an idea at least as old as Aristotle and Polybius. This ancient conception had won new sanction in the eighteenth century, which was dominated intellectually by the scientific work of Newton and in which mechanical metaphors sprang as naturally to men's minds as did biological metaphors in the Darwinian atmosphere of the late nineteenth century. Men had found a rational order in the universe and they hoped that it could be transferred to politics, or, as John Adams put it, that governments could be "erected on the simple principles of nature." Madison spoke in the most precise Newtonian language when he said that such a "natural" government must be so constructed "that its several constituent parts may, by their mutual relations, be the means of keeping each other in their proper places." A properly designed state, the Fathers believed, would check interest with interest, class with class, faction with faction, and one branch of government with another in a harmonious system of mutual frustration. . . .

Government, thought the Fathers, is based on property. Men who have no property lack the necessary stake in an orderly society to make stable or reliable citizens. Dread of the propertyless masses of the towns was all but universal. George Washington, Gouverneur Morris, John Dickinson, and James Madison spoke of their anxieties about the urban working class that might arise some time in the future—"men without property and principle," as Dickinson described them—and even the democratic Jefferson shared this prejudice. Madison, stating the problem, came close to anticipating the modern threats to conservative republicanism from both communism and fascism:

"In future times, a great majority of the people will not only be without landed but any other sort of property. These will either combine, under the influence of their common situation— in which case the rights of property and the public liberty will not be secure in their hands—or, what is more probable, they will become the tools of opulence and ambition, in which case there will be equal danger on another side."

What encouraged the Fathers about their own era, however, was the broad dispersion of landed property. The small landowning farmers had been troublesome in recent years, but there was a general conviction that under a properly made Constitution a *modus vivendi* could be worked out with them. The possession of moderate plots of property presumably gave them a sufficient stake in society to be safe and responsible citizens under the restraints of balanced government. Influence in government would be proportionate to property: merchants and great landholders would be dominant, but small property-owners would have an independent and far from negligible voice. It was "politic as well as just," said Madison, "that the interests and rights of every class should be duly represented and understood in the public councils," and John Adams declared that there could be "no free government without a democratical branch in the constitution."

In fact, the Fathers' image of themselves as moderate republicans standing between political extremes was quite accurate. They were impelled by class motives more than pietistic writers like to admit, but they were also controlled . . . by a statesmanlike sense of moderation and a scrupulously republican philosophy. . . .[2]

Review in your text and in your lecture notes materials relating to:

A. The political conflicts which immediately preceded, and which resulted in, the calling of the constitutional convention of 1787.

B. The delegates to the convention, including the social backgrounds from which they came, the main interests with which they were identified, and the ideas concerning government in which they believed.

C. The deliberations of the convention, the main decisions it made as to the structure and operation of government under the new Constitution, and the probable reasons or motivations for those decisions.

Now read the Constitution as originally written (without any amendments) and analyze it carefully in relation to the defense of "majority rule" in the *Packet* article.

For class discussion, or as a written exercise, prepare careful, well-thought-out, complete answers to the following questions:

1. To what extent and in what ways, both in the general structure of government and in particular provisions for its operation,

---

[2] From Richard Hofstadter, *The American Political Tradition and the Men Who Made It* (New York: Alfred A. Knopf, 1951), 5–15.

does the Constitution as framed at Philadelphia embody the views expressed in the *Packet* argument? To what extent, and in what ways, does it fail to embody them?

2. What particular provisions of the Constitution can be cited to justify the contention that the Constitution was an "economic document," serving particular economic interests, as the statement quoted from Beard maintains?

3. What particular provisions of the Constitution can be cited to justify the contention that the Constitution was the product of a "scrupulously republican philosophy," as the passage quoted from Hofstadter maintains?

PART III

THE SEPARATION OF POWERS

PROBLEM 7

Checks and Balances: Formal and Nonformal

The Constitution of the United States, as nearly everyone knows, includes a system of separation of powers and checks and balances. It is perhaps less clear, however, just what purposes the framers had in mind in devising such a system, and just what these concepts mean in operation. Fundamentally, the framers feared that the concentration of political or governmental power would result in what they called "tyranny"—the oppression, particularly, of minority groups or individuals. Moreover, they feared the possible tyrannical or oppressive exercise of power not only by officials acting *within* government, but also by interest groups or parties ("factions") acting *through* government, particularly if such groups constituted a *majority* of the population. For instance, if a *majority* of the voters were poor debtors, they might gain control of the government and wipe out their debt—which would mean serious injury to the minority, the creditors. The separation-of-powers, checks-and-balances system was established to guard against such "dangers," as the framers saw them.

Furthermore, the framers did not rest content with what James Madison called mere "parchment barriers" against oppressive power. That is to say, they did not rely solely on the legal or constitutional structure of government, such as the constitutional separation between legislative, executive, and judicial powers, and the legal checks among these "branches" of government, such as the president's veto. The framers also considered the possibility of relating the national government to the whole social and political system so that, in the conflict or interplay of many varied, widely dispersed groups or factions, the chance of any group or faction achieving preponderant power would be kept to a minimum. Thus, *within the government,* James Madison saw the prevention of tyranny depending not only on "the constitutional rights of the place" or office or "branch," but also on "the interest of the man" in office. As he put it, one officeholder's "ambition must be made to counteract [another officeholder's] ambition." In addition, outside the governmental structure, Madison saw another bulwark against possible tyranny in the interplay of "opposite and rival interests" in the whole field of politics, which would prevent any group or combination of groups from becoming strong enough to dominate the government. In short, the framers saw possible barriers to tyrannical power not only in the *legal structure of government,* but also in the action-and-reaction of day-to-day *politics.*

In this insight, Madison and others had hold of a fundamental distinction for all political analysis—the distinction between what we may call *formal* and *nonformal* power relations. Restraints on power provided by the separation of powers and checks and balances of the Constitution we may call *formal.* Restraints on power that depend primarily upon pitting persons against persons or groups against groups, upon the conflict of "opposite and rival interests" (either individual "ambition" countering individual "ambition" within government *or* the political action of one party or interest group counteracting the power of another group), we may call *nonformal. This important distinction should be held firmly in mind.* It should become clearer as you proceed with the analysis involved in this problem.

A classic statement of the over-all character of separation of powers and checks and balances, as the framers saw it, is contained in *The Federalist,* Essays 47, 51, and 10. Read thoughtfully, and pause to digest, the selections from these essays given below. These particular essays were written by James Madison.

From *Federalist* 47

No political truth is certainly of greater intrinsic value, or is stamped with the authority of more enlightened patrons of liberty, than . . . the political maxim, that the legislative, executive, and judiciary departments ought to be separate and distinct. . . . The accumulation of all powers, legislative, executive, and judiciary, in the same hands, whether of one, a few, or many, and whether hereditary, self-appointed, or elective, may justly be pronounced the very definition of tyranny. . . . In order to form correct ideas on this important subject, it will be proper to investigate the sense in which the preservation of liberty requires that the three great departments of power should be separate and distinct.

The oracle who is always consulted and cited on this subject is the celebrated Montesquieu [1689–1755]. . . .

The British Constitution was to Montesquieu what Homer has been to the didactic writers on epic poetry. . . .

On the slightest view of the British Constitution, we must perceive that the legislative, executive, and judiciary departments are by no means totally separate and distinct from each other. The executive magistrate forms an integral part of the legislative authority. He alone has the prerogative of making treaties with foreign sovereigns, which, when made, have, under certain limitations, the force of legislative acts. All the members of the judiciary department are appointed by him, can be removed by him on the address of the two Houses of Parliament, and form, when he pleases to consult them, one of his constitutional councils. . . .

From these facts, by which Montesquieu was guided, it may clearly be inferred that, in saying "There can be no liberty where the legislative and executive powers are united in the same person, or body of magistrates," or, "if the power of judging be not separated from the legislative and executive powers," he did not mean that these departments ought to have no *partial agency* in, or no *control* over, the acts of each other. His meaning, as his own words import, and still more conclusively as illustrated by the example in his eye, can amount to no more than this, that where the *whole* power of one department is exercised by the same hands which possess the *whole* power of another department, the fundamental principles of a free constitution are subverted. . . .

The reasons on which Montesquieu grounds his maxim are a further demonstration of his meaning. "When the legislative and executive powers are united in the same person or body," says he, "there can be no liberty, because apprehensions may arise lest *the same* monarch or senate should *enact* tyrannical laws to *execute* them in a tyrannical manner." Again: "Were the power of judging joined with the legislative, the life and liberty of the subject would be exposed to arbitrary control, for *the judge* would then be *the legislator*. Were it joined to the executive power, *the judge* might behave with all the violence of *an oppressor*." Some of these reasons are more fully explained in other passages; but briefly stated as they are here, they sufficiently establish the meaning which we have put on this celebrated maxim of this celebrated author. . . .

From *Federalist 51*

To what expedient . . . shall we finally resort, for maintaining in practice the necessary partition of power among the several departments, as laid down in the Constitution? The only answer that can be given is, that as [merely paper barriers] are found to be inadequate, the defect must be supplied, by so contriving the interior structure of the government as that its several constituent parts may, by their mutual relations, be the means of keeping each other in their proper places. . . .

In order to lay a due foundation for that separate and distinct exercise of the different powers of government, which to a certain extent is admitted on all hands to be essential to the preservation of liberty, it is evident that each department should have a will of its own; and consequently should be so constituted that the members of each should have as little agency as possible in the appointment of the members of the others. Were this principle rigorously adhered to, it would require that all the appointments for the supreme executive, legislative, and judiciary magistracies should be drawn from the same fountain of authority, the people, through channels having no communication whatever with one another. Perhaps such a plan of constructing the several departments would be less difficult in practice than it may in contemplation appear. Some difficulties, however, and some additional expense would attend the execution of it. Some deviations, therefore, from the principle must be admitted. . . .

It is equally evident, that the members of each department should be as little dependent as possible on those of the others, for the emoluments [pay] annexed to their offices. Were the executive magistrate, or the judges, not independent of the legislature in this particular, their independence in every other would be merely nominal.

But the great security against a gradual concentration of the several powers in the same department, consists in giving to those who administer each department the necessary constitutional means and personal motives to resist encroachments of the others. The provision for defence must in this, as in all other cases, be made commensurate to the danger of attack. Ambition must be made to counteract ambition. The interest of the man must be connected with the constitutional rights of the place. It may be a reflection on human nature, that such devices should be necessary to control the abuses of government. But what is government itself, but the greatest of all reflections on human nature? If men were angels, no government would be necessary. If angels were to govern men, neither external nor internal controls on government would be necessary. In framing a government which is to be administered by men over men, the great difficulty lies in this: you must first enable the government to control the governed; and in the next place oblige it to control itself. A dependence on the people is, no doubt, the primary control on the government; but experience has taught mankind the necessity of auxiliary precautions.

This policy of supplying, by opposite and rival interests, the defect of better motives, might be traced through the whole system of human affairs, private as well as public. We see it particularly displayed in all the subordinate distributions of power, where the constant aim is to divide and arrange the several offices in such a manner as that each may be a check on the other

—that the private interest of every individual may be a sentinel over the public rights. These inventions of prudence cannot be less requisite in the distribution of the supreme powers of the State.

But it is not possible to give to each department an equal power of self-defence. In republican government, the legislative authority necessarily predominates. The remedy for this inconveniency is to divide the legislature into different branches; and to render them, by different modes of election and different principles of action, as little connected with each other as the nature of their common functions and their common dependence on the society will admit. It may even be necessary to guard against dangerous encroachments by still further precautions. As the weight of the legislative authority requires that it should be thus divided, the weakness of the executive may require, on the other hand, that it should be fortified. An absolute negative [veto] on the legislature appears, at first view, to be the natural defence with which the executive magistrate [President] should be armed. But perhaps it would be neither altogether safe nor alone sufficient. On ordinary occasions it might not be exerted with the requisite firmness, and on extraordinary occasions it might be perfidiously abused. May not this defect of an absolute negative be supplied by some qualified connection between this weaker department and the weaker branch of the stronger department, by which the latter may be led to support the constitutional rights of the former, without being too much detached from the rights of its own department? . . .

There are, moreover, two considerations particularly applicable to the *federal system* of America, which place that system in a very interesting point of view.

First. In a single republic, all the power surrendered by the people is submitted to the administration of a single government; and the usurpations are guarded against by a division of the government into distinct and separate departments. In the compound republic of America, the power surrendered by the people is first divided between two distinct governments [federal, and state] and then the portion allotted to each subdivided among distinct and separate departments. Hence a double security arises to the rights of the people. The different governments will control each other, at the same time that each will be controlled by itself.

Second. It is of great importance in a republic not only to guard the society against the oppression of its rulers, but to guard one part of the society against the injustice of the other part. Different interests necessarily exist in different classes of citizens. If a majority be united by a common interest, the rights of the minority will be insecure. There are but two methods of providing against this evil: the one by creating a will in the community independent of the majority—that is, of the society itself; the other, by comprehending in the society so many separate descriptions of citizens as will render an unjust combination of a majority of the whole very improbable, if not impracticable. The first method prevails in all governments possessing an hereditary or self-appointed authority [king or dictator]. . . . The second method will be exemplified in the federal republic of the United States. Whilst all authority in it will be derived from and dependent on the society, the society itself will be broken into so many parts, interests and classes of citizens, that the rights of individuals, or of the minority, will be in little danger from interested combinations of the majority. In a free government the security for civil rights must be the same as that for religious rights. It consists in the one case in the multiplicity of interests, and in the other in the multiplicity of sects. The degree of security in both cases will depend on the number of interests and sects; and this may be presumed to depend on the extent of country and number of people comprehended under the same government. This view of the subject must particularly recommend a proper federal system to all the sincere and considerate friends of republican government, since it shows that in exact proportion as the territory of the Union may be formed into more circumscribed Confederacies, or States, oppressive combinations of a majority will be facilitated. . . .

In the extended republic of the United States, and among the great variety of interests, parties, and sects which it embraces, a coalition of a majority of the whole society could seldom take place on any other principles than those of justice and the general good . . . there being thus less danger to a minor from the will of a major party. . . .

From *Federalist 10*

Among the numerous advantages promised by a well-constructed Union, none deserves to be more accurately developed than its tendency to break and control the violence of faction [conflict of groups, and pursuit of total power by any group]. The friend of popular governments never finds himself so much alarmed for their character and fate, as when he contemplates their propensity to this dangerous vice. He will not fail, therefore, to set a due value on any plan which, without violating the principles to which he is attached, provides a proper cure for it. . . . The valuable improvements made by the American [state] constitutions on the popular models, both ancient and modern, cannot certainly be too much admired; but it would be an unwarrantable partiality, to contend that they have as effectually obviated the danger on this side, as was wished and expected. Complaints are everywhere heard from our most considerate and virtuous citizens, equally the friends of public and private faith, and of public and personal liberty, that our governments are too unstable, that the public good is disregarded in the conflicts of rival parties, and that measures are too often decided, not according to the rules of justice and the rights of the minor party, but by the superior force of an interested and overbearing majority. However anxiously we may wish that these complaints had no foundation, the evidence of known facts will not permit us to deny that they are in some degree true. . . .

There are two methods of curing the mischiefs of faction: the one, by removing its causes; the other, by controlling its effects. . . .

[But] the latent causes of faction are . . . sown in the nature of man; and we see them everywhere brought into different degrees of activity, according to the different circumstances of civil society. . . .

The inference to which we are brought is, that the *causes* of faction cannot be removed, and that relief is only to be sought in the means of controlling its *effects*.

If a faction consists of less than a majority, relief is supplied by the republican principle, which enables the majority to defeat its sinister views by regular vote. It may clog the administration, it may convulse the society; but it will be unable to execute and mask its violence under the forms of the Constitution. When a majority is included in a faction, the form of popular government, on the other hand, enables it to sacrifice to its ruling passion or interest both the public good and the rights of other citizens. To secure [make safe] the public good and private rights against the danger of such a faction, and at the same time to preserve the spirit and the form of popular government, is then the great object to which our inquiries are directed. . . .

From this view of the subject it may be concluded that a pure democracy, by which I mean a society consisting of a small number of citizens, who assemble and administer the government in person, can admit of no cure for the mischiefs of faction. A common passion or interest will, in almost every case, be felt by a majority of the whole; a communication and concert result from the form of government itself; and there is nothing to check the inducements to sacrifice the weaker party or an obnoxious individual. Hence it is that such democracies have ever been spectacles of turbulence and contention; have ever been found incompatible with personal security or the rights of property; and have in general been as short in their lives as they have been violent in their deaths. . . .

A republic, by which I mean a government in which the scheme of representation takes place, opens a different prospect, and promises the cure for which we are seeking. Let us examine the points in which it varies from pure democracy, and we shall comprehend both the nature of the cure and the efficacy which it must derive from the Union.

The two great points of difference between a democracy and a republic are: first, the delegation of the government, in the latter, to a small number of citizens elected by the rest; secondly, the greater number of citizens, and greater sphere of country, over which the latter may be extended.

The effect of the first difference is, on the one hand, to refine and enlarge the public views, by passing them through the medium of a chosen body of citizens, whose wisdom may best discern the true interest of their country, and whose patriotism and love of justice will be least likely to sacrifice it to temporary or partial considerations. Under such a regulation, it may well happen that the public voice, pronounced by the representatives of the people, will be more consonant to the public good than if pronounced by the people themselves, convened for the purpose. . . .

The other point of difference is, the greater number of citizens and extent of territory which may be brought within the compass of republican than of [a pure] democratic government; and it is this circumstance principally which renders factious combinations less to be dreaded in the former than in the latter. The smaller the society, the fewer probably will be the distinct parties and interests composing it; the fewer the distinct parties and interests, the more frequently will a majority be found of the same party; and the smaller the number of individuals composing a majority, and the smaller the compass within which they are placed, the more easily will they concert and execute their plans of oppression. Extend the sphere and you take in a greater variety of parties and interests; you make it less probable that a majority of the whole will have a common motive to invade the rights of other citizens; or if such a common motive exists, it will be more difficult for all who feel it to discover their own strength, and to act in unison with each other. . . .

Hence, it clearly appears, that the same advantage which a republic has over a democracy, in controlling the effects of faction, is enjoyed by a large over a small republic,—is enjoyed by the Union over the States composing it. Does the advantage consist in the substitution of representatives whose enlightened views and virtuous sentiments render them superior to local prejudices and to schemes of injustice? It will not be denied that the representation of the Union will be most likely to possess these requisite endowments. Does it consist in the greater security afforded by a greater variety of parties [or groups] against the event of any one party [or group] being able to outnumber and oppress the rest? In an equal degree does the increased variety of parties [or groups] comprised within the Union, increase this security. Does it, in fine, consist in the greater obstacles opposed to the concert and accomplishment of the secret wishes of an unjust and interested majority? Here,

Checks and Balances: Formal and Nonformal 77

again, the extent of the Union gives it the most palpable advantage.

The influence of factious leaders may kindle a flame within their particular States, but will be unable to spread a general conflagration through the other States. . . .

Review in your text and in your class notes materials relating to the formation of the Constitution, and particularly to the doctrine and practice of separation of powers and checks and balances. Read in your text also materials concerning the character and diversity of modern American society and concerning the interplay or action-and-reaction of interest groups and of parties in our two-party system.

As a written assignment or for class discussion:

1. Read carefully the Constitution of the United States, and LIST and DESCRIBE BRIEFLY every instance you are able to find of *formal* checks and balances or legally prescribed restraints on one branch or organ of government by another. In every case, cite the particular Article, Section, and Clause where each such check or restraint is prescribed.

2. Applying to modern conditions the ideas of James Madison concerning what we have called *nonformal* restraints on power (those that are NOT written down in the Constitution or prescribed by law), LIST and DESCRIBE BRIEFLY all such restraints you can identify, on the basis of your present knowledge, operating in American government and politics today.

Simply as suggestions, as take-off points for your own thinking, consider the following examples:

For Question 1, *formal* restraints: the president's authority to veto acts of Congress; the Senate's power to confirm certain presidential appointments.

For Question 2, *nonformal* restraints: personal rivalry or jealousy between a president on the one hand and congressional leaders on the other; two-party competition, with the "outs" ready to criticize the "ins."

PROBLEM 8

Separation of Powers and Delegation of Powers

One of the fundamental principles of the United States Constitution is that the power to govern must be divided among three coequal branches, the legislative, the executive, and the judicial. The three branches were not to be isolated in watertight compartments, but were intertwined in their relationships with each other in an elaborate fashion. Nevertheless, the basic separation of power between them was regarded by Madison, in *The Federalist,* Essay 47, as of the first importance in preserving liberty.

No political truth is certainly of greater intrinsic value, or is stamped with the authority of more enlightened patrons of liberty, than [this]. . . . The accumulation of all powers, legislative, executive, and judiciary, in the same hands, whether of one, a few, or many, and whether hereditary, self-appointed, or elective, may justly be pronounced the very definition of tyranny. . . .

Madison quoted Montesquieu approvingly:

"When the legislative and executive powers are united in the same person or body, there can be no liberty, because apprehensions may arise lest *the same* monarch or senate should *enact* tyrannical laws to *execute* them in a tyrannical manner."

To the Founding Fathers, tyranny meant arbitrary action by rulers. Although a tyrant might sometimes be benevolent, he could act as he pleased unrestrained by laws, customs, or constitutions. And such arbitrary authority, in the hands of any ruler, was always a threat to liberty.

Subscribing to this vitally important principle, the Founding Fathers were explicit and direct in writing the first sentence of each of the first three Articles of the Constitution:

> All legislative powers herein granted shall be vested in a Congress. . . .
> The executive power shall be vested in a President. . . .
> The judicial power of the United States shall be vested in one Supreme Court, and in such inferior courts as the Congress may from time to time ordain and establish.

Yet what *is* the *legislative* power as distinct from the *executive* power? Where *is* the line that *separates* one from the other? These questions may not have seemed difficult when the problems were those of writing down basic rules of government. But when it came actually to governing, the vagueness of many words such as "legislative" or "executive" became apparent. Furthermore, the social and economic conditions within which government operates have changed greatly, and with these changes the words of the Constitutional separation of powers, already unclear, have become even more clouded in their meaning.

In recent years the tendency has been for Congress to delegate to the president or the executive branch the authority to "fill in the details" of rather broad and sweeping declarations of legislative policy. This tendency has been regarded by some as a sensible adaptation of an eighteenth-century concept of separation of powers to twentieth-century needs. Others, however, have seen this delegation of power to the executive as the very threat to liberty that the Founding Fathers feared. Of course, intermingled in this debate about principle has been a variety of interests that are affected in one way or another by changes in the degree of authority and discretion to be exercised by the various branches of government. Thus some vigorous political conflicts have arisen over the question of the scope of authority each branch possesses, and the extent to which the Congress may authorize the President to make essentially legislative decisions.

Each of the following two paragraphs describes a situation in which Congress has authorized the President to carry out a program. The situations are not intended to be exact accounts of real events, although the first one is similar to a program which actually has been undertaken. The primary purpose of these paragraphs is to illustrate the problem of distinguishing between the legislative and executive functions. Each situation differs from the other in one or more of the factors relevant to the question of whether the delegation of power by Congress to the President is consistent with the idea of the separation of powers. The cases are different also in the circumstances that may account for Congress having taken this kind of action. Think about both aspects of this problem as you read.

A. Congress has enacted a law directing the President to carry out a program of supports for the prices of agricultural commodities. The law says that support prices are to be based on percentages of parity—the relationship at a given time between what a farmer pays for the things he buys and what he receives for the things he sells—and support prices may range from 75 per cent to 90 per cent of parity. The law specifies how parity is to be calculated. It also specifies that the President (or his subordinate) is to estimate in advance of each year's planting whether there is likely to be a surplus of each of several commodities. If he finds that a surplus is probable, he may at his discretion reduce the support price, but not to less than 75 per cent of parity. If, in contrast, he finds that a shortage is likely, he may raise the support price to not more than 90 per cent of parity. The statute specifies in detail the administrative procedures to be used in carrying out this program.

B. After a short paragraph which states that subversive organizations in the service of hostile governments threaten to undermine the nation, Congress authorizes and directs the President:

to determine whether any organization functioning in the United States is an agency of a hostile foreign government. If the President finds organizations to be serving the interests of hostile foreign governments, he may promulgate whatever regulations and take whatever action he deems necessary to prevent such organizations from accomplishing their purposes.

No other provisions are contained in the statute.

Review in your text and lecture notes the materials relating to the doctrine of separation of powers and to the problems of delegation of power by Congress to the President.

For written exercise or class discussion, prepare answers to each of the following questions:

1. In each of the two cases described, what factors do you think may have led Congress to decide that the President should make the decisions rather than Congress?

2. In what respects does the action taken in each case appear to be in keeping with the idea that the legislative and executive powers should be kept separate?

In what respects does the action taken in each case conflict with the doctrine of separation of powers?

3. The two statutes you have considered are not mere figments of the imagination. The first is an adaptation of an existing law, and they both put into concrete terms the kinds of actions performed by the two branches of government. Keeping these concrete examples in mind, prepare a brief statement distinguishing as carefully and as exactly as you can between the "legislative" and the "executive" functions of government. Make sure that your definitions are consistent with the tasks that the President and Congress actually perform.

4. In view of the vastly different conditions which confront governmental operation today, compared with the eighteenth century, how would you evaluate the present importance of separation of powers as a safeguard of individual liberty?

PROBLEM 9

Judicial Review and the Legislative Process

In the first session of the Ninety-first Congress the Republicans had a majority in both houses. The Republican party Congressional leadership, in accord with the party platform, sponsored a series of bills intended to deal with a recognized national crisis. This proposed legislation was designed to assure American scientific, educational, and cultural pre-eminence in a continuing race with the Soviet Union, which had followed its launching of an earth satellite in 1957 with further advances, to the detriment of American prestige in the international arena.

The bills were all passed by substantial majorities in both houses of Congress, though a small number of Republicans and a few more Democrats voted against them. They provided for federal financial aid in large quantities to state, municipal, and private universities and research undertakings, including a new Institute for Space Research at Winnemac State College in Zenith, and the Center for Advanced Social Science Research at the State University of Sunshine. They also provided funds to increase teachers' salaries in elementary and secondary schools, public and private, and in state and privately supported colleges and universities. In addition, they extended grants to qualified art centers and museums, music centers and symphony orchestras, and professional and community theatrical groups. In each case, however, an institution to qualify was required to satisfy the Secretary of Health, Education, and Welfare that it met certain detailed standards in terms of personnel, administration, curriculum, and program. These standards were specifically spelled out in the legislation.

Within the next year and a half, cases involving all these measures reached the Supreme Court. In each case the Court, by vote of five to four, declared the legislation involved unconstitutional, on the grounds that the federal government had no constitutional power to set specific standards for state institutions in the educational field, and that in so doing it was violating the Tenth Amendment. These decisions brought the new scientific, educational, and cultural program to a halt, while the Soviet Union continued to make remarkable and well-propagandized progress in all these areas.

In the off-year congressional elections, the Republican leaders in Congress decided to make the Supreme Court and its decisions an issue in the campaign. They charged that the Court was still living in the prespace age, and that "five justices who had barely heard of the atomic bomb" stood in the way of a "vital program to raise American prestige and win friends in the present critical world conflict." One of their spokesmen, Senator Thaddeus Spinner of Winnemac, built his campaign around a proposal for legislation to abolish the Supreme Court's power to review lower-court decisions in which the constitutionality of legislation in the scientific, educational, and cultural areas was challenged. He described such legislation as "merely taxing and spending to promote the common defense and the general welfare of the United States," a power granted to Congress in Article I, Section 8 of the Constitution. Other Republican candidates across the nation endorsed Senator Spinner's proposal. The balloting resulted in the re-election of Spinner, and in addition the Republicans gained four new seats in the Senate for a total of 56, and twelve new seats in the House for a total of 245.

Early in the first session of the Ninety-second Congress, Senator Spinner introduced a bill to abolish the Supreme Court's jurisdiction over cases in which the constitutionality of scientific, educational, and cultural legislation was challenged. The Spinner bill was endorsed and supported by the Republican leadership in the Senate; however, the President, Winfield MacArthur, a Republican, announced that he would leave the decision on Spinner's bill entirely to Congress. Substantially all the Democrats in the Senate opposed the Spinner bill strongly, with their leaders declaring that they objected to the bill not because they were against federal aid to scientific, educational, and cultural activities, but because they believed that the Spinner bill threatened the Constitution, the system of separation of powers, and judicial independence. By the middle of March, however, the Spinner bill was passed by the Senate, 54 to 39, with only three Republicans voting nay.

With the conflict transferred to the House, opponents of the Spinner bill marshaled their forces to make a strong stand against the measure. The major opposition to the bill came from the following groups:

1. The National Chamber of Manufacturers and the Association of American Merchants, whose stand was supported by the American Lawyers' Association and other business groups. They attacked the Spinner bill as a threat to "our Constitutional guarantees that the federal government shall be limited to its appropriate functions," and defended the Supreme Court as "our greatest bulwark" in this connection.

2. A group made up mostly of lawyers and professional people, called the Union for Constitutional Government, which had often defended individuals who claimed that their constitutional rights had been violated. The Union in a learned statement opposed the Spinner bill as "an improper way" to achieve "laudable" objectives, and as a threat to "the basic American constitutional tradition and structure."

The support for the Spinner bill among organized interest group associations was not as powerful as the opposition. Such support, however, included:

1. The American Education Association, which counted among its members thousands of primary, secondary, and university teachers across the nation.

2. Several large, politically active labor unions, whose spokesmen argued that the Supreme Court had acted in a "backward, undemocratic, and irresponsible fashion," and that it was likely to do so again on such matters as labor and welfare legislation, unless "the people, through their elected representatives in Congress," made it clear that the Court could not continue in the "error of its present, five-to-four, arbitrary ways."

3. The American League to Defend World Democracy, an active citizens' group particularly concerned with foreign policy issues. Spokesmen for the League declared that the Supreme Court's decisions, if allowed to stand, threatened American ability "to maintain its position in the contest with the USSR in the forum of world opinion."

The groups opposing the Spinner bill and those favoring it all engaged in widespread publicity campaigns and in active lobbying for their positions, utilizing all the legitimate means at their disposal. Reliable public opinion polls, which had shown large majorities favoring the original scientific, educational, and cultural proposals, now reported that 83 per cent of all persons interviewed had an opinion on the Spinner bill, and that 58 per cent of those who had an opinion favored the bill.

In the House, the Spinner bill was referred to the Judiciary Committee, whose chairman was Darius Greene. He soon secured a favorable committee report for the Spinner bill, unaltered; and, in consultation with other Republican leaders in the House, decided that the bill should be brought up for debate as soon as possible. They felt that it was necessary to act promptly, since pressure against the bill was rapidly increasing.

The scheduled course of the bill was upset by Martin Cockerell, Republican Chairman of the Rules Committee of the House. Representing a rural constituency in New York, and serving his fourteenth consecutive term, he had recently become chairman of the Rules Committee following the death of the previous chairman. He had opposed the original science-education-culture legislation. He now announced in a press interview that he had "documentary evidence" that the president and the executive secretary of the American League to Defend World Democracy had formerly been members of groups which were on the Attorney General's list of subversive organizations. The next day, two more of the seven Republican members of the twelve-member Rules Committee joined Chairman Cockerell in a public statement that there should be a "full investigation of the possible taint of Communism among the supporters of the Spinner bill," before the bill was called up for debate. Most Democrats in the House had opposed the Spinner bill from the beginning, as their Senate fellow-partisans had done, on the grounds that it was a threat to the American constitutional system. Now many Democratic leaders in the House joined in calling for "an investigation of possible sinister elements behind the bill."

It seemed possible, given all the forces, arguments, and pressures in the situation, that the Spinner bill might die in committee, or suffer defeat if it was called up in the House.

Review, in your text and in your class notes, materials relating to Congress, the legislative process, the judiciary and Supreme Court, separation of powers in the Constitution, and judicial review.

Assume that you are Distinguished Service Professor of Political Science at William Few University, in Washington, D.C. An English acquaintance of yours, Merriman Cooke, comes to you to ask for your help. He has just been sent to the United States as correspondent for the Manchester *Defender,* an outstanding liberal, internationally minded journal of news and opinion. He shows you an editorial that has recently been printed in the *Trumpet,* an influential London weekly:

The immediate issue before the American House of Representatives is whether to curb the irresponsible exercise of power by the Supreme Court in a critical situation. All sham stripped aside, the basic constitutional question involved is one that strikes at the heart of representative, democratic government: whether the elected representatives of the people shall have the power to determine the policy of the government.

The American people, after permitting the courts to veto policy decisions for many years, indicated in the last election that they do not think that a small group of men who are not responsible to the people should have that power. The intense campaign by various interest groups, and the distraction created by the present uproar over alleged Communism, do not alter the fact that the Republican party, after waging a campaign on this very issue, was given a clear mandate by the people to curb the Supreme Court, if necessary, in order to enact its program.

Nor should the House of Representatives let empty slogans and shibboleths, such as cries of separation of powers and judicial independence, obscure the real issue. Such notions are outmoded in the Space Age, in an era of world tension and danger in which democracy must act if we are to stand up to the threat of Russian tyranny. The people have spoken: their will must be obeyed. It makes, and should make, no difference whatsoever if some supporters of the Spinner bill have been Communists or "subversives."

The Republican leadership in the House knows this, and should use the full force of its party's disciplinary machinery to thwart whatever undemocratic, obstructive plan may be in the mind of the members of the Rules Committee. The individual congressman, when faced with the pressures and diversions created by the Spinner bill's opponents, will surely realize that the source of his authority derives from the majority of his constituents who elected him to Congress, and that that majority spoke quite clearly in the elections last November.

You read and ponder this editorial. Then Cooke tells you that he and his paper, the *Defender*, looked favorably upon the original scientific, educational, and cultural legislation as a model Britain might follow, and that he and his paper were distressed and rather surprised that the Supreme Court could block such a fine program. He has just received a long cable from his editor. It suggests that the *Trumpet* editorial, though perhaps on the "right side," may be based on provincially British misconceptions or erroneous assumptions about the American political tradition and political system and the way it works. It assigns Cooke to prepare a draft of an informed, thoughtful, balanced editorial-article, covering at least the following points:

1. A careful analysis of the *Trumpet* editorial, considering particularly in what ways, if any, it exhibits a misunderstanding of the nature and workings of the American political system;
2. Whether he, Cooke, approves or disapproves of the Spinner bill as a means to remove the obstacles to the scientific-educational-cultural program, and his *reasons in full* for approving, or disapproving;
3. Assuming that the bill might not pass, what other means, if any, are available within the American political system to remove the obstacles to the original scientific-educational-cultural legislation.

But, Cooke says frankly, he does not think that he as an Englishman new to the United States has as yet sufficient understanding of American government, constitutional structure, and politics to explain the questions involved in the current complicated situation to the English readers of his paper, the *Defender,* or enough background to form an intelligent judgment on the *Trumpet* editorial or the Spinner bill. He asks you to prepare a draft of the editorial-article his editor has assigned him to do.

As a written assignment, or for class discussion, work out, in a clear, orderly, and complete way, what you would say in such a draft, covering all three of the points above.

PART IV

THE FEDERAL SYSTEM

PROBLEM 10
The Nature of Federalism

A federal system is one in which the individuals in a particular area are subject to control by *two* governments—the central or national government and the state government or (as in Canada) the provincial government. Each government has certain powers allocated to it. Each can exercise its own powers without the other preventing it from doing so.

These powers are allocated to the national and state governments by the constitution of the country, and the allocation can be changed only by the process of constitutional amendment, a process in which both governments take part. In a nonfederal or "unitary" country such as Britain, there are of course local governments as well as a central government, but the powers of the local governments are granted and can be taken away by the legislative action of the central government's Parliament. In contrast, in a federal union such as ours a mere act of Congress cannot increase the central government's power or diminish the powers allocated by the constitution to the states. And, of course, no state legislation can alter the national government's powers.

Thus, in the United States, the national government has the power to establish post offices; no state, therefore, can pass a valid law prohibiting the national government from establishing post offices in that state. The state governments in the United States have the powers not specifically given by the Constitution to the national government: for instance, the power to establish mental hospitals in the state. If the State of Missouri passes a state law to build a new mental hospital, Congress cannot order that the hospital shall not be built.

Each government, within its own sphere of action, can control the individuals within its borders. If you tamper with a U.S. mailbox in St. Louis, Missouri, you are violating a national law and the national government can put you in jail. If you are caught breaking into a house in the same city with intent to steal, you are violating a state law and will be prosecuted in a state court.

In the U.S. Constitution, the powers of the national government are spelled out, particularly in Article I, Section 8. The powers of the state governments are not spelled out; the states simply have all governmental powers not specifically given to the national government and not denied to the states (Amendment X). However, if a country's constitution specifically expressed all the states' powers, and then said that all other (unspecified) governmental powers belonged to the national government, that country, too, would have a *federal* system. It would fit the conception of a federal system given in the first paragraph.

Suppose you are a member of a Convention assembled to draft a constitution for a new nation composed of people living on four large islands, each 100 miles distant from another. You have instructions from your island legislature to establish a federal system for this imaginary country. The drafting committee has presented the following proposals:

1. There shall be a National Parliament, consisting of six representatives from each island.
2. The National Parliament shall choose a Prime Minister, who shall be the Chief Executive and shall serve at the pleasure of the National Parliament.
3. There shall be a National Supreme Court, which shall decide controversies between the islands, but shall not have power to hold Acts of the National Parliament unconstitutional.

4. The National Parliament shall have authority to request each island to furnish men, ships, and airplanes to compose the National Armed Services.

5. The National Parliament shall have the power to levy taxes, but no Act of the National Parliament levying taxes shall be effective in any island if the island legislature passes a resolution prohibiting the collection of such taxes.

6. Each island legislature shall have power within its island to (1) establish public institutions of learning; (2) prevent crime; (3) promote sanitation and health, and preserve order; (4) impose taxes, including import taxes on any goods brought into the island; (5) establish courts of justice; (6) regulate industry and labor.

7. The National Government shall have exclusive power to make treaties with foreign nations.

8. The enforcement of all National and Island laws, treaties, and regulations in each island shall be the duty, exclusively, of the government of that island.

9. All proper governmental powers not specifically mentioned heretofore in this Constitution shall be vested in the National Parliament.

As a written exercise or for class discussion, prepare a report to the Convention, indicating what changes must be made in this draft in order to establish a federal system.

PROBLEM 11

Intergovernmental Relations

In 1953, at the suggestion of President Eisenhower, Congress established a temporary Commission on Intergovernmental Relations to conduct an intensive study of national-state-local relationships, especially those involving "federal aid" to state and local governments. The Commission issued its report in 1955. There follow excerpts from that report:

Federal Grants-in-Aid

The grant-in-aid device is used by central governments to assist smaller governmental units in practically all political systems, whether federal or unitary. Grants are found in a wide variety of forms. The common characteristic of all forms is that the central government provides aid without supplanting smaller units as the governments which bring the aided services to the public.

Grants made by the United States Government to the States are usually in the form of money, although the earliest grants were in land and at present some grants of agricultural commodities are being made. Most grants-in-aid are continuing arrangements; there have, however, been a few one-time grants.

At first glance existing Federal grant programs look like a hodgepodge. Purposes are not always clearly stated, the choice of activities seems haphazard, apportionment methods and controls vary widely. The Commission's study of past and present

Federal grant-in-aid programs showed plainly that the grants do not constitute a system, and indeed that they were never intended to make a system. Their varied characteristics are largely the natural outgrowth of their varied objectives and piecemeal development. This conclusion becomes apparent in examining the historical development of grants.

Evolution of the Grant-in-Aid

The National Government has used the grant-in-aid primarily to achieve some National objective, not merely to help States and local governments finance their activities. Specific objectives have been as varied as getting the farmer out of the mud, assisting the needy aged, providing lunches for school children, and preventing cancer. As a condition of financial assistance the National Government establishes requirements and provides administrative supervision.

The trend has been toward sharper definition of objectives, closer attention to conditions and requirements, more extensive administrative supervision, and recently, greater attention to relative State fiscal capacity. . . .

As a result of many developments, the grant has become a fully matured device of cooperative government. Its elements are well established: the objectives are defined; apportionment and matching formulas are laid down; conditions, minimum standards, and sanctions are prescribed; and provisions are made for administrative supervision. The maturing of the grant as a means of stimulating and shaping particular programs, as distinct from a subsidy device, is reflected not only in increasing legislative attention to conditions, standards, sanctions, and methods of supervision, but also in the evolution of National administrative machinery and procedures. The conditions attached to grants have not remained mere verbal expressions of National intent; National agencies have generally had funds and staff to make them effective.

In establishing grants-in-aid programs, the Congress has apparently regarded the disparities in fiscal capacity among the States as a matter of secondary importance. Almost all grants are available to all States, even the wealthiest; the formulas for allotting funds among the States and prescribing their matching expenditures do not usually reflect differences in State resources; and, further, many programs offer relatively small amounts of money.

During the past decade, however, the grant structure has been modified to recognize varying State fiscal capacity. In grants for hospital construction, school lunches, and public health, for example, the National Government assumes more of the financial burden in States of lesser fiscal capacity than in more prosperous ones. Thus Mississippi, with the lowest per capita income, receives for hospital construction four and one-half times as much per capita as New York does. . . .

While the traditional type of grant-in-aid is to be preferred to the subsidy, substantial improvement is desirable in determining both when and how to use it. The Commission advances the following broad principles for guidance:

1. A grant should be made or continued only for a clearly indicated and presently important national objective. This calls for a searching and selective test of the justification for National participation. The point has been made . . . that existence of a national interest in an activity is not in itself enough to warrant National participation. Related questions are the relative importance of the national interest and the extent to which it may be served by State and local action. Consequently, where the activity is one normally considered the primary responsibility of state and local governments, substantial evidence should be required that National participation is necessary in order to protect or to promote the national interest.

2. Where National participation in an activity is determined to be desirable, the grant-in-aid should be employed only when it is found to be the most suitable form of National participation. It is important to compare the strong and weak points of the grant-in-aid device with those of other forms of National-State cooperation as well as with those of other forms of direct National action. It is likewise important to consider the types of objectives and situations for which the grant is best adapted. The probable effect on State or local governments is an important consideration.

3. Once it is decided that a grant-in-aid should be made, the grant should be carefully designed to achieve its specified objective. This requires careful attention to the shaping of apportionment formulas and matching requirements, the prescription of standards and conditions, and the provision for administrative machinery and procedures. Objectives as varied as cancer control, old-age assistance, highway construction, and forest fire prevention call for imaginative use of varied types of standards, controls, and fiscal formulas. It is more important to shape these elements of the grant to a particular purpose than to achieve complete uniformity among the programs. At the same time, in order to ease the impact of grants-in-aid on State and local government, as much uniformity should be striven for as is compatible with the achievement of specific objectives. . . .

Where used effectively, the grant not only has increased the volume of State and local services, but also has promoted higher standards both in service and in administration. These gains have come through the conditions attached to the grants and from the administrative leadership and supervision of National agencies. Thus a study made for the Commission on the impact of grants-in-aid in one State concluded:

"Grants-in-aid programs have had a significant effect upon the administrative practices of the State departments. . . . Personnel management is distinctly better in Welfare, Health, Employment Security, and Highways than in the non-federally aided departments. Again, the necessity of preparing annual work programs for the review of Federal agencies has developed a concept of the work program which makes for more effective and better organized administrative performance within those departments. Similarly, the necessity of preparing monthly and annual reports for the review of the responsible Federal agency has improved the reporting practices of the State agencies concerned. This would appear to be in distinct contrast to the rather loose and general reporting practices of the non-federally assisted State agencies."

Comparable findings were reported from other States.

A good illustration of these effects is afforded by the highway grants that were first authorized in 1916. Automobiles were then swarming onto roads designed for the horse and wagon. Federal grants served both to increase the volume of construction and to introduce minimal standards and some interlocking of State systems. One of the major results was the speedy establishment of State highway departments in all States; before the grant became available, only a few States had set up this type of agency. Without the National standards, the States and localities in this early period could hardly have served the national interest in an adequate highway system. . . .

Notwithstanding its obvious usefulness, the grant-in-aid is not a panacea. Its limitations should be recognized along with its potentialities.

When only a few States are not providing reasonably adequate services, the grant-in-aid may be a costly way to stimulate these States. The National Government has not as yet developed a method of making grants that is flexible enough to meet such a limited objective. In this situation it remains to be explored whether National contractual services or loans, or direct National action on a limited basis, may be preferable alternatives to a grant.

Other limitations of the grant-in-aid are inherent in its complexity. It divides responsibility and offers ample opportunity to dodge it. There is joint provision of policy, finances, and administration, but National and State action do not mesh perfectly. The States must wait for Federal appropriations to plan their budgets for grant-aided activities; State policy must be geared to National standards and conditions; and State administrators must accept National supervision. In such a situation some friction cannot be avoided.

The Commission notes with concern that a number of State budget officers believe that grants-in-aid have distorted State budgets. Neither the nature nor the extent of the distortion, however, is entirely clear.

Almost of necessity, grants-in-aid in their early stages will induce State and local governments to adopt a pattern of expenditure in which the emphasis is somewhat different from that which would prevail in the absence of grants. Such an effect is indeed one of the major objectives of grants-in-aid, for the grant is intended to stimulate States and their localities to exert greater effort in aided programs than they presumably would exert without financial inducement from the National Government.

To say that States are not required to accept grants-in-aid is not a completely satisfactory answer. Although State authorities are not legally required to accept grants, they are under strong practical compulsion to do so.

It is questionable whether any State, today, spends more of its own funds on major activities supported by grants-in-aid than it would were there no Federal support of these activities. However, restrictions attached to the use of some Federal grants, particularly those in the fields of public health, vocational education, and highways, probably do affect the relative support of various special programs in some State budgets. This element of distortion could be eliminated or greatly reduced by giving the State more discretion in the allocation of grant-in-aid funds, as later recommended by the Commission. . . .

Mr. Burton (former Budget Director of New York State) observes: "The Commission has not emphasized sufficiently an inherent danger in the grant device. By this device the National Government spends money and exercises controls for programs which might not be supported if the National Government proposed to spend the money directly and exercise the control. In other words, the National Government does things indirectly which the public might not support if it attempted to do so directly." Governors Driscoll (New Jersey) and Thornton (Colorado) join in this view.

Governor Driscoll adds the following comment: "Woodrow Wilson once observed that we ought not to pit power against weakness. In the relationship between the National Government and the States, it is important that we maintain, as nearly as circumstances will permit, a reasonable balance between the collective powers and responsibilities of the States on the one hand and the National Government on the other.

"A grant-in-aid program should be the exception rather than the rule. Federal grants are not cloaked in magic. They derive their support from the same taxpayers that provide the wherewithal for all levels of government. If grants should become a part of every governmental activity, there is good reason to believe we would lose some of the substance of our present republican form of government and federal system. President Andrew Jackson foresaw this result in 1833, when he stated that Congress should not be the tax gatherer and paymaster for State governments. 'It appears to me,' he said, 'that a more direct road to consolidation cannot be devised. Money is power, and in that government which pays all the public officers of the States will all political power be substantially concentrated.'

"It is conceded that grants-in-aid have upon a number of occasions performed a useful service. This fact, however, does not invite indiscriminate expansion. It has been suggested that grants to support specific programs may be made without strings and that controls need not be a conspicuous feature of these grants. An examination of the facts discloses that the grant has frequently been used to establish the authority of the National Government over State policies. For example, in the Hayden-Cartwright Act the National Government seeks to compel the States to dedicate gasoline taxes—one of their major tax resources. The Hatch Act uses the grant as a device to prohibit reasonable, as well as unreasonable, civic and political activities by a major proportion of all State employees. In addition, the grant has been used as an entering wedge for a wide variety of administrative controls over State policies and administration.

"I do not question the right of the National Government to attach reasonable controls to its grants-in-aid. I do question the wisdom of adopting the costly and frequently confusing grant device as standard practice in government. A grant-in-aid program of all States, irrespective of relative need and ability to pay, is a cumbersome and expensive method of administration which negates many of the values of our American system of political decentralization.

"I find that grants-in-aid in practice result in a much greater impact of National policy on State budgets, administration, and policies than the Commission report indicates."

Governors Battle (Virginia), Thornton, and Peterson (Nebraska) and Mr. Burton join in this view.[1]

---

[1] The Commission on Intergovernmental Relations, *A Report to the President for Transmittal to Congress* (Washington, D.C.: Government Printing Office, 1955), 118–131 *passim*.

In your text and class notes, review material concerning federal grants-in-aid and intergovernmental co-operation.

Now assume that in the near future a new and disabling disease appears in the United States. It attacks chiefly tiny infants and people in the age group from twenty-five to forty-five. Little is known about its transmission, but in different areas at different times it assumes epidemic proportions. Some distinguished doctors announce the discovery of a vaccine which, they say, will protect most individuals from infection or at least mitigate the effects of the disease. Other doctors express doubts as to the vaccine's effectiveness; still others say that it will be fully effective only in cases where the people inoculated are less than thirty-five years of age. Limited experiments in mass inoculations give all three medical groups some evidence to support their different positions; but the most extensive experiment, on the Pacific Coast, has had such apparently good results that a widespread public demand has arisen for a national inoculation program. The arguments for a *public* and *national* program are that: (1) the vaccine is expensive, and unless it is provided by the government, poor people cannot afford it; and (2) the spread of the disease is not checked by state boundaries, so the problem is a national one.

Meanwhile,

A. California has enacted a compulsory inoculation law, applicable to all persons thirty years of age and older; to finance this program, the State has increased its income tax 2 per cent.

B. Wisconsin has enacted a voluntary inoculation law, under which people in the age group twenty-nine to thirty-five may be inoculated at state public health centers on payment of a $5 fee, people with low incomes being excused from paying any fee.

C. Inoculation bills, introduced in the legislatures of New York, New Jersey, Massachusetts, Connecticut, and Pennsylvania have been badly defeated. There have been few cases of the disease in that area. All those states (let us assume) have recently tripled their budgets for mental hospitals and clinics, and have sharply increased their tax rates accordingly. Many of the leading physicians in that region are openly dubious about the effectiveness of the new vaccine.

D. Two southern governors have issued a joint statement as follows: "The people of each of the States can meet this crisis themselves, and have a right to do so without dictation from Washington."

E. A bill has been introduced by Representative Claggett in the U.S. House of Representatives, providing that the United States should offer to match state appropriations up to $1,000,000 a year for any state, for a state inoculation program. To qualify for such a "matching grant" a state program, compulsory or voluntary, must (1) include free inoculation for all babies before the age of six months and all adults from twenty-five to thirty-five years of age; (2) provide for full monthly reports of health statistics to the U.S. Public Health Service on forms prescribed by the U.S. Public Health Service; and (3) provide that all nonmedical personnel employed in the program will be selected under a civil service or merit system approved by the U.S. Public Health Service.

Now assume that you are Assistant Secretary of the U.S. Department of Health, Education, and Welfare. Your chief, the Secretary, says to you: "The President has decided to make a televised address on this inoculation business. As you know, there's a grant-in-aid bill pending in the House. However, our party's leader in the House, Jim Keenan of Massachusetts, just telephoned me to urge that the Administration go slow on this. He expressed the hope that the President would merely express a faith in state action where needed, and keep the national government out of the picture except for any technical advice which the Public Health research teams may make available. He says there's some feeling that the federal government is getting too powerful. Senator Clow of Oregon, on the other hand, says that any state-by-state approach will be casual and ineffective, and demands one single over-all national program. He says some of the states will do a bad job if it's left to them.

"Now, what the President wants to do is to propose something that will be practical, will be consistent with our scheme of government, and will get this disease stopped if that's at all possible. Please prepare a memorandum that I can give to him to help him in writing his speech. Indicate the alternative possibilities, select the one that is most appropriate, and justify your choice of it. Explain why your plan meets most of the objections that may be raised. The President will have to mention the Claggett bill, so you'd better deal with that in some detail—whether you approve of the general scheme of the Claggett bill or not. The President realizes that he can't please everybody, but he wants to minimize the opposition. As you know, it's a general principle of his that any program, to be successful, must have wide public acceptance."

For class discussion or as a written exercise, prepare the requested memorandum.

PROBLEM 12

States' Rights: Slogan or Reality?

There has long been disagreement about what constitutes the reality of American politics. Some have seen the fundamental political issue as one in which the individual is pitted against big government in a struggle for freedom. Others have regarded this as much too simple a view, which ignores the fact that government too is people. Many political scientists have come to regard the various formal arrangements of government as essentially impersonal machinery which may be used by some people or groups to gain concrete advantage over others or, conversely, to protect advantages already won against opposing groups. Thus it might be argued that those who talk about the dangers of too much government are simply propagandizing to prevent changes which others wish to achieve by using the governmental mechanism. The question is not too much or too little government, but for whom and to what ends.

One of the formal arrangements of American government, federalism, has been particularly subject to such radically different interpretations. The impossibility of drawing clear lines between federal and state authority which would be final and binding for all time has meant that continuing controversy revolves around the extent of authority to be exercised by the nation and by the states as new problems and new programs come into existence. The cry of "states' rights" has been raised perennially by those who for whatever reason oppose a proposed federal action. On the other hand, it is clear that some groups find their objectives more readily achieved through Washington than through the state capitals. Each side may adduce a variety of arguments to support its position. Each may accuse the other of using loaded terms which have no real meaning. In any case, and however philosophical the argument may appear to be, real and quite specific conflicts of interests are involved. The job of the interested citizen in such controversies, and there are many, is to get as accurate a picture as possible of each side; which groups are involved, and what are their specific interests; and then to determine how these interests square with the citizen's own values. The arguments and counter-arguments must be examined in this light.

Review in your text and lecture notes the material relating to federalism and to major interest groups in the United States.

Now ponder well the following situation.

In the 1964 Olympics the USSR administers a sound whipping to American athletes, particularly in basketball and gymnastics. Defeat in gymnastics is not new to the United States, but the basketball loss shattered a long supremacy in international competition and is regarded as a serious blow to American pride and prestige. There has been considerable agitation to "do something" about the situation, and now in 1966 a bill has been introduced in Congress to remedy the deficiency. The bill provides that one billion dollars a year shall be granted by the federal government to the states to assist them in building up physical education. The money will be spent to train more recreation directors and physical education teachers, to enable cities to build gymnasium and outdoor recreation facilities, and to finance the expansion of compulsory physical training programs in the public schools. The states are to put up a total of half a billion dollars in order to qualify for the federal grants. The proposed bill also prescribes standards of administration that states must meet in order to receive grants. These standards primarily seek to assure that the money will be spent with reasonable efficiency for the purposes intended. The question is not at all clear, but there is a strong possibility that no state will be granted any aid for the construction of facilities that would segregate people on the basis of race. Some of those speaking on both sides of the bill have announced that they would expect the courts to interpret the law in this way even though the bill contains no specific language on the point.

On the floor of the House of Representatives the proponents of the bill have already spoken. Representatives from New York City, Detroit, and Los Angeles have spoken for the bill. The American Gymnastic Society, an organization based primarily in the eastern seaboard states, and the Physical Education Federation, with members in almost every city of over 50,000 in the country, have strongly supported the bill. A number of ethnic groups, including Scandinavian, Irish, Polish, and Italian, are favorably inclined. The bill provides for assistance to any group undertaking a physical training program that meets the standards set forth, and Catholic and Jewish youth organizations have testified in favor of the bill.

When the time allotted to those opposing the bill is at hand, several congressmen place a great deal of emphasis on what they call the dangers this bill poses to the continued existence of a federal system and the sovereign rights of the states. It is argued that this program should not be undertaken by the national government; each state should decide for itself whether to have such a program and should run its program its own way, without federal supervision. In the course of this debate one representative makes a rather abstract and general argument against the bill. His peroration consists of an excerpt from an article by Frank Chodorov, in *Human Events,* May 26, 1956:

> States' rights sprang from fear and distrust of centralized government. It was not just a political theory worked out in an ivory tower. The 1776 Americans rose in revolt against an impersonal, self-sufficient, and arbitrary government and were in no mood to countenance an American Government built along the same lines. As every schoolboy should know, there were delegates to the Constitutional Convention who favored a government of practically unlimited powers, and they dropped the idea because they knew the American people would make short shrift of a constitution that embodied it. The genius of the Americans was against centralism.
>
> But, why? Why did they favor State governments as against the newly proposed government? Simply because they knew from experience, and some from history, that their freedom was

less likely to be impinged upon by a government of "neighbors" than by one that was beyond their reach. One could keep one's eyes on the governor and the State legislature and, if need be, lay one's hands on them. The States cannot print money and there is a sharp limit to the deficit spending in which they can engage. Taxes could be held within reason, enforcement officers could not be arbitrary, the legislators would be more amenable to local customs.

Those early Americans knew what we have forgotten, that inherent in government, any government, is an insatiable appetite for power; that it could be contained only by the vigilance and opposition of the governed. But, how can you watch over and resist a government that is beyond reach, physically and fiscally? After all, one has enough to do to make a living. . . .

The recurring interest in States' rights in this country is but a version of the recurring struggle of the individual through history to attain a measure of freedom.

States' rights has nothing to do with sectional interests. It has nothing to do with the racial question or with the sedition laws of Pennsylvania. It has everything to do with freedom. It is a device invented by our forefathers to prevent the centralization of power, to the detriment of the individual. If the present enthusiasm for this doctrine is to be galvanized into a political movement, a movement to restore Article 10 to the Bill of Rights, it will be only because the spirit of freedom is not dead in this country.

Review in your text and lecture notes materials relating to the issue of centralization versus decentralization of government.

You are a newspaper reporter assigned to cover this debate in Congress. Your paper is a tabloid that likes to personalize the news, avoiding abstractions wherever possible, and reporting vague speeches in terms of the concrete interests and specific groups of people the speakers seem to be representing in their arguments.

The proponents of the bill are fairly clearly identified. Your task is to relate the arguments against the bill to the major groups in American politics which probably oppose it. This you can do in large part by analyzing what the bill would do and for whom, and by assuming that groups which have interests opposed to those of the proponents will probably oppose the bill. Be sure to include in your discussion the positions you think major labor, business, and farm groups will take, if any, as well as any others you think will be concerned.

In performing this task as clearly and specifically as possible:

1. Indicate specifically whether and in what respects the proposed bill represents, in your judgment, a genuine threat to the values that the quoted article argues are important.

2. Identify as many as possible of the interests that could be expected to oppose the bill, and show why each would oppose it.

3. Draw any generalizations which, on the basis of your understanding of American politics, seem to be justified, as to which groups of people would argue for or against "states' rights" on *other issues,* and explain the basis of your generalizations.

PART V

"LIBERTY AND JUSTICE FOR ALL"

PROBLEM 13

Freedom of Speech

"Congress shall make no law . . . abridging the freedom of speech. . . ."

These words of the First Amendment appear to recognize that everyone in the United States has a right to say whatever he likes. The Amendment prohibits Congress from interfering with that right; and by judicial interpretation of the Fourteenth Amendment, the individual's right of free speech is likewise protected against interference by State or local governments. Yet the question remains, *what is* "the freedom of speech" that cannot be "abridged" by government? It is not absolute liberty of expression. No person has the right with impunity to slander his neighbor, or to utter obscenities, or to conspire to commit a felony, even though all these activities involve "speech." In cases such as these, courts have had no difficulty in deciding that the right to free speech is a limited right. The really difficult cases are those in which the "speech" is not slanderous, or obscene, or conspiratorial, but where it is alleged to be "subversive" or "seditious." One of the basic reasons underlying the First Amendment is the belief that freedom to criticize the government is a necessary safeguard against tyranny.

And it is fairly easy to claim that severe criticism is itself "subversive" or "seditious." Therefore, laws punishing "subversive" or "seditious" utterance have been attacked as violating the very heart of the First Amendment. On the other hand, such laws have been defended as necessary to protect the country from foreign aggression or domestic violence. The right to freedom of speech, this argument contends, does not include the right to say things that weaken or endanger the national security.

In deciding such difficult cases, the courts have started with the assumption that freedom to criticize—even to dissent vehemently and to urge drastic changes in government—should be protected, unless there is a clear necessity for suppressing such kind of speech. The problem is to decide when such a "clear necessity" exists. In trying to meet this problem the courts have been faced with a difficult and never-ending problem of drawing lines; of deciding from case to case that this speech is protected or that speech may be restricted. These lines have come to be phrased in verbal formulae, which the courts then use to guide them in making future decisions.

Read carefully and thoughtfully the statements below in which are quoted four of the most famous and most often cited principles for deciding free speech cases.

> We admit that in many places and in ordinary times the defendants in saying all that was said in the circular would have been within their constitutional rights. But the character of every act depends upon the circumstances in which it is done. . . . The question in every case is whether the words are used in such circumstances and are of such a nature as to create a clear and present danger that they will bring about the substantive evils that Congress has a right to prevent. It is a question of proximity and degree. When a nation is at war many things that might be said in time of peace are such a hindrance to its effort that their utterance will not be endured so long as men fight and that no Court could regard them as protected by any constitutional right.[1]

> Those who won our independence by revolution were not cowards. They did not fear political change. They did not exalt

---

[1] Justice Holmes in *Schenck v. U.S.*, 249 U.S. 47 (1919).

order at the cost of liberty. To courageous, self-reliant men, with confidence in the power of free and fearless reasoning applied through the processes of popular government, no danger flowing from speech can be deemed clear and present, unless the incidence of the evil apprehended is so imminent that it may befall before there is opportunity for full discussion. If there be time to expose through discussion the falsehood and fallacies, to avert the evil by the processes of education, the remedy to be applied is more speech, not enforced silence. Only an emergency can justify repression. Such must be the rule if authority is to be reconciled with freedom. Such, in my opinion, is the command of the Constitution. It is, therefore, always open to Americans to challenge a law abridging free speech and assembly by showing that there was no emergency justifying it.[2]

In this case we are squarely presented with the application of the "clear and present danger" test, and must decide what that phrase imports. We first note that many of the cases in which this Court has reversed convictions by use of this or similar tests have been based on the fact that the interest which the State was attempting to protect was itself too insubstantial to warrant restriction of speech. . . . (But) overthrow of the Government by force and violence is certainly a substantial enough interest for the Government to limit speech. Indeed, this is the ultimate value of any society, for if a society cannot protect its very structure from armed internal attack, it must follow that no subordinate value can be protected. If, then, this interest may be protected, the literal problem which is presented is what has been meant by the use of the phrase "clear and present danger" of the utterances bringing about the evil within the power of Congress to punish. . . .

Obviously, the words cannot mean that before the Government may act, it must wait until the *putsch* is about to be executed, the plans have been laid and the signal is awaited. If Government is aware that a group aiming at its overthrow is attempting to indoctrinate its members and to commit them to a course whereby they will strike when the leaders feel the circumstances

---

[2] Justice Brandeis, concurring, in *Whitney* v. *California*, 274 U.S. 357 (1927).

permit, action by the Government is required. The argument that there is no need for Government to concern itself, for Government is strong, it possesses ample powers to put down a rebellion, it may defeat the revolution with ease needs no answer. For that is not the question. Certainly an attempt to overthrow the Government by force, even though doomed from the outset because of inadequate numbers or power of the revolutionists, is a sufficient evil for Congress to prevent. The damage which such attempts create both physically and politically to a nation makes it impossible to measure the validity in terms of the probability of success, or the immediacy of a successful attempt. In the instant case the trial judge charged the jury that they could not convict unless they found that petitioners intended to overthrow the Government "as speedily as circumstances would permit." This does not mean, and could not properly mean that they would not strike until there was certainty of success. What was meant was that the revolutionists would strike when they thought the time was ripe. We must therefore reject the contention that success or probability of success is the criterion.

[With respect to the "clear and present danger" test] . . . Chief Judge Learned Hand, writing for the majority below, interpreted the phrase as follows: "In each case (courts) must ask whether the gravity of the 'evil,' discounted by its improbability, justifies such invasion of free speech as is necessary to avoid the danger.". . . We adopt this statement of the rule. As articulated by Chief Judge Hand, it is as succinct and inclusive as any other we might devise at this time. It takes into consideration those factors which we deem relevant, and relates their significances. More we cannot expect from words. . . .[3]

The essential distinction is that those to whom the advocacy is addressed must be urged to *do* something, now or in the future, rather than merely to *believe* in something. . . . Mere doctrinal justification of forcible overthrow, . . . even though uttered with the hope that it may ultimately lead to violent

---

[3] Chief Justice Vinson in *Dennis* v. *U.S.*, 341 U.S. 494 (1951).

revolution, is too remote from concrete action to be regarded as the kind of indoctrination preparatory to action which [can legitimately be suppressed].[4]

Review carefully the materials in your text and lecture notes relating to problems of free speech.

You are a justice of the United States Supreme Court. The cases listed below have come before the court on appeal. In each of them the defendant was convicted as charged. Each defendant argues that the activities for which he is being punished are protected by the First or Fourteenth Amendment of the Constitution. You must decide whether to uphold the convictions or reverse them and set the defendant free. The statements quoted above are the legal rules you are to follow in determining what the First Amendment means.

A. The little town of Valleyville lies on the banks of the Blake River just below a large dam. Behind the dam is a reservoir large enough to flood the entire valley and easily wash Valleyville off the face of the earth. One evening James Jones raced through the town shouting "The dam is bust!" Appropriate sound effects were heard coming from the dam, and the frightened people ran for the hills without stopping to investigate. Before they could return, thieves looted the houses and made off with a sizable haul. Jones thought all this was a huge joke, which apparently was what he was after in the first place. There was no evidence linking him to the thieves. However, he was arrested and convicted of disturbing the peace, in violation of the following local law:

Any person who with intent to provoke a breach of the peace, or whereby a breach of the peace may be occasioned, commits any of the following acts shall be deemed to have committed the offense of disorderly conduct:
1. Uses offensive, disorderly, threatening, abusive or insulting language, conduct or behavior;

---

[4] Justice Harlan in *Yates* v. *United States,* 354 U.S. 298 (1957).

2. Acts in such a manner as to annoy, disturb, interfere with, obstruct, or be offensive to others; . . .[5]

B. The United States has recently been having repeated diplomatic difficulties with the new but large and potentially powerful nation of Graustark. In a public meeting a lecturer, one Orville Lyceum, reports that on a recent visit to Graustark he observed enormous strides being made in the economic and social development of that country. Lyceum suggests that the "Graustarkian way" is admirably suited to the rapid development of new nations. He concludes with the observation that congressional government is not well suited to the conditions of modern life, and that the United States could learn much from the methods of the new nation. Graustark is an absolute monarchy in which the king rules by divine right. The king owns all the property in the country, with which he may and does do exactly as he pleases. Many observers have disagreed with Lyceum's estimate of Graustarkian accomplishments, and since the diplomatic conflicts began, those who spoke in praise of Graustark have found themselves highly unpopular.

Lyceum is indicted and convicted under the following federal legislation:

> And be it further enacted, that if any person shall write, print, utter or publish, or shall cause to procure to be written, printed, uttered, or published, or shall knowingly and willingly assist or aid in writing, printing, uttering, or publishing any false, scandalous and malicious writing or writings against the government of the United States, or either house of the Congress of the United States, or the President of the United States, with intent to defame the said government, or either house of the said Congress, or the said President, or to bring them, or either of them, into contempt or disrepute; or to bring excitement against them, or either or any of them, the hatred of the good people of the United States, or to stir up sedition within the United States, or to excite any unlawful combinations therein, for opposing or resisting any law of the United States, or any

---

[5] Sec. 722 of the Penal Law of New York, quoted in Thomas Emerson and David Haber, *Political and Civil Rights in the United States* (Buffalo: Dennis & Co., 1952), 666.

act of the President of the United States, done in pursuance of any such law, or of the powers in him vested by the constitution of the United States, or to resist, oppose, or defeat any such law or act, or to aid, encourage or abet any hostile designs of any foreign nation against the United States, their people or government, then such person, being thereof convicted before any court of the United States having jurisdiction thereof, shall be punished by a fine not exceeding two thousand dollars, and by imprisonment not exceeding two years.[6]

C. John Alden, an elderly man of old New England family, has recently taken to making speeches on the causes and cures of the decline of New England. The essence of his argument is that New England has declined in economic and social influence because "the system" is rotten to the core. Otherwise, argues Alden, New England would have retained its dominance. Obviously the way to cure this evil is to destroy "the system." Alden is never very clear about what constitutes "the system" but he has made reference from time to time to "rascally rulers, state and national." He has advocated seizing property "owned by outsiders." Doctors have attested that Alden is not insane. Although he has often found his audiences sympathetic, particularly in mill towns and other places suffering from unemployment, Alden has no organized backing and he himself has always operated entirely on his own. There have been rumors of financial and moral support from abroad, but nothing more is known about this aspect of the case.

Alden is convicted under the following federal legislation:

It shall be unlawful for any person to knowingly or willfully advocate, abet, advise, or teach the duty, necessity, desirability, or propriety of overthrowing, or destroying any government in the United States by force or violence, or by the assassination of any officer of any such government.[7]

For each of the cases described:

1. Decide whether the defendant has in fact violated the statute in question. Has he really done things that the law forbids?

---

[6] 1 *Statutes* 570, sec. 2; cited in *ibid.*, 369.
[7] 54 *Statutes* 670–671, sec. 2 [A(1)]; cited in *ibid.*, 461–462.

2. Decide in each case whether the law can be applied to the facts without overstepping the limits of the First or Fourteenth Amendment.

3. As you reach your conclusions in (2), carefully and explicitly compare your decisions with each of the four precedent cases quoted. Does your decision "square" with each of these statements of principles? If not, why not?

PROBLEM 14

Due Process of Law: Procedural Safeguards

The Constitution protects individual rights by placing restraints on the use of power by both the federal government and the state governments. Twice it insists that when government coerces a person, it must do so only if its action is consistent with "due process of law." These are historic words, but what do they mean? That is the central question in this problem. You can come closer to answering it if you try to apply the general phrase, "due process of law," to a very specific human situation.

The Bill of Rights—the first Ten Amendments of the Constitution—spells out a number of "procedural safeguards" to which Americans are entitled; but these are protections for the individual against the *federal* government only. After the Civil War, however, the Fourteenth Amendment was adopted. The Fourteenth Amendment restrains *state* governments. Among other things, it says that no state shall "deprive any person of life, liberty, or property, without due process of law." In 1925, in *Gitlow* v. *New York,* the Supreme Court assumed that the "liberty" protected by the Fourteenth Amendment included the substantive "freedoms" of speech, press, assembly, and religion mentioned in the First Amendment.

A question remained, however, as to the meaning of the phrase "due process of law." With respect to procedure, does it simply mean "fair trial," as "fair trial" may be defined by particular judges at a particular time? Or does it mean a trial in which the defendant has all the procedural safeguards specified, for example, in the Fourth, Fifth, and Sixth Amendments? The Sixth Amendment, for instance, provides that a defendant being prosecuted in a federal court may have a jury trial. If, in a state court, he is not given a jury trial, is he being denied "due process of law"?

On this kind of question the justices of the Supreme Court have differed sharply among themselves. Various majorities (often only five justices out of nine) have held that the "due process" clause in the fourteenth Amendment only requires the state to provide a defendant with a fair trial, and that the Supreme Court itself must decide, on the basis of some general conception of fairness and justice, whether the trial has been fair or unfair. But articulate minorities have vigorously disputed this view. They say that if in a state court a defendant is deprived of any of the safeguards he would receive in a federal court under the Bill of Rights, the trial is unfair and the "due process" clause of the Fourteenth Amendment is violated.

Remember that most Supreme Court decisions have become settled law and have been followed, in later cases, for many years or always. However, remember too that occasionally when a particular majority of the Supreme Court interprets the Constitution one way, a later majority "overrules" the first decision and interprets the Constitution in a different way.

Now, read very carefully and thoughtfully the following statements:

A. From Charles Fairman, *American Constitutional Decisions* (New York: Henry Holt & Co., 1950), 378–383:

> The due process clause [of the Fourteenth Amendment] imposes a standard of decency and fairness in trials in state courts; it leaves to the states procedural details for securing fair judgment. The Court has felt that it ought not to go so far as to declare that due process necessarily involves the assistance of counsel in every criminal case. It has said that it would appraise "the totality of facts in a given case" and refrain from formulating "a set of hard and fast rules." *Betts* v. *Brady*, 316 U.S. 455 (1942). Justices Black, Douglas, and Murphy disagreed with this approach. They contended that just as the Sixth Amendment makes the right to counsel in criminal cases inviola-

ble by the federal government, the Fourteenth Amendment should be construed to impose the same flat requirement upon the states.

The rule in the trial of criminal cases in the federal courts implementing the Sixth Amendment is that

"If the defendant appears in court without counsel, the court shall advise him of his right to counsel and assign counsel to represent him at every stage of the proceeding unless he elects to proceed without counsel or is able to obtain counsel." Rule 44, Federal Rules of Criminal Procedure.

A consequence of the holding in *Betts* v. *Brady* is that cases keep arising wherein the Court must consider whether, in the light of the particular circumstances, the want of a lawyer's assistance deprived the accused of a fair trial. Betts was a man of 43, of ordinary intelligence. There was no question of the commission of the robbery with which he was charged: his defense was an alibi. The Court held that Maryland's refusal to provide him with counsel did not offend the due process clause. In *Uveges* v. *Pennsylvania*, 335 U.S. 437 (1948), the accused was a youth of 17, charged with four separate burglaries. He was not informed of his right to counsel nor was counsel offered him. He pleaded guilty to crimes that carried a maximum sentence of 80 years. The Supreme Court said that this was not good enough. Justice Reed's opinion explained that

"Some members of the Court [Black, Douglas, Murphy, and Rutledge, JJ.] think that where serious offenses are charged, failure of a court to offer counsel in state criminal trials deprives the accused of rights under the Fourteenth Amendment. They are convinced that the services of counsel to protect the accused are guaranteed by the Constitution in every such instance. Only when the accused refuses counsel with an understanding of his rights can the court dispense with counsel. Others of us think that when a crime subject to capital punishment is not involved, each case depends on its own facts. *Betts* v. *Brady*. Where the gravity of the crime and other factors—such as the age and education of the defendant, the conduct of the court or the prosecuting officials, and the complicated nature of the offense charged and the possible defenses thereto—render criminal proceedings without counsel so apt to result in injustice as to be fundamentally unfair, the latter group hold that the accused must have legal assistance under the Amendment whether he pleads guilty or elects to stand trial, whether he requests counsel or not. . . ."

The Fourth Amendment imposes the following limitation upon the United States Government:

"The right of the people to be secure in their persons, houses, papers, and effects, against unreasonable searches and seizures, shall not be violated, and no warrants shall issue but upon probable cause, supported by oath or affirmation, and particularly describing the place to be searched, and the persons or things to be seized."

How does a federal officer go about obtaining a warrant to search for, say, a thing believed to be in use as a means of committing an offense? Consult the Federal Rules of Criminal Procedure (prescribed by the Supreme Court under authority delegated by Congress), and turn to Rule 41, Search and Seizure:

"A search warrant authorized by this rule may be issued by a judge of the United States or of a state or territorial court of record or by a United States commissioner within the district wherein the property sought is located."

The Rule goes on to impose requirements implementing the constitutional provisions as to "probable cause," particularity, etc. The warrant is (save for exceptions) to be "served in the daytime"; it "may be executed and returned only within 10 days after its date."

Not every search without warrant is "unreasonable." Here is one situation where a search warrant is not essential:

"The right without a search warrant contemporaneously to search persons lawfully arrested while committing crime and to search the place where the arrest is made in order to find and seize things connected with the crime as its fruits or as the means by which it was committed, as well as weapons and other things to effect an escape from custody is not to be doubted. *Agnello* v. *United States,* 269 U.S. 20, 30 (1925)."

Again, "practically since the beginning of the government" it has been recognized that there is

"a necessary difference between a search of a store, dwelling house, or other structure in respect of which a proper official warrant readily may be obtained and a search of a ship, motor boat, wagon, or automobile for contraband goods, where it is not practicable to secure a warrant, because the vehicle can be quickly moved out of the locality or jurisdiction in which the warrant must be sought."

So as to vehicles, search may be made "upon probable cause, that is, upon belief, reasonably arising out of circumstances known to the seizing officer . . ." *Carroll* v. *United States*, 267 U.S. 132 (1925).

Do those principles seem clear? In practice they prove very difficult—so much so that "in recent years" this "has been a subject of almost constant judicial controversy. . . . In no other field has the law's uncertainty been more clearly manifested." Black, J., dissenting, in *United States* v. *Rabinowitz*, 339 U.S. 56 (1950). Consider the right to search "incident to arrest": is that a right to "rummage all over the house"? In Rabinowitz' case the officer after arresting him had searched the desk, safe, and file cabinets in a one-room office, finding forged stamps that were thereupon used to obtain a conviction. The majority held this search and seizure "reasonable." Three justices dissented. . . .

The matter really in issue, of course, in these cases is whether the thing "unreasonably" seized may be used as evidence. *Weeks* v. *United States*, 232 U.S. 383 (1914), held that the Federal Government could not use as evidence against an accused a thing "unreasonably" seized from him by a federal officer.[1] . . .

Does the Fourteenth Amendment—in particular, the due process clause—impose upon the several states the body of law we have just been deriving from the Fourth Amendment? That was the question in *Wolf* v. *Colorado* 338 U.S. 25 (1949). Wolf had been convicted in the state court on evidence unlawfully obtained. He asked the Supreme Court to say that the Fourteenth Amendment required Colorado to follow the rule that the Court had applied to the Federal Government in *Weeks* v. *United States, supra*—that is, to hold that the Colorado court must exclude evidence that the state had obtained by an "un-

---

[1] This assumes that the defendant makes a timely objection to the introduction of such evidence. (Ed.)

reasonable search." This the Supreme Court refused to do, three justices dissenting. Colorado had not made any law authorizing such unreasonable searches. It merely took the benefit of an unlawful search by a state officer. Must the evidence so obtained be rejected because of the misconduct of the trespasser? There are other means of deterring such official invasions. The victim could sue for damages. The officer might be disciplined by his superiors. At any rate, a survey showed that in 30 of the states the courts had rejected the federal rule in the *Weeks* case. The Court's conclusion was that for a state to rely upon these other sanctions without following the Weeks rule could not be condemned "as falling below the minimal standards assured by the due process clause. . . ."

We hold, therefore, that in a prosecution in a state court for a state crime the Fourteenth Amendment does not forbid the admission of evidence obtained by an unreasonable search and seizure.

B. In *Adamson v. California,* 332 U.S. 46 (1947) a defendant in a state court had not taken the witness stand. A California statute authorized any state judge to mention, to the jury, the failure of a defendant to testify in his own behalf. In this case, the judge did so. After being convicted, the defendant took the case to the U.S. Supreme Court, alleging that the California statute permitted a denial of that "due process of law" which is guaranteed by the Fourteenth Amendment. Defendant correctly asserted that the Fifth Amendment prohibits the *national* government from requiring a defendant to testify, and that, therefore, no *federal* judge can comment on his failure to do so. Defendant then argued that no *state* could force him to testify, nor any *state* judge comment on his failure to testify, because no state can punish him without "due process of law."

The Supreme Court divided, 5 to 4. The majority held that the Fifth Amendment "privilege against self-incrimination" can be asserted only against the national government; by itself it does not apply to *state* action. They held, further, that for a judge to comment on a defendant's voluntary silence was not a violation of "due process of law."

The dissenting judges said that the "due process" clause of the

Fourteenth Amendment incorporated all the procedural safeguards in the Bill of Rights. Thus they believed that any protection a defendant has in a trial in a federal court—such as the privilege against self-incrimination—he also has in a trial in a state court.

C. From John P. Frank, *Cases on the Constitution* (New York: McGraw-Hill Book Co., 1951) 252–253.

As *Adamson* v. *California* shows, justices are not agreed as to the extent to which the states must abide by the principles of the Bill of Rights. A minority believe that the entire Bill of Rights is binding on the states, but a majority hold instead that the states must accord only those particular rights in the Bill of Rights which are absolutely essential to free government.

That stand, of course, leaves the question of just what those "essentials" are. Among the provisions of the Bill of Rights over which there has been greatest controversy as to whether or not it is "essential" is the provision in the Sixth Amendment that "in all criminal prosecutions the accused shall . . . have the assistance of counsel for his defense."

The decisions hold that in federal criminal proceedings the defendant must have a lawyer if he wants one, and that the judge will appoint a lawyer for him . . . if he cannot afford to retain counsel himself. *Johnson* v. *Zerbst*, 304 U.S. 458 (1938). The states also are required to provide counsel in capital cases (cases involving a possible death penalty). *Powell* v. *Alabama*, 287 U.S. 45 (1932).

Here agreement stops. In noncapital cases, the majority has consistently held since *Betts* v. *Brady*, 316 U.S. 455 (1942), that counsel need not be provided if, under all the circumstances, the defendant has a "fair trial" without counsel.[2] The matter was fully reconsidered in *Bute* v. *Illinois*, 333 U.S. 640 (1948), and the same result reached by a vote of 5 to 4, Justices Black, Douglas, Murphy, and Rutledge dissenting.

In the *Betts* case, defendant Betts was charged with robbery in a Maryland state court. He lacked sufficient funds to retain a lawyer and asked the court to appoint one for him. The court

---

[2] In deciding whether the trial without counsel was "fair," the Court has considered such factors as the defendant's age, education, and mental condition, the complexity of the case, the clarity of the charge, etc.

refused. He then served as his own lawyer, calling his own witnesses and examining those of the state. The issue in this case is whether the state was required to appoint counsel for him. The Court, in an opinion by Justice Roberts, held that this was not required. Justices Black, Douglas, and Murphy dissented.

On August 2, 1942, Mr. Benjamin V. Cohen, a lawyer with many claims to fame, one of which was his prominence as one of President Roosevelt's most influential legal aides, and Dean Erwin Griswold of the Harvard Law School published the following letter in *The New York Times:* "Most Americans—lawyers and laymen alike—before the decision in *Betts* v. *Brady* would have thought that the right of the accused to counsel in a serious criminal case was unquestionably a part of our own Bill of Rights. Certainly the majority of the Supreme Court which rendered the decision in *Betts* v. *Brady* would not wish their decision to be used to discredit the significance of that right and the importance of its observance.

"Yet at a critical period in world history, *Betts* v. *Brady* dangerously tilts the scales against the safeguarding of one of the most precious rights of man. For in a free world no man should be condemned to penal servitude for years without having the right of counsel to defend him. The right to counsel, for the poor as well as the rich, is an indispensable safeguard of freedom and justice under law."

Now, assume that you are a lawyer called in to prepare an appeal for one Martin Morris, who has been convicted of burglary in the State of Winnemac. You ascertain the facts to be as follows:

Martin Morris, now 22 years of age, was the son of a prospector in the Rocky Mountains. When he was seven, his father took him on a prospecting trip to Mexico, and he lived with his father in various Mexican mining camps for fourteen years. Upon his father's death he returned, almost penniless, to the United States and got a filling station job in the city of Zenith, State of Winnemac. Though possessing no formal education, he appeared to be an intelligent, upright young man, of rugged but pleasing appearance.

At the filling station a new Chrysler drove in one day. Morris looked at the driver, Flora Flowers, 20, and it was love at first sight. But Flora was the daughter of wealthy Ferdinand Flowers, Judge of Winnemac District Court. The judge did not like the idea of his daughter marrying Martin Morris. After Martin Morris had called at the Flowers' home twice, the judge ordered him to leave, and declared that if he ever returned he would be prosecuted for trespass.

Flora secretly sent a message to Martin, telling him that her parents would be out until midnight on the night of January 15. Martin went to the Flowers' home when the filling station closed at 9 P.M. It was beginning to rain so he took his raincoat. At the Flowers' home, he hung it in the hall closet, where other coats were hanging. He promised Flora never to tell anyone that he had come to her home that night.

Just before midnight, Flora saw the lights of a car turning into the Flowers' driveway. Martin hastened to leave. He forgot his coat but Flora grabbed a coat from the closet and tossed it after him. As he ran out, he came in full view of the headlights and Mrs. Flowers, driving the car, recognized him.

Flora, terrified, denied to her parents that Martin had been in the house. When the judge went upstairs, he found that during his absence his study window had been forced and his safe cracked, and that securities worth $60,000 were missing. He called the police, who immediately went to Martin Morris's lodging house, entered his room, and arrested him for burglary. Just after the arrest, one policeman picked up a raincoat lying across a chair and noted on the inside collar a name tag: "Ferdinand Flowers."

Meanwhile Flora, realizing that she had given the wrong coat to Martin, hastened to the hall closet, took Martin's coat, and hid it in an old costume trunk in the attic. The next morning, Judge Flowers bought an airplane ticket for Flora and sent her off to spend several months with her aged aunt, who lived 2,000 miles away.

Martin Morris went on trial for burglary in Judge Flowers' court. He had no lawyer, nor did anyone tell him he should or could have one. He felt that he could not afford a lawyer, for he had lost his job and had no savings.

At the trial, Mrs. Flowers testified to seeing Martin running from the house. The policemen testified, introducing the judge's raincoat as evidence. A butler in the Flowers' home testified that on an earlier visit, Martin, with one of Flora's bobby pins, had expertly picked the lock of the door of a pantry cupboard that had been locked by mistake. The filling station owner testified that at 9 P.M. on January 15, Martin Morris had whispered to him: "I'm off now to put one over on that old so-and-so, Judge Flowers."

Martin, mindful of his promise to Flora, did not take the stand nor did he produce any witnesses. He did try to cross-examine the butler and the filling station owner, but was inexpert and failed to shake their stories.

Judge Flowers, in charging the jury, said that the jury could consider the fact that the defendant failed to testify as having some possible bearing on his guilt or innocence. The jury found Martin Morris guilty and Judge Flowers sentenced him to five years in State's prison.

Far away, Flora had won her aunt, romantic soul, over to her side. Her aunt gave her $5,000 and Flora secretly returned to Zenith, took a room at a hotel and retained you to appeal Martin Morris' case to the Supreme Court of Winnemac and, if necessary, to the Supreme Court of the United States.

The Constitution of Winnemac has a short bill of rights, consisting of two articles. Article I, in substance, is similar to the First Amendment. Article II provides that "No person shall be deprived of life, liberty, or property without due process of law; nor shall any defendant in a criminal case be compelled to testify against himself, but the prosecutor or the court may comment on his failure to take the witness stand."

Outline your argument for Martin Morris, indicating fully each point that you can reasonably make to show that his conviction was improper and should be set aside. Remember that this is an appeal on matters of law, not a trial of the facts of the case.

PROBLEM 15

Due Process: Protection against Arbitrary Legislative Action

The provisions of the Fifth and Fourteenth Amendments, protecting us from being deprived of "life, liberty, or property without due process of law," might seem to mean that we cannot rightfully be executed (life), imprisoned (liberty), or fined (property) without a proper judicial trial (due process). Actually it means more than this. The essence of "due process" is *reasonableness;* conversely, when a governmental action is unreasonable and arbitrary, and takes away our lives or our freedom or our property, it can be challenged as violating the "due process" clause. The governmental action may be an unfair trial, true enough; but it may also be a statute, a law which (for example) arbitrarily and unreasonably prohibits us from engaging in an occupation of our own choice or prevents us from making profitable use of our property. Questions concerning the fairness of a trial raise issues of what may be called "procedural" due process; when a statute is challenged as arbitrary and unreasonable, we have an issue of "substantive" due process.

Read and consider the following excerpts from a book published in 1942:

Shortly before the close of the last century the case of *Holden* v. *Hardy,* involving a statute of the state of Utah limiting the labor of workers in underground mines or in smelters to eight hours a day except in emergency, was appealed to the Supreme Court. The constitutionality of this progressive statute of the Mormons was attacked on the ground that it deprived both employer and worker of their freedom of contract, and thus, in effect, of their liberty and property without due process of law. This argument the Supreme Court rejected, upholding the law as a valid and reasonable exercise of the police power in view of its limitation to occupations admittedly hazardous and unhealthy. The Court said:

"These employments, when too long pursued, the legislature has judged to be detrimental to the health of the employes, and, so long as there are reasonable grounds for believing that this is so, its decision upon this subject cannot be reviewed by the Federal courts.

While the general experience of mankind may justify us in believing that men may engage in ordinary employments more than eight hours per day without injury to their health, it does not follow that labor for the same length of time is innocuous when carried on beneath the surface of the earth, where the operative is deprived of fresh air and sunlight, and is frequently subjected to foul atmosphere and a very high temperature, or to the influence of noxious gases. . . ."

Two justices dissented, believing that the statute was unconstitutional.

A few years later, a similar case, *Lochner* v. *New York*, involving a New York statute limiting the labor of workers in bakeries to sixty hours a week and ten hours a day, came before the Court. To our surprise we find the minority position in the Utah case becoming the majority decision in this case. Justice Peckham, one of the two justices who dissented in the earlier case, was the author of the majority opinion in the *Lochner* case. In a vitriolic opinion he denied that the law could possibly have any reasonable relation to the issue of public health and condemned it in no uncertain terms as a "mere meddlesome interference with the rights of the individual" and thus contrary to due process of law.

The decision was by the narrow margin of five to four, and two powerful dissenting opinions were written. That by Justice Holmes has become a classic. Adhering closely to the fundamental constitutional issue in the case, he made it clear that he thought the law in question was at least reasonably related to a perfectly valid purpose of governmental activity, the protection of health, and thus should not be considered a violation of the Fourteenth Amendment. Holmes said:

"The Fourteenth Amendment does not enact Mr. Herbert Spencer's *Social Statics*. . . .

"I think that the word liberty in the Fourteenth Amendment is perverted when it is held to prevent the natural outcome of a dominant opinion, unless it can be said that a rational and fair man necessarily would admit that the statute proposed would infringe fundamental principles as they have been understood by the traditions of our people and our law. It does not need research to show that no such sweeping condemnation can be passed upon the statute before us. A reasonable man might think it a proper measure on the score of health."

Moreover, it was the opinion of the minority justices that where there are reasonable grounds for the enactment of a police power statute the Court must accept the judgment of the legislature. Justice Harlan stated in his dissenting opinion that ". . . the State is not amenable to the judiciary, in respect of its legislative enactments, unless such enactments are plainly, palpably, beyond all question, inconsistent with the Constitution of the United States. . . ."

[In 1923] the Court by a five-to-three vote ruled in the case of *Adkins* v. *Children's Hospital* that a minimum wage law for the District of Columbia, limited to women and children, violated the due process clause of the Fifth Amendment. . . . The fact that the law was limited to women and minors, whose good morals and health might have been supposed to constitute a somewhat special problem, carried no weight. Justice Sutherland even made this remarkable statement: "It cannot be shown that well-paid women safeguard their morals more carefully than those who are poorly paid. Morality rests upon other considerations than wages; and there is, certainly, no such prevalent connection between the two as to justify a broad attempt to adjust the latter with reference to the former. . . ."

[In 1937] a minimum wage statute of the state of Washington, passed in 1913 and presumably rendered inoperative at the time of the *Adkins* decision in 1923, was resurrected and enforced by the state. The issue of constitutionality was raised in *West Coast Hotel Co.* v. *Parrish*. The Court . . . began to shift from its generally conservative attitude of the previous decade or so. By a five-to-four vote it upheld the statute and specifically reversed the decision in the District of Columbia [case]. . . .

[In a later decision, the Supreme Court upheld a national minimum wage law, saying]:

"Since our decision in *West Coast Hotel Co.* v. *Parrish*, it is no longer open to question that the fixing of a minimum wage is within the legislative power and that the bare fact of its exercise is not a denial of due process under the Fifth more than under the Fourteenth Amendment. Nor is it any longer open to question that it is within the legislative power to fix maximum hours. Similarly the statute is not objectionable because applied alike to both men and women."

What conclusion can be drawn concerning these cases in which the Supreme Court has endeavored to test the validity of wages and hours legislation in terms of the requirements of the two due process clauses of the Constitution? Can any other conclusion possibly be drawn than that these two clauses are sufficiently vague and ambiguous to enable any judge to read almost anything into them that he wishes to; and that in determining the constitutionality of wages and hours laws the individual justices have been enforcing not the Constitution but their own 'personal economic predilections?' Or in other words, have not the justices been consciously or unconsciously influenced by the claims and counterclaims of various pressure groups, some benefited by such legislation, some feeling themselves injured? If this be so is not the Supreme Court truly an active instrument of government sharing with Congress and the state legislatures the power to legislate? . . .[1]

---

[1] Robert K. Carr, *The Supreme Court and Judicial Review* (New York: Farrar and Rinehart, 1942), 150–159, *passim*.

Is Carr justified in implying that in refusing to strike down state statutes as "unreasonable," modern judges are upholding these laws because they approve of the laws themselves? Or do they uphold laws that they would have opposed if they had been legislators? One can imagine a judge who dislikes a statute yet refrains from denouncing it as "arbitrary and unreasonable," because he does not believe that a court should substitute its preferences for the considered judgment of the legislature. That this is the approach of most Supreme Court justices today is implied by Robert L. Stern:

> The 1937 decisions declared that regulatory legislation would not be found to violate the due process clause merely because it restricted economic liberty. Only restrictions which were in fact arbitrary, or not reasonably related to a proper legislative purpose, it was suggested, would be held unconstitutional in the future. Subsequently, in the Carolene Products case, the Court, through Mr. Justice Stone, stated:
>
> "[T]he existence of facts supporting the legislative judgment is to be presumed, for regulatory legislation affecting ordinary commercial transactions is not to be pronounced unconstitutional unless in the light of the facts made known or generally assumed it is of such a character as to preclude the assumption that it rests upon some rational basis within the knowledge and experience of the legislators. . . .
>
> "[B]y their very nature such inquiries, where the legislative judgment is drawn in question, must be restricted to the issue whether any state of facts either known or which could reasonably be assumed affords support for it. . . ."
>
> Since it is difficult to conceive of any statute for which some rational basis may not be found, this test means that the due process barrier to substantive legislation as to economic matters has been in effect removed—although it still stands in theory against completely arbitrary legislative action. . . .
>
> Although there is no longer doubt as to how the Court will decide cases of this sort, it cannot be said that the Court has limited the due process clause to procedural matters and repudiated the concept of due process as a bar to sufficiently arbitrary or irrational substantive legislation. . . . The Court has cer-

tainly not so stated in express terms, and the opinions still continue to examine legislation under attack to see whether it has a rational basis or is 'substantially related to a legitimate end sought to be attained.' . . .[2]

Review in your text and class notes material concerning "substantive due process."

Now: consider each of the following three situations, all of which arise in the State of Winnemac.

1. A great forest fire breaks out in the hills of northern Winnemac, destroying all the buildings and burning all the trees in beautiful Mishemokwa State Park. A reporter on a crusading newspaper, the Zenith *Scimitar,* is sent to "cover" the fire, and writes a sensational front-page story saying that the fire was started by the negligence of employees of the Great Hills Lumber Company, who left campfires untended on company property just east of the border of the park when a strong east wind was blowing. This story is printed on the morning of May 29, the final day of the regular session of the State Legislature. It arouses great indignation against the Great Hills Lumber Company, which is the largest of five lumber companies operating in the State. A bill is immediately introduced (with special permission of the legislature, as required for the introduction of bills late in the session), prohibiting every owner of a tract of woodland (defined as an area of not less than fifty acres, more than half of which is classified by the State Conservation Department as "forested") from lighting any outdoor fires for any purpose on such property, with heavy (specified) fines to be imposed on the owner if any such fires are lit with or without his permission. At present, most of the "forested" tracts, privately owned, are the property of the five lumber companies, and most of these tracts are adjacent to state parks and state wild life preserves. The bill, introduced in the House, is referred to the committee on conservation, which holds a hurried meeting and gives it a favorable report; it is then brought before the House, and passed by unanimous vote, without debate. The same process

---

[2] Robert L. Stern, "The Problems of Yesteryear—Commerce and Due Process," 4 *Vanderbilt Law Review* 466 (1951).

occurs in the Senate, except that in the Senate, Senator Zachary, a hunting-shooting-fishing enthusiast, makes a brief speech about the beauties of nature and the tragic effects of forest fires. Then the Senate passes the bill unanimously, at 4 p.m. One hour later the legislature adjourns; its five-month regular session, as prescribed by the state constitution, is over.

The Governor of Winnemac must either sign the bill or give it a "pocket veto," allowing it to die without his signature. You are his executive assistant. The Governor tells you that he doesn't particularly want to sign the bill, but that public opinion is so aroused that he cannot simply give it a "pocket veto." If he does not sign it, he must, he feels, issue a statement explaining his position. Because of the uproar, he would prefer that any statement avoid giving any impression that he condones the carelessness of the Great Hills Lumber Company; indeed, he does not wish to appear to be friendly to the lumber industry at all. He asks you for your help, saying that if you cannot furnish him with "a way out" he supposes that he will have to sign the bill. Would he be justified, he asks, in rejecting the bill on some "technical, constitutional ground?" "I don't know much about that stuff," he says, "but I don't want to do anything wrong. If the bill is all right, I don't want to call it unconstitutional. Please, now, give me a memorandum, showing me why the bill may be valid, but also showing me why it may be invalid. Give me both sides, briefly, and then I'll make up my mind."

Prepare the requested memorandum.

2. The State legislature, after lengthy hearings and debate, enacts a law providing that in all business, industrial, and commercial establishments, the regular work day shall not exceed six hours, and that any employee who works more than six hours shall be paid for such overtime work at three times his regular hourly rate of pay. In a time of economic recession, an employer refuses to make such triple-overtime payment. He says, with good reason, that he would go bankrupt if he did so. All his employees agree with him; at his suggestion, they sign an agreement to work for him, overtime, at their regular hourly rates of pay. But this becomes known outside his plant, and soon he is officially charged with violating this law. He says that the law is unconstitutional because it

arbitrarily deprives him and his employees of both liberty and property, and asks the court to dismiss the complaint accordingly.

As the judge, what is your decision, and why?

3. A statute has been passed, after due legislative deliberation, requiring that drug stores be operated only by licensed pharmacists. On the appeal of a druggist who is not a licensed pharmacist, the seven-member State Supreme Court, by a vote of 4 to 3, invalidates the law on the ground that it has deprived such druggists of their livelihood without due process of law, and therefore violates the Fourteenth Amendment.[3] Shortly thereafter, prescriptions improperly filled in the complaining druggist's store result in the death of several leading citizens. A resolution is introduced in the legislature to impeach the four "majority" justices on the ground that they had willfully usurped the legislative power and had decided the case unreasonably and arbitrarily, and hence had failed to live up to the standard of "good behavior" specified by the state constitution's provision that they should hold office "during good behavior."

Indicate those arguments, both for and against this impeachment resolution, which relate specifically to the Court's decision in the druggist's case.

---

[3] Note: The U.S. Constitution is the supreme law of the land. *All* courts, state courts as well as federal courts, are sworn to uphold it and to give effect to the restraints it imposes.

PROBLEM 16

Equal Protection of the Laws

Equality of all men before the law is one of the cardinal principles of justice as that word has come to be defined and applied in the United States. "Equal rights for all, special privileges for none," and other similar aphorisms by which American government has traditionally been characterized drive home the point that no rules of a society that calls itself free can impose prejudicial restrictions on some of its people or reserve special privileges for others. Thus when the Fourteenth Amendment provided that no state shall "deny to any person within its jurisdiction the equal protection of the laws," the Constitution was made entirely consonant with the going concepts of justice.

Of course, equal protection does not require that all men be treated with literal equality by government. Persons are constantly being classified by governmental actions for one purpose or another. Few men receive exactly the same treatment from public officials because few men find themselves in exactly similar circumstances of life. But the great significance of the equal protection clause is that it permits only "reasonable" classifications to be made. Rich men pay higher taxes than poor men because there is a reasonable connection between the ability to pay and the obligation to pay. Therefore, government may choose to classify men on the basis of income for purposes of allocating the tax burden. On the other hand, there is no reasonable relation between the color of a man's hair and any legitimate purpose of government, so a state could not impose special literacy requirements for voting on all redheaded men.

Not only must the classification meet the test of reasonableness, but the purpose of the classification must be one properly within the authority of government. Thus while a reasonable classification for purposes of taxation is permitted, even a reasonable classification for the purpose of suppressing newspapers would be invalid.

Review the material in your text and in your lecture notes dealing with equal protection of the laws.

In each of the following four cases a claim is made that a person is suffering from discrimination which is unjust and which denies to the individual the equal protection of the laws as guaranteed by the Fourteenth Amendment.

1. Jay Hanna claims that his eighteen-year-old son has failed a civil service examination with a score four points under the minimum passing mark set by the Catawba State Civil Service Commission. As a result of failing the examination, young Hanna has not been able to secure a job as a file clerk with the State Department of Finance, on which his heart was set. Young Hanna says that the reason for his failure was his inability to handle higher mathematics, but upon investigation it appears that the questions were fairly simple arithmetic problems.

2. J. A. Jakasian, President of the Armenian-American Federation, claims that his son's application for admission to Winnemac State University has been turned down along with the applications of every other prospective student of the past several years whose name ended in the letters "ian," the usual ending for Armenian names. In each case the University has claimed that lack of housing facilities was the reason for denying the applications, but Jakasian has data showing that the rejected applicants' grades on the entrance examinations were satisfactory and that other male applicants have invariably been admitted provided their grades were adequate. Jakasian also has some press clippings in which the President of the University Board of Trustees is reported as having made insulting remarks about Armenians.

3. The State University of Catawba provides that all undergraduate male students must take military training if physically able to do so. Any prospective students who claim religious scruples against such training are admitted to the University but are required to attend an extension branch in another city during their first two years. The extension branch offers only a two-year program, and its academic standing is far below that of the world-famous Catawba U. William Penn, a Quaker and a pacifist, claims that he has been "shunted off to a second-rate school" in violation of his constitutional rights.

4. John Wright, a Negro, has been refused admission to the examination given by the State of Winnemac for the licensing of architects. The state board of examiners claims that Wright's academic preparation is inadequate for admission to the examination. Wright graduated in 1946 from Winnemac A. & I., the only state-supported college for Negroes, where he took all the courses available that related to architecture. Admittedly, however, these courses were not on a par, in quantity or quality, with those of other colleges providing architectural training. At the time Wright attended school, Winnemac A. & I. was the only state college Negroes were allowed to attend.

As a written exercise or for class discussion, for each of the four cases:

A. Outline all the arguments that might be used to support the claim. Show in what respects it may be argued that the person is suffering an injustice, and in what ways this injustice violates his constitutional right to equal protection of the laws.

B. Outline the counterarguments that might be used.

C. Decide whether the equal protection clause of the Fourteenth Amendment has or has not been violated. Explain fully the reasons for your decision.

PART VI

THE POLITICAL ARENA: PARTIES, INTEREST GROUPS, ELECTIONS

PROBLEM 17

Distortion of the Representative System

Read carefully the following selections from Gordon Baker, *Rural Versus Urban Political Power.*

In 1955 inequality of legislative representation is solidly entrenched in all but a handful of the forty-eight states. Most urban areas are discriminated against in at least one house of their state legislature, and in many cases in both houses. This situation can be explained by two major causes—constitutional provisions and legislative failure to reapportion properly.

Reasons for Unbalanced Representation

Constitutional Restrictions on Populous Areas. In the first place, a number of state constitutions provide for representation of area regardless of population. This takes various forms. Extreme cases are the town representation provisions for the lower houses of the legislatures in Vermont and Connecticut. In the latter state, Hartford's 177,397 residents send two representatives, as does Union town, with a population of only 261. In Vermont, 49 inhabitants of Victory town enjoy the same share of the lower house as Burlington's 33,155. . . .

Other frequent methods of limiting larger urban areas are: formulas and ratios which allow progressively less representation to more populous communities; provisions against dividing counties into districts; minimum representation for each county; maximum limits for populous counties and cities. For instance, Iowa's constitution ensures a double advantage to rural areas by limiting any one county to a single senator and by guaranteeing a representative to each of the state's 99 counties, regardless of size. Since the lower house is limited to 108 seats, the restrictive ceiling on the nine most populous counties is obvious.

In a number of cases constitutional barriers are an accidental remnant from apparently convenient arrangements in the eighteenth and nineteenth centuries, set before the growth of urban centers resulted in an increasingly undemocratic situation. In an earlier day when population was spread less unevenly and the total number of counties in a state remained fairly small, provisions for minimum representation could be justified. Later on, however, shrewd politicians in some states found a handy advantage in creating many additional counties as a means of increasing legislative strength. Also, special limitations on the growing populous areas became frequent as rural forces modified constitutions in many states while they could still command a majority.

As a result by 1955 there were only twelve states with no constitutional restrictions of any consequence upon a democratic pattern of representation in both houses. . . .

A second—though less extensive—cause of unrepresentative state legislatures is the failure of the lawmaking bodies to keep districting arrangements abreast of population changes. Most state constitutions call for periodic reapportionment of one or both houses, usually after every federal census. This requirement, however, is often more honored in the breach than in the observance. Framers of state constitutions were wise in providing for future shifts in representation to keep pace with newer population patterns; but they were either optimistic or naïve in leaving such a function to the very body affected by the change.

This unhappy fact has been demonstrated convincingly by the record in all but a few states, so that even when there have been no constitutional barriers to democratic representation, inequalities have resulted from legislative inaction. Tennessee elects a law-making body that reflects population patterns of 1900. Minnesota's present apportionment dates back to 1913, Indiana's to 1921. Washington last reapportioned in 1930, and then only when an aroused urban electorate employed the popular initiative to overcome thirty years of inaction by the legislature. Failure to reapportion is the sole source of inequitable representation in six states and contributes substantially (in addition to constitutional restrictions) to a distorted picture in about ten more.

Since reapportionment has been so frequently stipulated in state constitutions, one might assume that these requirements could be enforced. However, numerous appeals have found state courts traditionally reluctant to interfere with the legislatures, even though judges have consistently held that reapportionment is a "mandatory duty." While the judiciary has not hesitated to invalidate positive acts of malapportionment (especially when flagrant abuses of legislative discretion are evident), it has left untouched the more serious negative process of "silent gerrymandering" caused by inaction. Judicial caution is partially understandable, since forcing a coordinate branch of government to perform a positive constitutional duty is more difficult than merely invalidating an unconstitutional act. However, it does seem that a problem so crucial to the very basis of government might have impelled courts to find ways of enforcing legislative obligations. . . .

The reasons for such a widespread failure of legislatures to live up to state constitutional redistricting requirements are not difficult to find. In almost any reapportionment a number of legislators would be personally affected through the abolition or consolidation of districts. A legislator naturally finds the *status quo* under which he was elected to be satisfactory and usually dreads the prospect of a new and unknown constituency. Also, many refuse to move because their particular party would lose strength. In almost all cases a dominant consideration has been the increasing disparities in rural and urban popular strength, with legislators from smaller communities showing a hostility to growing cities. Finally, interest groups benefiting from the *status quo* have fought reapportionment.

A point deserving emphasis is the fact that while opposition to reapportionment is more frequent among rural legislators, not all of their city colleagues are eager for a change. While urban areas have consistently outgained rural regions in population, these gains do not occur evenly within cities. Within some large urban areas, many districts gain at the expense of others. For example, Cook County (Chicago) has for decades been grossly underrepresented in a rural-dominated state legislature. Yet until 1955 the five smallest and hence most overrepresented districts were not found, as might be expected, in the downstate region, but were located in declining areas of Chicago. Cook County districts varied in size from 39,368 to 700,325.

Extent of Unbalanced Representation

As might be expected, the largest city within most states is the primary target of discriminatory representation. New York, Chicago, Los Angeles, St. Louis, Detroit, Baltimore, Atlanta, Birmingham, and Providence are all well-publicized examples. The list could be extended to include most principal cities. . . .

In addition to cities proper, fast-growing suburban areas are often among the most severely underrepresented constituencies. As once-sparsely-settled districts increase in population manyfold, additional inequalities arise. . . . It is significant that political equality went long unnoticed by some state legislatures until growing suburban areas began to feel the pinch of inadequate representation. This is doubtless due to the fact that political sentiment in suburbia is generally conservative and often quite compatible with rural views on how the state should be governed. . . .

Consequences of Unbalanced Representation

The far-reaching effects of rural legislative advantage are not always sufficiently appreciated. Whenever "rotten borough" situations have aroused publicity the problem is often treated in isolation, as though the controversy concerned only cities versus farmers. Such a view obscures the widespread ramifications of urban-rural representation. One of the most important effects of a distorted legislative pattern concerns the political party balance. In a number of states the party split bears a high correlation to the extent of urbanism. As a general rule, the Democratic Party in the North and West is stronger in city districts, while Republicans usually find most solid support in rural and suburban regions. However, in some border states—Oklahoma, Kentucky, Maryland, and Delaware are examples—Republican support is often weaker in rural than in urban and suburban areas. This is becoming increasingly true also in some parts of the South, though the real contests in that region result from Democratic intraparty differences, with liberal elements usually stronger in urban areas. In fact, the hard core of Southern conservatism lies in the rural "black belt," where a small white minority, grossly overrepresented in state legislatures as well as in other political institutions of the section, exercises enormous power.

With this general situation in mind, it is obvious that a representative system allowing urban areas less legislative strength than their populations merit gives an immediate advantage to the political party or faction that is stronger in smaller towns and rural areas. The imbalance varies from state to state, but it exists at least to some degree in most of them. This can result in legislative control by the actual minority party, even in states which vote heavily in the opposite direction. In other instances, even if the successful party represents a popular majority, its legislative strength is often greatly bloated due to a monopoly of rural seats. . . .

While political parties in many states are not noted for having a high degree of internal cohesion or unity of purpose, there are often issues on which the party balance can make a decided difference. This is particularly true when the governorship is held by a popular leader who has dramatized certain matters of public policy. Yet a misrepresentative legislature (or even one house) can nullify whatever attempt is made to embody into law a program apparently endorsed by the electorate. Even a governor's choice of his own cabinet and other important appointive posts must often meet the approval of a hostile upper house. . . .

The overrepresentation of rural areas means that organized agricultural interests are usually in a favorable position to influence state legislation. At the same time the system places certain urban interest groups at a disadvantage. However, those urban interests whose policies are compatible with the general outlook of rural representatives are in a more favorable position.

This fact helps explain the behavior of some urban business interests that staunchly defend inequitable representation for their own areas. These groups apparently find greater representation for their political outlook among rural delegates. The alliance is not surprising in view of the frequent similarity in attitudes held by both interests. In addition, representatives from rural constituencies are often not farmers, but small-town lawyers and business men. On many issues they share a natural community of interests with city groups representing a similar social and economic outlook. By contrast, other urban interests, notably labor groups, seldom find support from rural representatives. . . .[1]

The state of Winnemac fairly well typifies the political situations described in the selection you have read. Winnemac is located in the Midwest. In the past it has been a predominantly agricultural state, settled for the most part by people from New England. In one corner of the state—known as "Rebel Corner"—the people are of Southern origin. "Rebel Corner" once was fairly densely populated and just after the Civil War contained about one fourth of Winnemac's population. Its soil is largely exhausted today, however, and the area has lost population steadily since 1900 until now only about 8 per cent of the people of the state try to eke out an income from the badly eroded hills of "Rebel Corner."

Elsewhere in Winnemac farms are generally large and prosperous, producing corn, hogs, beef cattle, and dairy products. The farming portions of the state have virtually no other sources of income than agriculture and the trading and banking that depend upon agriculture. The political life in this part of the state usually revolves around the courthouses and the commercial leaders of the many small towns that serve as market centers for the agricultural community.

For nearly a century after the settlement of Winnemac in the

[1] Gordon E. Baker, *Rural Verus Urban Political Power* (New York: Random House, 1955), 11–14, 18–19, 21, 23–24.

1840's the only city of any size was Zenith. Zenith was a major center of finance and distribution for the whole agricultural region of which Winnemac is the heart. Yet in 1870 the city contained only 12 per cent of the state's population. After 1900 heavy industry in the form of steel and automobile manufacturing was added to the economic base of Zenith. With the steel and auto plants came a substantial growth in population. Heavy Catholic immigration into Zenith from 1900 to 1920 provided the basis for Democratic party dominance of the city's political life. This dominance has been maintained in recent years by the strong labor unions that have been organized in the manufacturing and distribution industries of the city. Today Zenith has about one third of the population of Winnemac. Since the war, however, the most striking growth has been in the suburban areas around the city where upper middle and middle income groups have sought refuge from the industrialized city. This metropolitan area outside the city has grown from 1 per cent of the state population eighty years ago to nearly 10 per cent today.

Since World War II two Winnemac towns, Middletown and Plainville, have been transformed with remarkable rapidity from marketing centers of a few thousand (2 per cent of the population in 1870) to burgeoning centers of industry, and each now has about 10 per cent of the population of Winnemac. Middletown has become a center of airplane manufacturing. Workers have come in from all over the country, and the plants are strong centers of the same union that is one of the most powerful in Zenith. Plainville is now the site of several food-processing plants. The labor force for these plants has come primarily from "Rebel Corner," and these workers are not unionized.

Most of the time the statewide elections in Winnemac are very closely contested by the two major parties. The Democrats, relying primarily upon labor support, normally produce about a two-to-one majority in Zenith and do nearly as well in Middletown. In Plainville the Democrats receive about 55 per cent of the vote. The rest of Winnemac, including the suburban areas around Zenith, gives about 60 per cent of its vote to Republican candidates. Rural Democratic strength is found chiefly in "Rebel Corner," and tends not to be particularly sympathetic to the labor-oriented Democratic elements in the urban centers.

The Winnemac state constitution was adopted in 1870 and provides as follows:

The legislature shall apportion the state every ten years beginning with the year 1871 by dividing the state into 100 districts which shall be formed of contiguous and compact territory, bounded by county lines unless a county is entitled to more than one representative, and which shall contain as nearly as practicable an equal number of inhabitants.

(Provisions for state senatorial districts are similar except that 50 districts are established rather than 100.)

The last reapportionment in the state of Winnemac occurred in 1871, and the courts have declined to compel reapportionment.

The governor and four other administrative officials of the state are elected by popular vote from the state at large.

For written exercise or class discussion:

A. Calculate the approximate strength in the state legislature of the two parties. What would be the strength of each party in the legislature, if reapportionment had occurred in accordance with the constitutional provision?

B. The urban business community, the more prosperous farmers, and organized labor are the major active interest groups concerned with the decisions of the state government of Winnemac. For each of these groups, indicate whether the governor or the legislature would usually be more sympathetic to the group's goals. Explain your answer.

C. Consider the following two proposals for state legislative action and, for each proposal, answer three questions: (a) What stand would each of the three major interest groups take on the issue? (b) Will the proposal get more support from the governor or from the legislature? (c) What effect, if any, would the failure to reapportion the legislature have on the chances for passage of each proposal?

   1. A proposal to establish a four-year college in Zenith, to be supported by state revenue substantially derived from

taxes on real estate. The college will provide technical vocational training leading to skilled employment in industry and the standard liberal arts curriculum. Tuition charges will be low, and no dormitory facilities are planned.
2. A bill to provide a state "right-to-work" law, forbidding collective bargaining contracts that provide for a "union shop." The effect of this bill would be to make it more difficult for labor unions to organize or to maintain their existing membership.

PROBLEM 18

Political Action by an Interest Group

In the State of Winnemac (one of the United States) state-wide elections have, for years, been very closely contested between the Republicans and the Democrats. Each party, moreover, is badly split within itself, each having two "wings" or "factions" with rival leaders.

The laws of Winnemac provide for nominations to be made by "recognized" parties at either a party convention or state-administered primary elections on the second Tuesday of September. To be a "recognized" party, entitled to have its name on the ballot, either (1) the party's candidate for governor must have received at least 10 per cent of the total vote cast at the previous election, or (2) in the case of a new party, petitions must be filed by August 1 of an election year, signed by at least 3 per cent of the registered voters of the State. In Winnemac, this means that a new party can be effectively established only if 45,000 registered voters petition for its "recognition."

The Fuertes Association of Winnemac is composed of 1025 ardent bird watchers, of whom 800 live in Zenith County. Normally, they are more interested in birds than in politics, but almost all of them, traditionally, vote the Republican ticket.

The Fuertes Association adopted a resolution urging the Winnemac legislature to pass a bill requiring that all cats should wear bells. Such a bill was passed by both Houses but was vetoed by the Governor, a Republican, who wrote a humorous and somewhat derisive veto message. The House overrode the veto. In the Senate, composed of 30 members, a roll-call vote was taken on the question of overriding the veto. The Winnemac Constitution requires that a bill that was vetoed must receive a two-thirds vote in order to be enacted despite the veto.

As the roll was called in the Senate, the result became more and more in doubt. The name of Senator Zachary, Republican, of Zenith County was the last name on the roll of Senators. Before his name was called, the vote stood 19 to override the veto, 10 to sustain it. But shortly before the Senate clerk reached his name, Senator Zachary arose, said, quite audibly: "I've got to leave; I've got a date to go duck-shooting down on the Wamusquett marshes," and walked out of the Chamber. The final vote, therefore, was 19 to 10, or less than two to one; and so the veto was sustained and the bill was killed.

The members of the Fuertes Association were disappointed and angry. They were especially angry at the Governor, many of them expressing the hope that he would be defeated in the next election. However, they were still determined to have their bill enacted, another year.

Review in your text and class notes material on the political techniques of interest groups and read and consider the following passages pertaining thereto:

> When pressure organizations attempt to direct upon a legislator influence from his constituency, they have a choice of two broad sorts of pressure: the "rifle" type and the "shot-gun" type. . . .
>
> The "shot-gun" type of pressure campaign encourages all and sundry to wire their Congressmen. Often this sort of effort is but an incident in a short-term campaign designed to build up public favor for or against a particular piece of legislation. The object may be to panic Congress into action by promoting the appearance of a universal and insistent public demand. The opposing strategy will be to delay action until the dust settles in order that considerations other than the volume of artificially induced clamor may govern. The pressure organization may,

indeed, in some of these campaigns on particular pieces of legislation succeed in activating a latent public sentiment to the service of its cause.

Letters and telegrams have some effect on some legislators on some bills, but a safe guess would be that most of these missives fall on fallow ground. Legislators speak with disdain of a flood of communications similar in phraseology and obviously stimulated by some interested party. Even if a legislator is disposed to be guided by these instructions, he soon finds that advice is offered often in ignorance of the parliamentary situation, at an untimely moment, or without an understanding of the details of the bill. Legislators, however, speak with tears in their voices of the influence of the letter written in pencil on a low-grade paper without complete mastery of the rules of English composition.

Pressure-group lobbyists may play a role in shepherding a bill through the legislative mill. The processes of legislation are intricate and the channels can become clogged at many points. Lobbyists may give a push at this point and that to keep their bill in motion and may serve both as gadflies and strategic advisers to their legislative friends. If the purpose is to defeat a bill, their skill and attention may be even more effective. The procedure of legislatures gives great advantage to those who seek to prevent action. At many stages, from committee consideration to executive approval, a bill can be killed, and an alert legislative counsel may perhaps carry the day at one step if not at another.

Implicit in the importunities of a lobbyist may be the threat that his organization will at the next primary or election throw its strength against the legislator who does not vote right. Historically the most impressive example of this type of persuasion has been the Anti-Saloon League which had enough of a following to determine the results of many elections. Most groups that have a numerically large membership analyze the voting records of legislators and inform the membership of the candidates' stands on issues of concern to them. Such operations may affect some votes, but it is doubtful that most legislators need have much fear of such activity. The number of voters who know both the name of their Congressman and how he voted on any measure are quite small, and, of those, the candidate may gain as much by his vote on one measure as he loses on another. Moreover, often the admonitions of a pressure group only re-enforce other pressures on a legislator. A Representative from a working-class district may have his back stiffened by a word from the AFL-CIO but he need not fear a candidate backed, say, by the state manufacturers' association. On the other hand, a Representative from a suburban Republican district who consistently supports labor measures has no right to be astonished if he faces primary opposition financed by those interests against whose wishes he has voted. In any case, it is not so much the rank-and-file legislator who receives the attention of pressure groups in campaigns as it is the conspicuous advocate or opponent of measures. The legislator who spearheads a movement that touches some interest in the pocketbook should give close attention to his political fences. . . .

What estimate is to be made of the significance of pressure-group representations in the determination of a legislator's votes? The unsatisfactory answer is that it "all depends." It depends in part on the strength of other factors bearing on legislative behavior and those factors vary from bill to bill, from time to time, and from legislator to legislator. The strength of party leadership may at times offset group pressures; the insistent but inarticulate demands of constituency may outweigh group representations. Another variable is the nature of the group itself. One group may be able to guide some legislators along the desired direction and another may be completely powerless. Still another variable may be the type of bill. All these factors and others are mixed in proportions that vary from legislator to legislator as well as from roll call to roll call. Such complexities warn against the easy generalization that Congressmen are invariably pushed around by lobbyists. . . .[1]

Now assume that the officers of the Fuertes Association consult you, as an impartial expert in political science, and ask your advice as to how they should proceed. It is April of an election year. They suggest that:

---

[1] V. O. Key, *Politics, Parties, and Pressure Groups* (New York: Thomas Y. Crowell Co., 4th edition, 1958), 149–153 *passim*.

A. They might try to prevent the governor's renomination in the Republican primary.

B. They might form a new party, hold a convention, and nominate their own candidate for governor.

C. They might ignore the contest for governor and devise other methods designed to gain their main objective of belling the cats.

1. Prepare as a written exercise or for class discussion a report, advising them with respect to the strong and weak points of each of these three suggestions, and specifying the methods you believe they should utilize.

2. Would your advice be the same, if the governor were a Democrat?

PROBLEM 19

More "Responsibility" in Political Parties?

Review in your text, and in your class notes, materials relating to democracy, interest groups, and political parties.

Read, thoughtfully, the following statements about two important American interest group associations.[1]

The National Association of Manufacturers, an influential business interest group, claims a membership of 15 per cent of all manufacturing firms in the United States employing eight or more workers. It depends particularly on large firms, which tend to dominate its policy. It has been interested in a minimum of government regulation of the economy; government policies providing particular benefits to business (usually large business); and government policies to regulate, limit, or diminish the power of organized labor. Its political tactics include the expenditure of large sums of money, aimed at exerting more indirect and unpublicized than open or public influence in government. It has operated largely through attempts to mold a public opinion generally favorable to business objectives, as an indirect influence on government; and through skilled lobbying, emphasizing direct contacts with congressmen and other government officials, testimony before congressional committees, and written statements or briefs for its position. It has stressed public relations, and undertaken expensive propaganda campaigns as major tools of influence. It does

---

[1] Statements prepared by the authors, 1958.

not directly endorse candidates for Congress or other government offices, though it has provided its member firms with congressional voting records and other information about the actions of government officials. Officials of its member firms are often very influential in their communities, or nationally.

The combined American Federation of Labor-Congress of Industrial Organizations encompasses some 15,000,000 members in various skilled trades and industries. Its members thus comprise about one third of all nonfarm workers currently employed in the U.S. It is interested in considerable government intervention in the economy, particularly in relation to regulation of business and to wages and hours standards; in government policies to improve working conditions and uphold labor union organization and promote union bargaining power; it is also interested in promoting social security measures, public housing programs, and other "welfare" policies. It seeks to mobilize its mass membership, through local unions and in election districts, to register, to work and canvass actively in election campaigns (including primary elections), and to vote. It may directly endorse, usually through its local branches, often on the basis of information from the national headquarters, candidates for Congress and other public offices, both in primary and in general elections. Thus, its political tactics stress mass, public action, although it also engages in direct lobbying and in some general propaganda.

Read and analyze the following recommendations concerning political parties, proposed by a Committee of the American Political Science Association in 1950.

> We propose a Party Council of 50 members. Such a Party Council should consider and settle the larger problems of party management, within limits prescribed by the National Convention; propose a preliminary draft of the party platform to the National Convention; interpret the platform in relation to current problems; . . . consider and make recommendations to appropriate party organs in respect to congressional candidates; and make recommendations to the National Convention, the

National Committee, or other appropriate party organs with respect to conspicuous departure from general party decisions by state or local party organizations. . . .

Establishment of a Party Council would do much to coordinate the different party organizations, and should be pressed with that objective in mind. . . . Local party organizations should be imbued with a stronger sense of loyalty to the entire party organization and feel their responsibility for promoting the broader policies of the party. This can be done by fostering local party meetings, regularly and frequently held, perhaps monthly. The national organization may deal with conspicuous or continued disloyalty on the part of any state organization. Consideration should be given to the development of additional means of dealing with rebellious and disloyal state organizations. . . .

There has been much difference of opinion as to the exact binding quality of a platform. All of this suggests the need for appropriate machinery, such as a Party Council, to interpret and apply the national program in respect to doubts or details. When that is done by way of authoritative and continuing statement, the party program should be considered generally binding [on party leaders and on party members in Congress and other government offices]. . . . Party platforms should be formulated at least every two years. National platforms should emphasize general party principles and national issues. State and local platforms should be expected to conform to the national platform on matters of general party principle or on national policies.[2]

This proposal for a co-ordinating, directing party council is aimed at bringing about one major purpose. This goal is what the APSA Committee called "more responsible" political parties in the United States—that is to say, parties that would commit themselves to relatively clear-cut positions of program or policy on national issues; parties that would support this national program in a relatively united or cohesive way at both national and local

---

[2] Committees on Political Parties, American Political Science Association, *Toward a More Responsible Two-Party System* (New York: Rinehart and Company, 1950), 5–7.

levels; and parties that would bind their leaders and their members in government office, especially Congress, to work for the national program. The proposal raises two questions. The first is whether, given the way in which the American political system as a whole generally operates, merely setting up a Party Council as a piece of formal party machinery would *in fact* result in "more responsible," more "programmatic," more "disciplined" parties, as the APSA Committee believes it would. This question entails a *prediction*, based on a factual analysis of American political life—and while political science cannot match the natural sciences in assurance of prediction, some effort along this line is possible. Next, *assuming* that the proposed party council *would* produce "more responsible" parties, the second question is whether such a development would be considered *desirable* or *undesirable*. This question involves the *value judgments* that various participants in American politics might make concerning the assumed results of the proposal, and the *grounds* on which these judgments of "good" or "bad" would rest.

Prepare as a written exercise or for class discussion, thoughtful answers to the following:

1. Decide, on the basis of what you know about American politics, interest groups, and parties,

    (a) whether you think the APSA Committee proposal to include a Party Council as a part of the formal machinery of American parties is one which *in fact* could be put into effect in the near future; and

    (b) whether you think the establishment of such a council would *in fact* result in a "more responsible," more "programmatic" party system in the United States.

Consider carefully the *evidence* and *analysis* upon which you base your predictions in (a) and (b).

2. Now, regardless of your own conclusions in Question 1, (a) and (b), above, *assume* that the establishment of a party council along the lines of the APSA Committee proposal would *in practice* result in "more responsible," more "programmatic" American parties. On the basis of this assumption, decide whether you

would favor or oppose the APSA Committee recommendations, *if* you were an intelligent, well-informed person who is:

(a) a state *Democratic* party leader in Mississippi;
(b) a local *Republican* party leader in a working-class district in a major northern city, like New York or Chicago;
(c) a *Democratic* Congressman from a northern city district in which the population is approximately half Negro;
(d) a national official of the National Association of Manufacturers;
(e) a national official of the AFL-CIO.

3. For each of the five "roles" in Question 2 above, consider carefully the particular *grounds* on which, in each case, you would base your support for or opposition to the APSA Committe proposal for a party council. Give attention both to the probable relevant facts which would be involved in each case, and to the special group, party, or factional interests you would probably, in each position, like to see served.

PROBLEM 20

Availability and Presidential Nominations

The nomination of candidates for President of the United States takes place amid the colorful and sometimes spontaneous, sometimes contrived hoopla of the national party conventions. But behind the flamboyant oratory and the frenetic demonstrations of enthusiasm and confidence, much careful calculation goes on. The main objective of the party in convention assembled is to nominate the man, fit for the presidency, who is most likely to win the election. The various interests to which the party leaders look for support and the principles to which they subscribe cannot be ignored. But the primary concern of all the delegates is usually the desirability of electoral victory.

From the point of view of the convention delegates, the candidate should be the man with the widest and most powerful positive appeal to voters, and with the fewest drawbacks and negative attributes. He must be able to pull wavering adherents away from the opposition, and win a large bloc of the uncommitted voters to his banner without alienating any large groups that usually support his party. If a candidate is too closely identified with a particular interest, he may alienate another competing interest whose support is necessary to win the election. Identification with a racial or religious minority has often been regarded as a severe handicap in seeking an electoral majority. Political eminence itself may be a handicap, since a man in political office must constantly make decisions, and while these decisions may win support from some groups, they may also dissatisfy others. Thus many Republicans feared that Senator Robert A. Taft could not win election as President in 1952, largely because the definite positions he had taken in the Senate had made him too many enemies. This seems to be one factor that makes it more difficult for senators—who must vote on many issues of national controversy—to win the nomination than it is for governors, whose unavoidable commitments take place in one state only, and who seldom if ever have to make actual decisions on national issues.

Yet a candidate must stand for something. Otherwise there would be no positive reason for anyone to support him. He should have accomplished something in his life that attracted favorable national attention. Though in rare cases this accomplishment may not have had anything to do with politics, the number of businessmen or professional soldiers who have sought the nomination successfully is rather small. Normally, the most likely candidates are men who have taken positive steps in their political careers to win strong backing from some major groups in the country, while holding their enemies to a minimum. No candidate can reasonably be expected to win unanimous approval; some enemies are unavoidable. But any serious aspirant for the nomination needs to win the support of a majority of the convention delegates, and he is unlikely to do so unless they are convinced that he will prove to be a strong vote-getter in the national election.

The likelihood that a candidate can win on election day is often related to his strength in particular key states. The man from a state with a large bloc of electoral votes is often in a better position to fight for the nomination than a man from a small state. Even more important, an aspirant who has demonstrated his vote-getting ability in a state that may give its electoral vote to either party—a politically "marginal" state—is more likely to be nominated than a man from a state where the vast majority of voters is firmly wedded to one party. Thus, since the Civil War, twenty-five of the forty-two nominees of the major parties have been residents of New York or Ohio, states that have been both large in electoral vote and marginal as to party. An aspirant from such a state often has the large convention delegation from his own state behind him, and wins the support of other delegates because he seems likely to be especially popular in his own state with its big electoral vote. Furthermore, if he has already proved his vote-getting ability locally by getting elected governor or senator by a big majority, he will probably be popular elsewhere, especially in those states where the dominant interest groups are similar to those that are the chief source of his popularity in his home state.

Of course, every presidential convention presents a picture that is unique in some respects, and the factors that are crucial in determining one nomination may be less important in another year. But the characteristics usually decisive can be summed up in the term "availability." The delegates to each convention ordinarily assess the candidates and try to select the "most available"—the most likely to win. This does not mean that they tend to choose unfit men; except in very rare instances when a party feels either smugly confident or utterly hopeless, the delegates refrain from nominating a candidate who is obviously unsuitable for the presidency, because he is unlikely to win. But among the suitable aspirants, the term "availability" sums up the factors that usually decide the nomination.

Assume that in a preconvention campaign four men have been mentioned as the leading candidates for the presidential nomination of their party. Assume, too, that six states where party strength is approximately equal seem to hold the key to success in the election. The other states are regarded as reasonably safe for one party or the other, and each party can count on receiving just about half of these safe electoral votes. Thus the delegates to the convention will try to nominate the man who, in the November election, seems most likely to win a majority (sixty-eight or more) of the total electoral votes of these key states. The six states and the number of electoral votes in each state are:

California 32 votes   Massachusetts 16 votes   Ohio 25 votes
Illinois   27 votes   Minnesota   11 votes   Texas 24 votes

Consult your text and lecture notes for any material relating to the general patterns of politics in these states. Pay particular attention to the interests that might affect the political decisions of residents of these states. Additional data may be obtained in *The World Almanac, The Encyclopedia Americana,* and *The Congressional Quarterly Almanac.* Your instructor may be able to direct you to more extended treatments of the politics of these states.

Availability and Presidential Nominations 159

The four most likely nominees and the known relevant facts concerning each are as follows:

A. Joseph O'Keefe: Fifty-four years old, Catholic, married, six children; first-term Governor of Massachusetts, having won an upset victory over the previous incumbent; formerly head of the state AFL-CIO; state senator for several years and national committeeman from Massachusetts before becoming governor, early supporter of previous party nominee for President; as governor has actively promoted expansion of school construction and public housing and has vigorously enforced existing legislation designed to eliminate racial discrimination in employment; in speeches during preconvention campaign has placed most emphasis on attacking foreign aid and advocating higher protective tariffs, arguing that the United States must follow a more self-sufficient foreign policy.

B. Robert Ballard: Fifty-five years old, Episcopalian, bachelor; President of Ballard Electric, a comparatively small company in Ohio which under Ballard's leadership has been highly successful as a manufacturer of electronic equipment; never has run for elective office or been closely identified with the party organization; recently served as chairman of President's Bipartisan Commission on Governmental Reorganization and was widely acclaimed in newspaper editorials for his impartial public service; has fostered friendly relations with the union in his company; has taken no pronounced stands on any of the leading controversial questions of the day, except to plead for greater co-operation between the United States and other nations of the free world and urge that foreign aid be increased.

C. Peter Hansen: Forty-six years old, Lutheran, married, no children, severely wounded in World War II; Governor of Minnesota in second term, having won large majorities in each election; former congressman who served on Agriculture Committee in House of Representatives; an outspoken advocate of high price supports for farm commodities, especially for wheat and dairy products; as governor permitted a "right-to-work" bill to become law without his signature, thus making it more difficult for labor unions to maintain their memberships; has concentrated all his preconvention fire on the farm issue; is regarded as somewhat independent of his state party organization, preferring to act in his own name rather than that of his party, frequently ignoring his party's candidates during election campaigns and rejecting the party organization's patronage requests in the state government.

D. James Jonas: Sixty-four years old, Presbyterian, married, two grown sons and six grandchildren, handsome and gifted orator; Senator from Washington, former professor of economics at the state university, author of several books on world economic problems; first man of his party to win election to the Senate from his state in several decades; emphasized in his senatorial campaigns the need for massive federal construction of electric power facilities in the Northwest and the need to expand expenditures for air power and aircraft carriers; in the Senate has continued to stress these issues and has been very critical of the leadership of both parties on these matters; during four years in the Senate has become a leading spokesman on questions of economic policy and taxation and is regarded by many senators of both parties as the leading expert in public life on the intricacies of these problems, has generally opposed large-scale tax reduction, particularly in the upper income brackets, but would reduce taxes on low incomes in time of recession; has recently become a member of the Senate Foreign Relations Committee and has attracted favorable international publicity for his speeches on foreign policy problems, in which he has advocated greater international efforts to control thermonuclear weapons.

As a written exercise or for class discussion:

You are a newspaper columnist covering the convention. On the basis of the available information, you are to predict whom the delegates will nominate as they seek to name the man most likely to win a majority (sixty-eight or more) of the electoral votes in the November election from the six key states indicated. In so doing, follow these procedures:

1. As accurately as you can—complete confidence is not possible—assign each key state to the candidate with the greatest positive appeal to the interests in that state, explaining fully your reasons for each assignment. Remember that the electoral votes of each state must be assigned as a bloc and no state's electoral vote can be divided among two or more candidates.

2. If, at first, no candidate seems able to win a majority, some compromises and second choices will have to be made. Take the votes of the candidate receiving the least support in your first calculation and assign these votes to the remaining candidate or candidates with the next greatest appeal to the interests in the state or states involved. Continue this process until one candidate has a majority. Explain your reasons for each assignment.

3. On the basis of your understanding of the two major parties in the United States, would you rank the candidates differently for the Republican nomination than for the Democratic nomination? Explain your answer.

PROBLEM 21

Presidential Nominating Procedures

It is not easy to define an American political party. Edmund Burke's description of a party as "a body of men united . . . on some particular principle in which they are all agreed" hardly fits either the Republicans or the Democrats. But we can say that whatever else parties may be or do, they play one recognizable and central role in the political process. They bring about the nomination of candidates for public office. There is usually a place on the ballot for "third party" and independent candidates, but most major elections in the United States are really contests between the *nominees* of the Republican party and the Democratic party.

In the old days, party nominations were made by small assemblies: first a caucus of office-holders, and later a convention of elected delegates. Early in the present century, however, there was a wide-spread demand for more democratic nominating procedures. State after state adopted the *direct primary* system, in which the voters themselves select their party's candidates. Today, almost all party nominees for Congress, governor, and membership in the state legislatures are selected in regular party primaries, established by state law.

In most states, a voter in a primary is given a ballot containing the names of those who seek one party's nomination for various officers; and the voter, to be eligible to vote in that party's primary, must give some indication of his own affiliation with that party. Again in most states, the winner of the party's nomination for, say, governor is that aspirant who receives the largest vote. There might be four persons, A, B, C, and D, aspiring to that nomination. If A gets 40 per cent of the vote, B 30 per cent, and C and D each 15 per cent, A has a plurality: he wins the nomination and becomes the party's candidate for governor. In some Southern states, however, where for many decades it was assumed that whoever won the Democratic nomination was sure to be elected, a *clear majority* is required: if in the first primary no one receives more than 50 per cent of the vote, the two with the largest vote (A and B, in our example) are matched against each other in a "run-off primary" that decides who the nominee shall be.

Although the system of nomination by popular vote is widespread, it has never been used in the selection of party candidates for president and vice-president of the United States. Instead, national party conventions, each attended by more than a thousand delegates, make the nominations. How are these delegates chosen? In more than half the states, they are selected by official party committees. In the rest, they are chosen by the voters in what are loosely called "presidential primaries." *These are contests for the position of delegate.*[1] One contender may announce that he is "pledged" to support Jones for president, and another that he is "pledged" to support Robinson for president. A "presidential primary" may help one aspirant for the presidential nomination to gain some support in the convention; it also provides a clue as to the relative popularity of the major aspirants. Thus in the winter and spring of 1956, Adlai E. Stevenson and Estes Kefauver both sought the Democratic nomination. In a few states, there were electoral contests between those who wanted to go to the convention to support Stevenson and those who wanted to go to the convention to support Kefauver. Several of these "presidential primaries" resulted in the election of delegates favoring Stevenson; whereupon Kefauver stopped campaigning, and the national convention promptly nominated Stevenson for president.

However, in most states the delegates are not popularly elected, and so it is not always necessary for an aspirant for the presidential nomination to prove his popularity in "presidential primaries." In-

---

[1] Notice that the ordinary direct primary is a contest for nomination: the winner is the party's candidate for office. The so-called "presidential primary" is not a contest for nomination; it is really an election of delegates, the winners gaining the right to participate in the national convention.

deed the convention sometimes nominates a man even though in the "presidential primaries" not a single candidate for delegate was pledged to support him. Thus the Republican convention in 1916 nominated Charles Evans Hughes, and the Democratic convention in 1952 nominated Stevenson, despite the fact that neither of their names was put even indirectly before the voters in the delegate elections.

In 1912, when enthusiasm for more "direct democracy" was high and states were adopting the regular primary system, Woodrow Wilson proposed that presidential nominations, like the nominations of governors and senators and representatives, should be made directly by the voters. He urged the establishment of a nationwide presidential primary—a real nominating primary, not just an election of delegates. This idea has been advanced from time to time since Wilson's day. But it has never been adopted by either party. The national conventions still choose the candidates.

Criticisms of the convention system are many. The chief one seems to be that it is not sufficiently democratic. Too few persons have any effective voice in making presidential nominations. Even in states where delegates are popularly elected, the party leaders often are able to arrange that the strongest candidates for delegate shall run "pledged" to a local favorite who is not a serious aspirant for the presidency; this "favorite son" receives a "complimentary vote" on the first ballot taken at the convention, and then gratefully withdraws his name, leaving the delegates free to vote for some better-known contender. It is often complained that the "party bosses" control most of the delegates and hence can dictate to the convention, and that the party's nominee is chosen by these politicians in a "smoke-filled room."

On the other hand, the proposal for a single, simultaneous nationwide primary raises many difficulties, including the terrific inroads it would make on any serious aspirant's energy and pocketbook. And defenders of the *status quo* argue that while a nationwide primary could split the party into irreconcilable factions, the convention system makes compromises possible and thus fosters party unity.

Assume that you are a United States Senator from Missouri. Your party is to nominate a presidential candidate next year. Already two men have announced their candidacy for the nomination. One of them, Governor Jones of Georgia, is a fire-eating orator who makes violent speeches every week in favor of racial segregation and "white supremacy"; he calls the Supreme Court "a bunch of dam' Yankee Communists," and arouses great enthusiasm in some Southern audiences. Another, Senator Smith of Michigan, is a former labor leader. In the Senate, he has urged the passage of new labor laws, higher taxes on corporations, and public ownership and operation of the steel industry. In his speeches he denounces big businessmen as "robber barons," and farmers as "wealthy beggars." He has many ardent supporters in Detroit, Cleveland, Pittsburgh, and some other large industrial cities. Other well-known men in the party, who have been widely mentioned as "presidential timber" but have not yet announced their candidacy, are former Governor Brown of New York, who has a high reputation as an able administrator; General Robinson, war hero and now President of the University of California; and Ambassador Bow, a resident of Pennsylvania and a realistic, experienced, and able diplomat. A Gallup Poll among the voters of your party reports that, today, they would favor the nomination going to:

Smith	28%
Jones	22
Brown	12
Robinson	12
Bow	9
Others, or Undecided	17

A bill is introduced in Congress to require the nomination to be decided at a nationwide popular primary, the candidate receiving the largest vote at the primary to be the party's nominee for president. (After this primary, the parties would be free to hold a convention at which the party platform could be adopted.)

You are a loyal party man who believes that it is important for the country that your party should win the next presidential election. In the debate on the bill, you are the final speaker. You oppose the bill.

Outline for class discussion or as a written exercise prepare your speech, basing your arguments on your understanding of the roles of political parties and interest groups in American political life. Stress FACTUAL ARGUMENTS *and thoughtful* ANALYSIS; *do* NOT *engage in windy oratory, and do* NOT *express your personal agreement or disagreement with the views of any candidate. Remember that you must answer the arguments made by previous speakers who favor the bill, as well as state why you oppose the bill. Organize your speech as follows:*

1. By summarizing the strongest arguments FOR the bill its proponents might be able to make.

2. By offering the best answers to these arguments you can.

3. By giving the best additional arguments you can develop for your position AGAINST the bill.

PROBLEM 22

An Informal Experiment in Voting Prediction

People like to say that they "make up their own minds" in political matters, and of course in a certain sense they do. Yet there are certain *regularities* in the way people behave in politics —for instance, in their decisions to vote for one candidate or party rather than another.

One of the fundamental aims of science is to make *general statements* that "sum up" such regularities. Another aim is to make *predictions,* if possible, on the basis of such statements. In the social sciences, various attempts at such precise generalization and prediction have been made, and measurement, quantitative statements, and mathematical analysis are increasingly used. So far such efforts at prediction in the social sciences fall short of the achievements of most of the natural sciences. But any prediction better than chance, if it is based on some systematic understanding, represents some advance toward a more scientific analysis of human behavior. Recent efforts along these lines have been particularly marked in studies of voting behavior.

Review in your text and in your class notes materials relating to voting behavior patterns. Then consider the following propositions concerning factors involved in voting behavior analysis adapted from a summary in Bernard R. Berelson, Paul F. Lazarsfeld, and William N. McPhee, *Voting: A Study of Opinion Formation in a Presidential Campaign* (Chicago, 1954), Appendix A.

Factors	Propositions
1. Family Background	1.1 In 80 per cent or more of all cases, voters and their immediate family agree in the way they vote, i.e., agree in favoring one candidate rather than another. 1.2 Young people tend strongly to vote in the way their parents did.
2. Personal Associations (Friends and Co-workers)	2.1 People generally agree in their voting behavior with their friends, and with the people they work with (co-workers); and this tendency to agreement is slightly higher among friends, who are self-chosen, than it is among co-workers.
3. Age	3.1 A higher percentage of younger people vote Democratic in comparison with older people.
4. Region	4.1 There are no appreciable differences in voting behavior tendencies from region to region in the United States, except for the strong Democratic vote in the South.
5. Expectations as to Who Will Win	5.1 There is a positive connection (correlation) between a voter's idea as to who will win an election on the one hand and his intention as to whom he will vote for on the other.
6. Ethnic or Religious Background	6.1 Protestants tend to vote Republican in higher proportions than do Catholics or Jews. 6.2 Persons of German, Scandinavian, and Scotch-or-English descent tend to vote Republican in higher proportions than persons of Irish, Italian, and Polish origins, and Negroes.

Factors	Propositions
7. Socioeconomic Status—Social Standing, or Class Position	7.1 The higher a person's social or class status or position is, the more likely he is to vote Republican. 7.2 The higher a person's or family's income is, the more likely that person or family is to vote Republican. 7.3 The "higher" a person's occupation or occupational standing is, the more likely he is to vote Republican.
8. Residence (Size of Community)	8.1 Urban residents, or city-dwellers, tend to vote Democratic in higher proportions than rural residents do. 8.2 However, residents of metropolitan areas and of open country (farms), tend to vote Democratic in higher proportions than residents of small or middle-sized towns or cities do.
9. Opinion of Consequences of Election	9.1 Both Democrats and Republicans believe that the two parties disagree on certain issues, particularly, for example, rich-man/poor-man issues. 9.2 Republicans think their party would be better for the whole community, and Democrats think their party would be better for everyone except the rich.

A moment's thought will reveal that different factors in voting behavior may operate, as it were, in different directions. For example, an individual might be a Catholic, an Italo-American, and live in a metropolis like Chicago, factors which would indicate a Democratic vote; but at the same time, he may be a high business executive, who earns $25,000 a year, and whose friends and co-workers are mostly Republican, all factors which would indicate a Republican vote. Such a person is said to be subject to *cross-pressures*. The following statements adapted from Berelson, Lazarsfeld, and McPhee relate to the important factor of cross-pressures.

Factor	Propositions
10. Cross Pressures	10.1 The more cross-pressures a voter is subject to, the longer he is likely to delay his final decision as to whom to vote for.
	10.2 The more the members of a family disagree in their political views, the more a member of the family is likely, during a campaign, to be uncertain about whom to vote for.
	10.3 The more he and his friends or co-workers agree about politics, the stronger an individual's conviction in support of a particular candidate will be; conversely, the more such personal associates disagree in their political views, the more an individual is likely, during a campaign, to be uncertain about whom to vote for.
	10.4 The more cross-pressures a voter is subject to, the less interest he is likely to take in an election.
	10.5 The more cross-pressures and inconsistencies a voter is subject to, the more likely he is to be uncertain about his voting preference during a campaign.

It must be borne in mind that these generalizations are based on studies conducted in the period 1940–1952, *and there may be some important changes in dominant patterns of voting behavior today.* All the above statements should be thought of as "hypotheses," that is, generalizations subject to further testing.

Early voting behavior studies tended to stress what we may call *situational* factors, that is to say, aspects of the social environment or social situation in which the voter lives and behaves. The propositions above refer almost entirely to such situational factors. A pioneering voting behavior study, Paul F. Lazarsfeld, Bernard Berelson, and Hazel Gaudet, *The People's Choice* (New York, 1944), placed particular emphasis on situational elements:

> There is a familiar adage in American folklore to the effect that a person is only what he thinks he is, an adage which reflects the typically American notion of unlimited opportunity, the tendency toward self-betterment, etc. Now [in voting behavior in the presidential election of 1940] we find that the reverse of the adage is true: *a person thinks, politically, as he is, socially. Social characteristics determine political preference.*

More recent investigations, however, have tended to stress another set of factors that must be borne in mind. These have been called *motivating* factors in such studies as Angus Campbell, Gerald Gurin, and Warren E. Miller, *The Voter Decides* (Evanston, Illinois, 1954)—an inquiry into voting behavior in the 1952 presidential election. Here the focus is on the ways in which an *individual personality* perceives and responds to the environment. In their 1952 election study, Campbell, Gurin, and Miller found three motivating factors to be particularly significant in explaining the outcome of the election:

(a) party identification—that is, the way in which a person thinks of himself or identifies himself as "a Democrat" or "a Republican";
(b) issue orientation—a person's ideas about, attitudes toward, or reactions to current domestic or foreign policy issues which he sees as being involved in the election contest; and
(c) candidate orientation—a person's perceptions of, attitudes toward, or feelings about the personality of a particular candidate or candidates.

Though situational and motivational factors are presumably related, a stress on motivating factors would indicate that *prediction* is unlikely to be very reliable unless the *motivating* as well as the situational factors are taken into account. Like situational factors, motivational factors may also develop cross-pressures within an individual. For example, a person may (a) identify himself with the Democratic party, and (b) agree with Democratic policy perspectives on most issues; but at the same time (c) be so strongly and favorably oriented toward the personality of a Republican candidate like Dwight D. Eisenhower that he votes Republican. He may do this despite the fact that situational factors would indicate a Democratic vote.

The difference between the situational and motivational approaches to analysis and prediction may be summed up in a pair of diagrams. The situational approach seems to assume a causal connection between social situation and political behavior, thus:

The motivational approach, on the other hand, stresses the importance of "psychological variables" between situation and behavior. As a hypothesis, we may then indicate that the causal connection must involve both situation and motivation (solid line), with situation and behavior thus only loosely related:

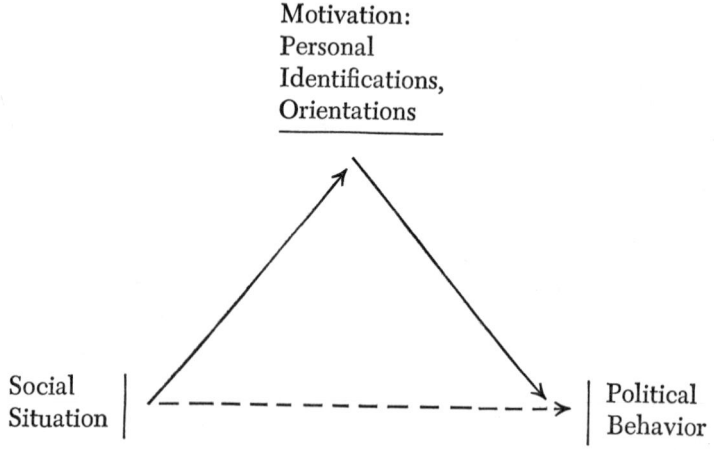

If this representation is at all accurate, prediction from both situational and motivational factors (solid lines) would have a higher chance of success than prediction from situational factors alone (dotted line). Still, some degree of prediction along the path of situational analysis should be possible.

It must also be borne in mind that patterns of voting behavior may change through time, from election to election. Thus during the 1930's and to a lesser degree during the 1940's, when economic and "rich-man/poor-man" issues seemed central in the minds of many voters, "social characteristics" may have "determine[d] political preference" to a high degree. In the 1950's, with economic, occupational-group, and class issues less dominant, such factors as candidate orientation and concern with different issues might play a larger part in ultimate behavior. In the 1952 and 1956 presidential elections, a movement toward Eisenhower was apparent in substantially *all* economic and social groupings or groups, including, for example, wage-earners and labor union members. Thus, factors that might seem to provide an adequate basis for prediction in one period might clearly fail to do so in another.

A short "Voting Profile" designed to provide some prediction of voting behavior was recently published by Eugene Burdick in a popular magazine. It is reproduced here, in slightly revised and adapted form, with a form for Tally Sheets and a Scoring Chart. This simple twenty-question schedule was not designed for refined professional use, but was rather presented as part of a popular article discussing the possibilities of prediction in voting behavior. Furthermore, while efforts at prediction in professional studies are concerned with statistical tendencies in large numbers or aggregates of voters, this Voting Profile is aimed at predicting the probable vote of a *particular individual*—a considerably riskier business. Again, asking the Voting Profile's twenty questions of a dozen quite unscientifically selected persons is by no means the same as interviewing a much larger number of persons in a scientifically designed sample. These warnings and qualifications should be kept in mind. The twenty questions, however, are based on many of the findings of recent voting behavior research, and should provide a usable and useful tool in an informal experiment aimed at achieving some understanding of voting behavior and of the possibilities and difficulties of prediction in this area. In this informal experiment, the Voting Profile itself is subject to testing as to its usefulness as a predictive instrument and to subsequent analysis of its strengths and weaknesses.

Undertake the following informal experiment and prepare the results for class discussion or a written report.

1. Analyze carefully the Voting Profile, to see what factors associated with voting behavior it includes, what factors it stresses, and what possibly important factors it fails to include.

2. Give the Voting Profile to twelve people, if possible people whose voting intentions you do not know in advance. Half of your respondents should be students; the other half should be nonstudents, not more than two of them teachers or members of your immediate family. Review the questionnaire thoroughly before you start interviewing, to make sure that you can ask the questions smoothly and clearly. Never express any approval or disapproval of answers you get during an interview. Make up a tally sheet for each interview, based on the Form given after the questionnaire.

3. After you have given the Voting Profile, ask each person how he voted, or would have voted, in the most recent presidential election. On the basis of this information, you will be able to judge how successful the Profile was in predicting how the people you interviewed voted, or would have voted.

4. Where the Profile failed to predict voting accurately, question the respondent further to find out why he voted or would have voted as he indicated, in order to find out if possible why the Voting Profile failed in that case—what factors it left out, overemphasized, or underemphasized, and so on. On the back of your tally sheets, make notes of the answers to these additional questions.

5. If the Voting Profile was more successful in predicting the behavior of the nonstudents of voting age you interviewed than it was in predicting the behavior of fellow students, analyze the possible reasons for this result.

6. On the basis of your findings in Steps 3, 4, and 5, make what general statements you can about the strengths and weaknesses of the Profile as a tool for prediction. Relate your generalizations to what you have discovered from your reading and this experiment about the factors involved in voting behavior.

Voting Profile

Adapted from Eugene Burdick
"How You'll Vote This Fall,"
This Week Magazine, *May 16, 1956*

INSTRUCTIONS. Items in Roman type are questions to ask respondent. Items in *italics* are instructions for the interviewer. Ask respondents to answer questions quickly. Use separate tally sheet for each respondent, following the Form indicated after the questionnaire. If an item is not appropriate, or the respondent cannot give an answer, leave space on tally sheet blank.

1. Is (*if living*) was (*if deceased*) your father a Democrat or a Republican? *Put 5 points under column of father's party, if father voted or identified self regularly or usually with one party.*

2. Is (*if living*) was (*if deceased*) your mother a Democrat or a Republican? *Put 5 points under column of mother's party, if mother voted or identified self regularly or usually with one party.*

3. *If respondent's father and mother are (were) of the same party, put 5 additional points under that party.*

4. *If father and mother are (were) of different parties,* CROSS OUT *the figures entered after Questions 1 and 2.*

5. (*If married*) Is your (wife) (husband) a Democrat or a Republican? *Put 15 points under the party which respondent's spouse usually supports.*

6. Just quickly and "off-the-cuff," do you think most of your friends are Democrats or Republicans? *Put 10 points under the party which most of respondent's friends support or favor.*

7. Now as to your age; are you thirty or younger, or are you over thirty? *If respondent is thirty or younger, put 4 points in the Democratic column.*

8. *If respondent is older than thirty years of age, put 4 points in the Republican column.*

9. *If respondent is regularly a resident of one of the following states, put 6 points in the Democratic column: Alabama, Arkansas, Florida, Georgia, Lousiana, Mississippi, North Carolina, South Carolina, Virginia.*

10. Which party do you think will win the next presidential election, regardless of which party you prefer? *Put 2 points in the column of the party respondent thinks will win.*

11. Do you read a foreign language newspaper regularly? *If YES, put 3 points in the Democratic column.*

12. Are you of Scandinavian, German, or Scotch-or-English ancestry? *If YES, put 2 points in the Republican column. If NO ask:*

13. Are you of Irish, Italian, or Polish ancestry? *If YES, put 2 points in the Democratic column.*

14. What is your occupation, or the kind of work you do? *List occupation briefly on tally sheet. If respondent is a factory worker, put 4 points in the Democratic column.*

15. *If respondent is regularly a resident on a farm, or in a suburb, or in a town smaller than 40,000, put 3 points in the Republican column.*

16. *If respondent is regularly a resident in a city larger than 50,000 put 3 points in the Democratic column.*

17. Regardless of which party you prefer, under what party do you think you personally, or your immediate family, will be better off in an economic sense? *Put 10 points under the column of the party respondent names.*

18. Can you quickly and "off-the-cuff" think of a person older than yourself whom you know, and whom you respect very highly? Which party do you think this person belongs to or supports? *Put 10 points under the column of that party.*

19. Can you recall the last time you talked about politics with a group, whether large or small, as long as it included people outside your own family? Did you have the impression that the group was mostly Republican or mostly Democratic? *Put 4 points under the appropriate column.*

20. Is (your) (your family) income more, or less, than $5,000 per year? *If LESS than $5,000 per year, put 4 points in the Democratic column.*

Form for Tally Sheets

	REPUBLICAN	DEMOCRATIC
Question 1		
2		
3		
4		
5		
6		
7		
8		
9		
10		
11		
12		
13		
14		
15		
16		
17		
18		
19		
20		
Add columns—Totals		
Subtract smaller total from larger		
Result—Net voting preference		

Scoring Chart

On Tally Sheet for each respondent, figure for Net Voting Preference will appear in either Republican or Democratic column, or at 0. Locate Net Voting Preference for respondent at appropriate point on "continuum line," below.

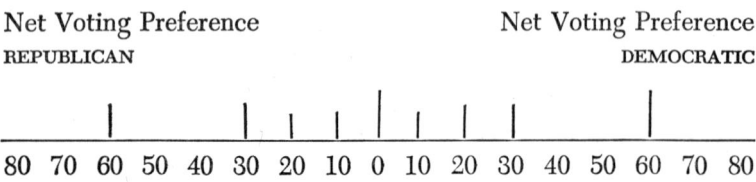

Net Voting Preference
REPUBLICAN

Net Voting Preference
DEMOCRATIC

80 70 60 50 40 30 20 10 0 10 20 30 40 50 60 70 80

Between 60 and 80—almost certain to vote for party indicated.

Between 30 and 60—ten-to-one will vote for party indicated.

Between 20 and 30—better than even chance will vote for party indicated.

Ten or less either way—an Independent or Undecided voter.

PROBLEM 23

Propaganda Strategy in a Congressional Campaign

The Third Congressional District in the State of Sunshine has a population of approximately 300,000, and covers nine counties. Quentin, the largest city, has a population of about 65,000. A dozen lesser cities, ranging in size from 5,000 to 10,000, have a combined population of 95,000. Some 65,000 people live in small towns or other rural nonfarm areas. About 15,000 farms of various sizes account for the remaining 75,000 of the population, some 5,000 of these being farm laborers, concentrated on a few relatively very large farms.

Three dams that provide sources of cheap hydroelectric power have recently been constructed in the area, as part of a federal government development program. Mills and factories, attracted by the supply of cheap electricity, have been established in many of the small towns and cities during the past few years. Industry now accounts for about one fifth of the employment in the district outside of Quentin, and for about half of the employment in Quentin. The new industries have brought with them a significant boom in building construction, in which many local contractors and their employees have benefited.

Until the recent growth of industry, the region had been overwhelmingly agricultural. The farming is diversified, with wheat, corn, and cotton accounting for 59 per cent of the agricultural income. Most of the farms in the area are family farms, and most of the farmers own their land. Of the 15,000 farms in the District, about half yield annual gross incomes of $5,000–$10,000, with a few exceeding $10,000. The new dams have resulted in inundating some valuable farm land, and forced some farm families to give up their homes. Some have established themselves on other farms; some have gone to Quentin or to smaller towns and taken jobs in industry. On the other hand, the new industry and the new population it has brought with it have resulted in some enlargement of the local market for farm products, particularly for cotton to supply new textile mills and for poultry, vegetables, dairy products, and eggs sold for local consumption. Few farmers in the area belong to farm organizations, though some units of the American Farm Bureau Federation and the National Farmers' Union exist.

There has been some talk of using the water reserves building up behind the federal dams for irrigation purposes. The *New Era,* the leading newspaper in Quentin, has suggested a federally financed irrigation system to bring water to dry-land areas and increase farm productivity in the region, but nothing has been done toward irrigation development. Some farmers are wary of irrigation proposals as a threat to their old way of life, while others, generally the more successful, favor an irrigation project as a way toward progress. Substantial dry-land areas do exist in the District, many of which could be brought under cultivation by irrigation.

The federal dams, the cheap electricity they provide, and the growth of industry have begun a basic transformation in the lives of most of the people in the district, particularly in the smaller cities and towns. A typical case is that of Jonesville, where two paper mills have been established, each employing about 500 workers. The town's population increased sharply in a short time, and is now nearly 6,500. The new mills were built by companies whose headquarters are in New York, and the mill executives and supervisors were sent to Jonesville from other plants owned by the companies. There has been a real estate boom in Jonesville as a result of the population increase, and many new houses are now under construction. Bonds have been levied for a new school building to relieve the crowded classrooms. There is full employment in Jonesville, and the people are more prosperous than they have ever been before. The first chain supermarket, an A&P store, was established in Jonesville two months ago. Rumor is circulating that a Sears Roebuck store will soon be built on the vacant lot across the street from the courthouse. Many merchants who welcomed the increase in trade are now beginning to fear that the arrival of chain stores will destroy their businesses.

Another result of the coming of industry has been the growth of labor unions in an area which had been traditionally "open shop," and often actively opposed to unions. Much of the new management in the area has been quite ready to sign union contracts in order to guarantee stable labor conditions, so important to getting the new plants into production. Employers longer established in the District, however, have resisted labor organization, often bitterly. Shortly after the new mills were built in Jonesville, for example, a newly organized union in one of the older-established shops voted overwhelmingly to strike for wages comparable to those being paid in the new mills. The company fought the strike; after four months, the workers went back to their jobs without their pay raise, and with their union practically destroyed. Many of the "Old Timers" in Jonesville agreed with the local newspaper, the Jonesville *Courier*, that the strike was caused by "the grasping tendencies of the labor leaders, who won't let the men be satisfied when they're well off." The AFL-CIO unions in the area, faced as they are with the problems of getting organized and negotiating with management, have not so far undertaken any significant degree of political action.

The pattern of social and political leadership in Jonesville is changing. People who have moved to Jonesville to manage the new plants have begun to emerge as leaders in the city's social life. Two men who did not live in the area two years ago have been elected to the city council.

The picture in Jonesville is similar to that in most of the small towns in the District. The economy has changed greatly in a short time. Established patterns of living and thinking are being challenged. The status and prestige of old community leaders is being threatened. On the other hand, most people have derived financial advantage from the industries, and the Chambers of Commerce in many of the towns are working actively to attract more industry. There is no open hostility between the old and the new, but there is much latent dissatisfaction. This is voiced from time to time by "Old Timers" who see their way of life threatened.

The congressional seat for the Third District will be vacant next term, as a result of the retirement of the incumbent congressman. He has announced that he will take no part in the election to choose his successor. The Republicans always carry the District, and the Republican primary is thus the effective election. Because of this one-party dominance, party organization as such is weak, and candidates find it necessary to an unusual degree to conduct their own campaigns and build their own organization and following. A hard-fought congressional primary is likely to bring out a total vote of 65,000 to 80,000.

One candidate has already filed for the congressional nomination in the Republican primary. He is Mike Brown, a fifty-seven-year-old druggist from Jonesville. He has lived all his life there, is energetic, has many friends, and has been an important figure in his city and in the District for many years. He has served as mayor of Jonesville and as state senator. He is well known for his leadership of an effort in the state legislature of Sunshine to get better highways for the area. Mr. Brown is basing his campaign on an appeal to local, independent businessmen, to old-established residents in the towns, and to farmers. He attacks the new industrial concerns and their officials from outstate as "foreigners" and "carpetbaggers," and denounces the "monstrous expansion of federal government power" in the District, particularly as represented by the federally built dams and hydroelectric generators and by the proposals made by the Quentin *New Era* for federal aid to public schools in the region. At the same time, Brown calls for more federal aid to farmers, as well as for laws to "restrict unfair competition from chain stores," and for new federal labor legislation to "curb the union bosses." He reminds his audiences of the uncomplicated "good old days" before the dams were built and new industry and labor disputes came into the area. He says that he will work in Congress "to keep old-fashioned sunshine in the hearts of the people of the Sunshine state." The Jonesville *Courier* is supporting Brown vigorously, by running news stories and editorials reflecting Brown's campaign themes, and by picturing Brown as an ideal person to represent the District.

Only one other person, Harry Trout of Quentin, has announced for the Republican nomination. A youthful thirty-nine, he is vigorous, has an attractive personality, possesses a wide circle of friends in Quentin and in Quentin County, and has often spoken on public affairs, particularly international affairs, at church and lodge meetings, and over Quentin's TV station and local radio stations.

He has an attractive, intelligent, red-haired wife and three small children. A life-long resident of Quentin, he is not nearly as well known in small-town and rural areas as Brown is. He is a lawyer who has been active in Republican politics, and has served as prosecuting attorney of Quentin County. In the past his chief support has come from a group of businessmen in Quentin, who have not been affected by the recent changes as have the people in the smaller communities. While he has always been a businessman's lawyer, Trout has never taken a position on the questions that are currently agitating many people in the Third Congressional District, such as the federal dams, irrigation proposals, the influx of new industries, farm price supports, union activity and labor legislation, federal aid to education, and the like. Thus most people in the District have no clear picture of him, in terms of his personality, or of his stand on issues.

Though he knows he faces a tough fight, Trout thinks he can win, IF he can devise a campaign that will appeal effectively to people or groups in the District who might be brought, for various reasons, to support him or to oppose Brown.

Review in your text and in your class notes materials relating to the role of public opinion, candidates, and propaganda in election campaigns, and review any supplementary material you can find. Particularly useful materials may be found in Stephen K. Bailey and Howard D. Samuel, Congress at Work *(New York: Henry Holt and Company, 1952), Chapter 2; Stanley Kelley Jr.,* Professional Public Relations and Political Power *(Baltimore: The Johns Hopkins Press, 1956), 26–38, and Chapter II; and Vance Packard,* The Hidden Persuaders *(New York: David McKay Company, 1957), Chapter 17. This last book should be taken with a few grains of salt.*

Assume that you work in Quentin as a member of a public relations firm. Mr. Trout has come to you for advice on the substance and methods of publicity (propaganda) that would be most effective, given all the circumstances, in his campaign for the nomination. As a public relations specialist, you know that one of the most important jobs in a winning campaign would be to build up, in the minds of as many voters as possible, a favorable "picture" or "image" of Harry Trout as a *personality* and as a *candidate*. You know that there are many ways in which such a picture or image can be built up: for example, by carefully painting Trout's public personality in a certain way; or perhaps by contrasting his general background, character, and outlook with that of Brown; or by trying to connect or identify him in the minds of the voters with certain groups or leaders in the District; or by developing and stressing positions he may take on certain "important" issues; or perhaps merely by identifying him in the minds of the voters with some general slogan or slogans. You also know that a favorable picture or image of Trout may be built up by a careful *combination* of various possible approaches, including those listed above, or others. At the outset of his consultation with you, Mr. Trout lists six possible alternative ways to focus his campaign that have been suggested to him, and asks for your criticism of these six ways. They are:

A. Pitch the campaign toward the union members in the District, urging amendment of the Taft-Hartley Act so as to prohibit states from passing "antiunion" or "right-to-work" laws. Exploit Brown's opposition to unions, paint yourself as a "friend of labor," and try to get the solid backing of labor, which, it is argued, can give you organized and therefore effective support.

B. Wage an "anti-Brown" campaign. Frequently assert that Brown is reactionary, a petty man who lives in the past, an "Old Fogey," a person who is not abreast of modern developments. Accuse him of being a tool of "vested interests" in the small towns, and paint yourself as a "progressive" leader.

C. Conduct a high-level campaign and rationally discuss the issues. Do not allow yourself to engage in mud-slinging, even if Brown does. Point out to the people the fallacies in Brown's arguments in regard to industry and to unions. Agree with him on the farm issue, disagree on the education issue. "Talk sense" to the people, taking specific positions on issues of concern to people in the District.

D. Concentrate on important issues facing the nation, rather than on issues of local interest. Take a stand on foreign affairs. Mention local issues, but subordinate them to "the national interest." Appeal, as a broad-gauge "statesman," to the better nature of the people to elect a congressman who has the vision and the courage to make the nation as a whole his chief concern.

E. Appeal for the support of the new industries and their employees, and the new-industry leadership in the Third Congressional District, by denouncing Brown's "carpetbagger" charges, and painting these new business leaders in the area as the agents of progress and prosperity. Paint yourself as a "forward-looking" man who can work with these new leaders.

F. Conduct a highly general campaign around the slogan "Progress or Decay? The people must choose!" Support "progress," and identify yourself with "progress" in general terms.

As a public relations expert, give Mr. Trout:

1. Your ESTIMATE of the probable success or failure of *each* of the *six* possible propaganda strategies described above; and

2. Your own RECOMMENDATIONS as to the most effective publicity or propaganda strategy for his campaign, which might be an elaboration of one of the six strategies already suggested to him; or some combination of two or more of these; or a new strategy line, which might or might not incorporate within it one or more of the six ideas already suggested.

Be as clear and specific as you can.

In both Questions 1 and 2, above, *develop as fully as you can your* REASONS *for your estimates or suggestions.* Base your analysis and argument throughout on, first, your knowledge of factors that apparently influence the outcome of primary (nominating) elections in general, and second, on the situation in the Third Congressional District as it has been described.

Remember, your objective is to plan a winning propaganda strategy, or at least the best possible strategy to help Mr. Trout get the Republican nomination.

PART VII

THE LEGISLATIVE POWER

PROBLEM 24

The Legislator's Choice

Read and ponder the following excerpts from a book about Congress and congressmen by Senator John F. Kennedy of Massachusetts:

> Senators, we hear, must be politicians—and politicians must be concerned only with winning votes, not with statesmanship. . . .
>
> Walter Lippmann, after nearly half a century of careful observation, rendered in his recent book a harsh judgment both on the politician and the electorate:
>
> "With exceptions so rare they are regarded as miracles of nature, successful democratic politicians are insecure and intimidated men. They advance politically only as they placate, appease, bribe, seduce, bamboozle, or otherwise manage to manipulate the demanding threatening elements in their constituencies. The decisive consideration is not whether the proposition is good but whether it is popular—not whether it will work well and prove itself, but whether the active-talking constituents like it immediately."

I am not so sure, after nearly ten years of living and working in the midst of "successful democratic politicians," that they are all "insecure and intimidated men." I am convinced that the complication of public business and the competition for the public's attention have obscured innumerable acts of political courage—large and small—performed almost daily in the Senate Chamber. I am convinced that the decline—if there has been a decline—has been less in the Senate than in the public's appreciation of the art of politics, of the nature and necessity for compromise and balance, and of the nature of the Senate as a legislative chamber. And, finally, I am convinced that we have criticized those who have followed the crowd—and at the same time criticized those who have defied it—because we have not fully understood the responsibility of a Senator to his constituents or recognized the difficulty facing a politician conscientiously desiring, in Webster's words, "to push [his] skiff from the shore alone" into a hostile and turbulent sea. Perhaps if the American people more fully comprehended the terrible pressures which discourage acts of political courage, which drive a Senator to abandon or subdue his conscience, then they might be less critical of those who take the easier road—and more appreciative of those still able to follow the path of courage.

The *first* pressure to be mentioned is a form of pressure rarely recognized by the general public. Americans want to be liked —and Senators are no exception. They are by nature—and of necessity—social animals. We enjoy the comradeship and approval of our friends and colleagues. We prefer praise to abuse, popularity to contempt. Realizing that the path of the conscientious insurgent must frequently be a lonely one, we are anxious to get along with our fellow legislators, our fellow members of the club, to abide by the clubhouse rule and patterns, not to pursue a unique and independent course which would embarrass or irritate the other members. We realize, moreover, that our influence in the club—and the extent to which we can accomplish our objectives and those of our constituents—are dependent in some measure on the esteem with which we are regarded by other Senators. "The way to get along," I was told when I entered Congress, "is to go along."

Going along means more than just good fellowship—it includes the use of compromise, the sense of things possible. We should not be too hasty in condemning all compromise as bad morals. For politics and legislation are not matters for inflexible principles or unattainable ideals. Politics, as John Morley has acutely observed, "is a field where action is one long second best, and where the choice constantly lies between two blunders"; and legislation, under the democratic way of life and the Federal system of Government, requires compromise between the desires of each individual and group and those around them. . . .

The question is how we will compromise and with whom. For it is easy to seize upon unnecessary concessions, not as means of legitimately resolving conflicts but as methods of "going along.". . .

All of us in the Congress are made fully aware of the importance of party unity (what sins have been committed in that name!) and the adverse effect upon our party's chances in the next election which any rebellious conduct might bring. Moreover, in these days of Civil Service, the loaves and fishes of patronage available to the legislator—for distribution to those earnest campaigners whose efforts were inspired by something more than mere conviction—are comparatively few; and he who breaks the party's ranks may find that there are suddenly none at all. Even the success of legislation in which he is interested depends in part on the extent to which his support of his party's programs has won him the assistance of his party's leaders. Finally, the Senator who follows the independent course of conscience is likely to discover that he has earned the disdain not only of his colleagues in the Senate and his associates in his party but also that of the all-important contributors to his campaign fund.

It is thinking of that next campaign—the desire to be re-elected—that provides the *second* pressure on the conscientious Senator. It should not automatically be assumed that this is a wholly selfish motive—although it is not unnatural that those who have chosen politics as their profession should seek to continue their careers—for Senators who go down to defeat in a vain defense of a single principle will not be on hand to fight for that or any other principle in the future.

Defeat, moreover, is not only a setback for the Senator himself—he is also obligated to consider the effect upon the party he supports, upon the friends and supporters who have "gone out on a limb" for him or invested their savings in his career, and even upon the wife and children whose happiness and security—often depending at least in part upon his success in office—may mean more to him than anything else. . . .

The *third* and most significant source of pressures which discourage political courage in the conscientious Senator or Congressman—and practically all of the problems described in this chapter apply equally to members of both Houses—is the pressure of his constituency, the interest groups, the organized letter writers, the economic blocs and even the average voter. To cope with such pressures, to defy them or even to satisfy them, is a formidable task. All of us occasionally have the urge to follow the example of Congressman John Steven McGroarty of California, who wrote a constituent in 1934:

"One of the countless drawbacks of being in Congress is that I am compelled to receive impertinent letters from a jackass like you in which you say I promised to have the Sierra Madre mountains reforested and I have been in Congress two months and haven't done it. Will you please take two running jumps and go to hell."

Fortunately or unfortunately, few follow that urge—but the provocation is there—not only from unreasonable letters and impossible requests, but also from hopelessly inconsistent demands and endlessly unsatisfied grievances. . . .[1]

Review in your text and class notes materials relating to Congress, members of Congress, and pressures on congressmen.

Assume that the President sends a special message to Congress, urging the passage of a bill to authorize the granting of large sums to the states for education, with a condition that no state will be eligible for such aid if any public schools in the state are "segre-

---

[1] John F. Kennedy, *Profiles in Courage* (New York: Harper and Brothers, 1955), 3–10.

gated" on the basis of color.[2] In his message, the President calls improvements in education a matter of national concern; he also stresses that his program would still vest administrative responsibility and educational policy-making in the local school districts of the country. The next night, speaking at a party banquet, the President returns to the same subject. He points out that the recent party platform pledged "giant steps to make American education, already the finest in the world, still better," that it called for respect for the Supreme Court, and that it said: "This party stands firmly for that great American principle, equality of opportunity."

As a written exercise or for class discussion:

For each of the following situations, A through D, assume that you are the member of Congress described. For each case, separately,
1. Analyze the situation carefully.
2. Select and evaluate, in terms of their importance in the situation as you see it, the specific factors that would lead you to take a specific position with reference to the President's proposal.

Assume throughout that the President's party has a majority in both houses of Congress.

A. You used to be a professor of international relations; now you are beginning your fourth term as U.S. Senator from a Southern state. In your state, most schools remain segregated; but the schools of the state's largest city have been voluntarily and peaceably desegregated. On this issue, you have long urged patience and moderation, without being specific about what steps, if any, should be taken. In the recent primary, you narrowly defeated an aspirant who preached race hatred and said that the Supreme Court justices should be impeached. Your chief interest is in foreign affairs. You are of the President's party, and for the last few years have been an eloquent senatorial supporter of his foreign policy. Right now you know that there will soon be a close battle

---

[2] Despite the Supreme Court's "desegregation" decision of 1954, most schools in the South are still segregated. The Supreme Court directed merely that its ruling be complied with, in each such school district, "with all deliberate speed"; and thus far, there has been much more deliberation than speed.

in the Senate over ratification of a treaty that the President has made with Ruritania. You feel that the ratification of this treaty is of vital importance to the country; you know, too, that ratification is ardently desired by the tobacco growers in your state, who expect to profit by renewed trade with Ruritania. The outcome may well depend on the votes of a dozen other Southern senators, ten of whom have regularly sought your advice and followed your lead in voting on foreign policy questions, but have thus far remained silent about the treaty.

B. You are a 29-year old lawyer and U.S. representative, from a district in a Northern metropolis, serving your first term in the House. Last fall, you were elected as the nominee of the President's party, receiving 80,020 votes to 77,153 for your opponent. About 19,000 voters in your district are Negroes; the ward where most of them live gave you a 3-to-1 advantage. The chief financial contributors to your campaign were leaders (including your uncle) in the local Chamber of Commerce, which has just adopted a resolution calling for lower taxes and condemning additional federal expenditures. In the House, you have been assigned to the Committee on the District of Columbia. This bores you; you are anxious to be assigned to the Committee on the Judiciary, where an early vacancy is likely. Committee assignments are made by a group of fourteen senior congressmen of your party, seven of whom are southerners. You are not very happy in Congress, partly because your wife and small children did not accompany you to Washington. Your secret ambition is to become a federal judge.

C. You are of the same party as the President; but when you were fighting successfully to be renominated last year for your second term in the U.S. Senate, the President openly endorsed your primary opponent, a former member of his cabinet. You come from a small Western state. It is rich in natural resources and its people are justifiably proud of their public schools. Many wealthy men live in the state. By profession, you are a journalist. Before 1954, you wrote several syndicated articles deploring the effects of segregation. Since that year, most of your articles have centered on the question of whether federal dams should be built on western rivers. You favor such dams; the President opposes them. On the Senate floor, you have criticized the President very sharply for his stand against the dams. He has taken offense and neglected "accidentally" to invite you to a recent White House reception for Western Senators.

D. You are one of the senior U.S. representatives in the minority party. Your district is in a rather poor border state, where schools used to be segregated but were all voluntarily desegregated in 1955. You have won re-election by smaller and smaller margins, the last time by only 2,000 votes. Conservative business interests regularly support you, because you agree with them on tariff and labor questions. Organized labor is strong in your district. Its leaders have long opposed you. They favor the President's education proposal. So does a small branch of the N.A.A.C.P. In past years, before Sputnik, you have strongly and sincerely opposed federal aid to education, on the ground that financial aid would soon be followed by federal control of the schools' programs. Among your closest friends and supporters are the owners of a television station, who are seeking Federal Communications Commission approval of their application for a new channel. There is a vacancy on the bipartisan F.C.C., which, by law, must be filled by the presidential appointment of a member of your party. You have been urging the appointment to this post of your able nephew, for whom you have great affection and admiration. A presidential assistant has told you that your nephew seems well qualified and "appears to be in the lead for that job."

PROBLEM 25

Strategic Pressure Points in the Legislative Process

There are many ways of approaching the process by which Congress makes laws. Some may wish to evaluate the congressional process in terms of the extent to which it meets the needs of the contemporary international situation, some in terms of the extent to which Congress conforms to a model of democratic government, and others in terms of the extent to which Congress satisfies particular political or economic interests. Prior to any such evaluation, however, must come a thorough understanding of how Congress operates to achieve its results; of the procedures it follows, of the relationships between the presidency and Congress, of the impact of party leadership, and of the relationships between congressmen and their constituents. To further this understanding the student is here thrust into the role of a leader of an interest group with an important stake in the fate of a bill in Congress and is asked to calculate as thoroughly and fully as possible all the possible steps one might take in order to influence the course of the legislation.

There are perhaps five general techniques one might use in order to influence legislation. *Direct lobbying*, in which the interest group representative personally contacts legislators and tries to persuade them of the virtue of his case, is the most obvious. *Indirect lobbying* may also be useful as the group tries to stimulate public opinion through a propaganda campaign, hoping that the opinion so generated will be fed back from constituents to the congressmen and affect their thinking. Many interest groups have *spokesmen* for their point of view who are members of Congress.

These *spokesmen in Congress* need no particular convincing on an issue, but only data and arguments from the interest group in order to make the best possible case within Congress. Fourth, an interest group may try to use its *voting strength* to reward its political friends and punish its enemies. And finally, a group may try to work through *party leadership*, both inside and outside Congress, with whom they have sympathetic associations in order to get the leaders to exert whatever influence they may possess on other congressmen. On any particular major issue it is likely that the experienced interest group will use all these techniques in one way or another to develop the maximum influence.[1]

Another point to be borne in mind is that to the legislative agent of an interest group there are a number of strategic agencies in Congress, such as the standing committee, strategically located congressmen such as committee chairmen, and strategic points on the legislative track where a bill may be halted or run off the rails. It is of particular importance for these points of decision and these persons to be influenced. Thus the lobbyist will not try indiscriminately to persuade any and all congressmen, all the time, but will concentrate his attention on those who can be of the most service at a critical time.

You are the registered lobbyist for the AFL-CIO and are responsible for planning and carrying out the actions necessary to persuade congressmen to accept the AFL-CIO position on legislation of interest to labor. You have a large though not unlimited budget, and you can call upon the nationally known leaders of your organization and the labor press whenever it seems appropriate.

In the second session of the Eighty-eighth Congress (1964) a bill has been introduced which seems to have substantial support in Congress and which the leaders of your labor group interpret as a very serious threat to the health of the labor movement. This bill has been introduced following a long and widely publicized congressional investigation of several labor unions. This investigation emphasized the fact that corruption and racketeering were rife in some unions, and the many headlines produced by the investigaion have helped create an unfavorable image of labor generally in

[1] Cf. selection from V. O. Key, Jr., *Politics, Parties, and Pressure Groups,* in Problem 20, "Political Action by an Interest Group."

the minds of much of the public. The AFL-CIO has itself taken disciplinary action against the unions demonstrated to be corrupt, but the public image of labor—insofar as this image is reflected in the nation's press—has not been much affected by these measures.

The bill itself provides that labor unions will be fully subject to the antitrust laws, thus repealing the substantial exemption from such laws that has been in the statutes since 1914. Before 1914, liability of unions to prosecution under the antitrust laws effectively prevented unions from improving the economic position of labor through action designed to compel collective bargaining. Whether this liability would be reimposed by the proposed legislation is not clear since the bill does not repeal other federal statutes that guarantee collective bargaining rights to unions. Although the effects of the proposal are unclear, the bill's proponents have made effective use of the symbol of "labor monopoly" as they argue that all they propose is to restore antimonopoly controls over labor unions just as they apply to business corporations.

The Democrats have majorities in both houses of Congress. In the Senate, largely because of the persuasive skills of Majority Leader Whitson, the Democrats have exhibited substantial party unity. Whitson and a few other Democratic leaders have been able to mobilize about 75 per cent of their party members in support of almost any position on which they take a strong stand, and when Democratic leaders outside Congress (for example, former presidential candidates) also agree, nearly 90 per cent of the Democrats vote together. On the bill in question many Democratic leaders outside Congress have voiced strong opposition to the bill, but so far neither Whitson nor the other prominent Democratic senators have publicly taken a position.

In the House, Democratic party leaders are not nearly as influential. Speaker Blackburn is usually able to command the support of twenty or thirty Democratic congressmen and other congressmen are influential with small groups, but no strong man or group of men can successfully "deliver" the House Democrats.

In both houses of Congress the Republicans have shown little unity. Again, as with the House Democrats, particular leaders have a few followers, but except when the Republican President takes a strong stand, most Republicans are apt to make up their minds on an individual basis rather than look to their party leaders. So far the President has adhered to the position he took in a press conference a year ago when he said that he had no particular opinion on the question and would bring no pressure on Congress, one way or another. Some but not all of the Republican leaders in Congress have announced their support of the bill, while none of the most influential Democrats in House or Senate has taken a stand.

In the House there are 235 Democrats and 200 Republicans. Speaker George Blackburn presides; he is a faithful party wheelhorse whenever the interests of the party, as he sees them, are involved in legislation. Perhaps 120 Democrats in the House regularly support the interests of organized labor, while about 40 Republicans usually can be counted on for such support. The AFL-CIO classifies about 140 Republicans and 50 Democrats as "usually antilabor." The rest of the members are publicly uncommitted on the bill, and their voting tendencies on labor questions are uncertain.

The thirty members of the House Education and Labor Committee include seventeen Democrats and thirteen Republicans. Eight of the Democrats are opposed to the bill and three are for it. Nine Republicans on the committee support the bill and two oppose it. The remaining eight members are uncommitted. The six uncommitted Democrats include the chairman, Walter Garden. Garden is regarded by labor, and everyone else, as "unpredictable." He professes to make up his mind on most questions of public policy in terms of whether the proposed policy squares with his religious convictions. The other five uncommitted Democrats normally follow the lead of Garden, who rules his committee with a very firm hand. Policies that Garden opposes have small chance of reaching the floor of the House. Garden's district contains no significant organized labor groups, and his political support back home is such that he has been unopposed in either primary or general election for the past four elections.

In the Senate there are 50 Democrats and 48 Republicans. Thirty-two of the Democrats can probably be counted on to oppose the bill and eight have indicated that they were sympathetic to its purposes, leaving ten uncommitted. The best estimate of Republican sentiment places thirty-four for the bill and eight against, with the remaining six neutral. Senator John Sanders is one of the Republican "neutrals," and his opinion on labor matters is valued by many other Republicans including some of those who have indicated sympathy for the bill. Sanders is from a state that until recently had little industry or labor, but since World War II automobile factories have been built in his state and a rapidly growing organized labor movement is becoming a political force that Sanders must reckon with.

The Senate committee that will consider the bill is composed of seven Democrats and six Republicans. The chairman is one of the bill's sponsors, and one other Democrat has announced his support of the proposal. Three Democrats oppose the bill. Three Republicans on the Committee have spoken in favor of the bill while the others, including the ranking Republican, Sanders, are uncommitted.

Review the material in your text and lecture notes relating to Congress and the legislative process, and relating to the techniques of interest groups.

For class discussion, or as a written exercise:

Prepare a full plan of strategy to defeat the proposed bill. Do not concern yourself with the substance of the proposal unless you intend to use this in some way in your campaign.

In preparing your plan, consider carefully each of the following:

1. List the strategic points in the congressional process where you might attempt to have the bill killed. Include not only the strategic agencies and strategically located congressmen, but also the major rules of procedure in each house which might be used to your advantage.

2. Evaluate your chances, considering carefully the resources or pressures you have available, of successfully killing the bill at each strategic point. Explain the reasons for your evaluation in each case.

3. Show specifically how you would use particular techniques of influence or pressure at the particular strategic points that seem most promising to you, so as to give you the best chance of defeating the bill.

NOTE: Regardless of whether you think you can kill the bill at any one point or use successfully any particular technique of influence, consider explicitly all the available alternatives.

PROBLEM 26

The Seniority Rule

In the United States Congress, almost invariable custom decrees that the chairman of a standing committee of the House or Senate shall be that member of the majority party who has the longest uninterrupted period of service on that committee.

Read what your text has to say about congressional committees (especially committee chairmen) and the "Seniority Rule," and review your class notes on these subjects. Then read the following excerpts:

1. Just as the standing committees control legislative action, so the chairmen are masters of their committees. Selected on the basis of seniority, locally elected and locally responsible, these "lord-proprietors" hold key positions in the power structure of Congress. They arrange the agenda of the committee, appoint the subcommittees, and refer bills to them. They decide what pending measures shall be considered and when, call committee meetings, and decide whether or not to hold hearings and when. They approve lists of scheduled witnesses, select their staffs and authorize staff studies, and preside at committee hearings. They handle reported bills on the floor and participate as principal managers in conference committees. They are in a position to expedite measures that they favor and to retard or pigeonhole those they dislike. Strong chairmen can often induce in executive sessions the kind of committee action that they desire. In the House of Representatives, where debate is limited, the chair-

man in charge of a bill allots time to whomever he pleases during debate on the floor; he also has the right to open and close the debate on bills reported by his committee; and he may move the previous question whenever he thinks best. In short, committee chairmen exercise crucial powers over the legislative process. In his little classic on *Congressional Government,* written sixty-eight years ago, Woodrow Wilson described our form of government in a single phrase by calling it "A government by the chairmen of the standing committees of Congress." So far as Congress is concerned, this description is, in a large sense, still true.[1]

2. To become chairman of a committee, a Senator or Representative must be assigned to the committee in the first place. If he is re-elected enough times, and if he lives long enough, and if his party comes into power, sooner or later he is bound to become a chairman. Once chairman, he is regarded as having the right to continue in his chairmanship so long as he continues to be re-elected and continues to live. This is the famous—or rather, infamous—seniority system. Luce comments:

"It is a dangerous system, for sooner or later the man who has started at the tail end of a committee, if re-elected enough times, will knock at the door of the chairmanship. He may be unqualified to preside over meetings or at hearings. He may have no capacity for defending committee reports on the floor. He may be a man whose reputation for honor is questioned—there are black sheep in every legislative flock." [2]

The seniority system has often been mistakenly attacked on the ground that it puts too much power in the hands of old men. This argument misses the real implications of the seniority system. Age alone does not cause diminution of mental vigor, alertness, and leadership ability. Nor does it mean that a man becomes more conservative. Some of the outstanding liberals in Congress have been old men who have fought valiantly despite the other handicaps of age. Witness Senator Norris, Senator Wagner, Senator Murray, and Representative Sabath.

---

[1] George B. Galloway, *The Legislative Process in Congress* (New York: Thomas Y. Crowell Co., 1953), 289.

[2] Robert Luce, *Legislative Procedure* (Boston: Houghton Mifflin Co., 1922) 120–121.

The significant effect of the seniority system is that it tends to concentrate political power in the hands of members from "safe and solid" areas of the country, areas where there is very little real competition between the two major parties. This tends to insulate committee chairmanships from the real meanings and mandates of national electoral conflicts. It tends to undermine the ability of party leaders to carry out campaign pledges. Above all, it tends to bring a greater number of conservatives than of liberals into committee chairmanships.[3]

3. Seniority influence is not unique or original in the Congress. . . . It works in the local lodges and grand lodges of every order. It is especially strong in the national meetings of a number of church organizations. However, it is particularly noticed in the Congress and commented upon because the Congress is more or less a permanent working body of long standing and represents all the people of our country.

Legislation is unquestionably much influenced by the men who have served long and occupy these important places in the organization of the House. Greater influence in and with the departments is certainly enjoyed by those who have had the advantage of knowledge and acquaintance gained by years on the job. Long service in the House brings members in contact with the personnel of the several departments and helps them to be of service in many little and some big ways to their constituents back home. Seniority or length of service in the House of Representatives is a large factor in giving a member position and influence in the Congress and in Washington.

In the course of a memorial oration before a joint session of Congress on February 27, 1882, in commemoration of the life and death of President James A. Garfield, Senator James G. Blaine made this interesting comment on service in the House of Representatives:

"There is no test of a man's ability in any department of public life more severe than service in the House of Representatives; there is no place where so little deference is paid to reputation previously acquired, or to eminence won outside; no place

---

[3] Bertram Gross, *The Legislative Struggle* (New York: McGraw-Hill Book Co., 1953) 278.

where so little consideration is shown for the feelings or the failures of beginners. What a man gains in the House he gains by sheer force of his own character, and if he loses and falls back he must expect no mercy, and will receive no sympathy. It is a field in which the survival of the strongest is the recognized rule, and where no pretense can deceive and no glamour can mislead. The real man is discovered, his worth is impartially weighed, his rank is irreversibly decreed." [4]

Now read and consider the implications of the following statement:

Perhaps the most important standing committee of the U.S. House of Representatives is the Committee on Ways and Means. To it are referred all tax bills. These include tariff bills, and even such seemingly irrelevant measures as Social Security bills—because the Social Security Act imposes special payroll taxes. Hence many Representatives would like to serve on this powerful committee. Especially, Democrats want to serve on it; for the Democratic members of "Ways and Means" themselves constitute the Democratic Committee on Committees. They assign new members to particular committees; they can accept or reject an older member's request for a transfer from a committee that bores him to one that would interest him.

When a Democratic vacancy occurs on the Ways and Means Committee the Democratic caucus, a meeting of all Democratic representatives, selects a Democrat to fill the vacancy. Sometimes there is hot rivalry between members who want to fill the vacancy.

Some years ago, by a close vote, the Democratic caucus elected Representative X of an eastern state to the Committee on Ways and Means. A few months later, a new tax bill was voted on, in the House. The Democratic President, the party leadership in the House, and virtually all eastern Democrats were against the bill; most western Democrats and Republicans were for it. Although he was an easterner and usually a faithful follower of the President, Representative X voted for that bill. Astonished, his friends asked him why. He replied: "I'm sorry, but I had to. I didn't like the bill.

---

[4] George Galloway, *op. cit.*, 368–369.

But back in January, when the caucus met, I wanted to get on Ways and Means. To get a majority in the caucus I needed some western votes. To get them, I had to promise those fellows from the West that I would vote for this tax bill when it came up."

Now assume that you have been elected a member of the state Senate of Aloha, a brand-new state just admitted to the Union. Over the Senate, according to the new Aloha Constitution, presides the Lieutenant-Governor; he is a Republican. The newly elected Senate itself, however, has a Democratic majority.

You and your fellow-senators are engaged in drafting a body of senate rules, including rules relating to the establishment, composition, and chairmanship of standing committees. Aged Senator James Hamilton, who served in the U.S. Congress from Illinois 40 years ago but moved to Aloha and became one of its leading citizens, urges that the Aloha Senate adopt a specific rule of seniority (like the unwritten rule in Congress) to govern the selection of committee chairmen.

Examine his proposal, and then as a written exercise or for class discussion prepare a speech that you will deliver in the Aloha Senate, criticizing Senator Hamilton's plan, and proposing and defending a different plan to replace the seniority system.

PROBLEM 27

Congressional Investigations

Speaking to a witness in 1948, Representative J. Parnell Thomas, then the chairman of the House Committee on Un-American Activities, said:

> The rights you have are the rights given you by this committee. We will determine what rights you have and what rights you have not got before the committee.[1]

In 1924, Felix Frankfurter, then professor at the Harvard Law School, wrote a magazine article that included the following paragraph:

> The procedure of congressional investigations should remain as it is. No limitations should be imposed by congressional legislation or standing rules. The power of investigation should be left untrammeled. . . . The safeguards against abuse and folly are to be looked for in the forces of responsibility which are operating from within Congress, and are generated from without.[2]

In 1927, the U.S. Supreme Court decided the case of *McGrain v. Daugherty*, 273 U.S. 135. Mr. Justice Vandevanter's opinion (for a unanimous Court) including the following language:

---

[1] Quoted by Telford Taylor, *Grand Inquest* (New York: Simon and Schuster, 1955), 240.

[2] Felix Frankfurter, "Hands Off the Investigations," *The New Republic*, May 21, 1924.

We are of opinion that the power of inquiry—with process to enforce it—is an essential and appropriate auxiliary to the legislative function. . . .

A legislative body cannot legislate wisely or effectively in the absence of information respecting to conditions which the legislation is intended to affect or change; and where the legislative body does not itself possess the requisite information—which not infrequently is true—recourse must be had to others who do possess it. Experience has taught that mere requests for such information often are unavailing, and also that information which is volunteered is not always accurate or complete; so some means of compulsion are essential to obtain what is needed. . . .

The contention is earnestly made on behalf of the witness that this power of inquiry, if sustained, may be abusively and oppressively exerted. If this be so, it affords no ground for denying the power. The same contention might be directed against the power to legislate, and of course would be unavailing. We must assume, for present purposes, that neither house will be disposed to exert the power beyond its proper bounds, or without due regard to the rights of witnesses. . . .

Now read and consider carefully the following quotation from Erwin N. Griswold, *The Fifth Amendment Today:*

Is not the due process clause technical lawyers' stuff? Was it not on the basis of the due process clause that the Supreme Court held that New York could not fix the length of hours that bakers might work, and that Congress could not fix a minimum wage for women in the District of Columbia? What do such decisions have to do with the struggle to obtain and to maintain liberty? The answer I would give is Very Little. They are only eddies in the stream which carries on the great idea. For the idea of due process, of "the law of the land" is a great idea, and one of our greatest heritages from the past. It is something of the spirit, something that gives life to our political institutions. In very large part we take it for granted in our day-to-day relations with our fellow men and with the several governments with which we deal. It is so deeply ingrained in us all that it is rarely violated; and many of the violations which do occur are naturally of the more or less technical sort with which courts deal.

In the long run, ideas are more powerful than more tangible weapons. And the idea of due process has been a very fruitful and pervading one in our history. What does it mean? Can it be defined? Many people feel the need for a rather precise sort of a definition of concepts with which they deal—but this is not that sort of an idea. This is an idea born out of the hearts of men. It has great capacity for development and growth, and yet a rather clear basic content. Perhaps the essential thought can be put by saying that due process has some application wherever men feel a sense of injustice. Thus it becomes a chief source of support for individual liberties. What is liberty? Is it not freedom or protection of the individual against arbitrary or improper exercise of the organized power of the state? What is a tyrant? Is he not a man who exercises the collective power of the state in an arbitrary, capricious, or purely selfish manner? Such words as "arbitrary" and "capricious" are difficult words. They may not in fact mean much more than "unreasonable," and that in turn may mean in substance "not customary," or not what we are accustomed to. Perhaps it may be said that we are accustomed to decent treatment from our public officers, and that our hearts and minds recoil when that custom is broken. It is with this sort of thing that the idea of due process, of "the law of the land" is concerned.

Now let us turn to the question which has been constantly recurring in recent days. Does this basic idea have any application to legislative investigations? Do these investigations always measure up to our ideal of due process of law? I think it fair to say that a large section of the public has from time to time felt "a sense of injustice" with respect to some of these hearings; and if they have, then there is a situation where the ancient ideal of due process is involved. A failure to appreciate the intimate relation between sound procedure and the preservation of liberty is implicit, may I say, in that saddest and most short-sighted remark of our times: "I don't like the methods, but. . . ." for methods and procedures are of the essence of due process, and are of vital importance to liberty. As Mr. Justice Brandeis wrote some thirty years ago, "In the development of our liberty insistence on procedural regularity has been a large factor." More recently Mr. Justice Frankfurter has put the same truth in these words: "The history of liberty has largely been the history of observance of procedural safeguards."

The complaint against the Star Chamber was chiefly one of bad procedures. Torture is a procedure, and inquisition without charge, forcing a witness to testify against himself, and the other things which were standard practice in the infamous Star Chamber would all fall into the category of procedure. Liberty is established and preserved by the development and maintenance of proper procedures. It is, in last analysis, only through procedural rules that the individual is protected against arbitrary governmental action. And, as we have seen, the very essence of liberty is the protection of the individual against arbitrary application of the collective power of the state.

Do not misunderstand me. I am not opposed to legislative investigations. They clearly have a proper place in our governmental structure. The fact, though, that they can be useful and necessary, does not mean that they should not be properly conducted, and under proper safeguards and procedures. Nor does it mean that when not properly conducted they may not violate our basic and fundamental conceptions of due process, rooted so firmly in Magna Carta. In my opinion, for what it is worth, some recent legislative investigations have been clear violations of due process. If so, why have the courts not so held? The answer is easy. The courts do not have the sole responsibility for the proper conduct of our government. As Mr. Justice Stone once said: "Courts are not the only agency of government that must be assumed to have capacity to govern." At this point another important governmental doctrine comes into play—the separation of powers. The courts have their responsibilities, but so do the executive and the legislative branches of the government. All are sworn to uphold the Constitution, including the due process clause of so ancient and vital origin.

The responsibility for the proper conduct of legislative investigations is clearly in the legislature. In the case of investigations by the federal legislature, the responsibility is clearly in Congress and its two Houses. Has this responsibility been fully met? [3]

Now assume the existence of the following situation:

Senator Josiah Strong is the junior senator from his state and a member of the Senate Committee on Interstate and Foreign Commerce. His party controls the Congress, the opposition holds the presidency. In a speech on the Senate floor Senator Strong charged that he had evidence of infiltration of American industry by foreign capital. This infiltration is alleged to have occurred in much heavy industry in the United States; particularly oil, steel, and chemicals. Strong charged that in some cases these industries are now under the effective control of foreign owners and in two cases of foreign governments. He said that the governments of Saudi Arabia and Kuwait are using royalties received from oil to expand their industrial power, and that Ahmed Haifa, ruler of Saudi Arabia, was using political contributions from the firms he controls to pressure the American government to support him in his efforts to unite the Arab states and revive the attempt to conquer the world for the religion of Islam. Strong also charged that West Germany now effectively ran the United States chemical industry and would use this control to prevent the United States from interfering with German plans for territorial expansion. He demanded that an investigation be launched into this entire matter, and soon after he was appointed chairman of a five-man subcommittee of the Interstate Commerce committee that was authorized "to inquire into the extent and character of foreign ownership and control of American industry and to recommend appropriate legislation concerning such matters."

Senator Strong represents a state in which a large labor vote is prepared to react against such international capitalism at least to the point of relieving from public office a political party under whose leadership this situation came about, and there are rumors to the effect that Senator Strong may be catapulted by the publicity from this issue into contention for his party's presidential nomination.

Over the opposition of the two minority party subcommittee

---

[3] Erwin N. Griswold, *The Fifth Amendment Today* (Cambridge: Harvard University Press, 1955), 36–40.

members, Senator Strong selected the entire committee staff, and this staff works only at his direction. Strong decided when and where hearings should be held, whether the hearings would be open to the press and public, and who should testify and on what subjects.

Subpoenas were issued to the leading executives of the corporations involved, and the executives were ordered to produce all financial records of the companies for the previous ten years as well as minutes of board meetings for a like period.

Two weeks prior to the beginning of the hearings, Strong announced to the press that the earlier evidence of foreign domination of American industry had been confirmed as "not only true but fantastic beyond all belief." Strong told the press that the facts were plain that American industry could not longer act upon its own initiative, and that, in the event of another war, far from equaling the production records of World War II, we would be "shackled to the whims of foreign despots." He further asserted that the administration appeared to be encouraging these developments and that some officials "very close to the top" were benefiting financially.

Public hearings were begun in Washington with a series of witnesses whose testimony in every case tended to corroborate Strong's charges. One witness, former vice-president in charge of sales for a firm in question, testified under oath that in his experience decisions that affected international trade had to be "cleared" with officials in other countries. Three former middle-level executives for financial houses handling the business of these companies testified that they were instructed to give preference to prospective purchasers of stock when those purchasers represented foreign investors. A professional economist testified that it was common knowledge that the companies concerned were part of a giant international cartel that allocated markets and fixed prices of the products throughout the world. Nine other witnesses, all former wage earners in some capacity with one of the companies under scrutiny, testified that they always understood that no employee of these companies was permitted to speak disparagingly of the Islamic countries of the Middle East. Finally, records were produced demonstrating that close relatives of two cabinet members have large holdings of stock—the value of which has increased rapidly—in firms in question. No further evidence concerning the administration is made public or even alluded to.

For two weeks the testimony of these witnesses produced sensational headlines throughout the nation. When they had been heard in public hearings and it was time for the business firms to be questioned, the subcommittee decided to hold secret hearings and went into executive session. The companies protested violently at this and so did the minority members of the subcommittee, but Senator Strong said that he did not wish to divulge secret information to others about the firms' business practices or competitive situations, and for their own protection he insisted that the businesses be questioned privately. Each business firm or its representative was questioned for one day, and each day was spent in a different city. Because of the uncertainty about when and where hearings were to be held and because Strong, by interrupting or pounding his gavel, usually prevented them from participating in the examination of witnesses, the other members of the subcommittee did not attend the meetings. The testimony of the business representatives was not made public, but after each session Senator Strong gave a resume of the testimony to the press. After each day's hearing much the same report was given; that the witnesses had denied the charges, that they had asked for the opportunity to cross-examine the earlier witnesses, that they had insisted on an open hearing in which to reply to the charges that had been made. Strong each day assured the press that the witnesses had not denied the evidence that had been taken earlier, that they were most contemptuous of democratic processes of government, that they demonstrated an un-American disregard for the necessary and proper authority of Congress to investigate matters that might require legislation, and that, finally, facts were piling up to support the original allegations made against the business firms. These daily interviews with Strong were given extensive coverage in the mass media, and while the business firms tried to condemn Strong and to insist that the facts were on their side their position got much less publicity than the other.

In order to counteract the publicity advantage possessed by Strong, several of the business firms pooled resources and ran full-page advertisements in nearly two thousand newspapers throughout the country over a period of six days in which they attempted to refute Senator Strong's charges, and in which they charged particularly that the early witnesses who testified in support of the Senator were not reliable. Senator Strong immediately called another session of his subcommittee and ordered the business representatives to reveal the names of all those who contributed to this "unconscionable slur upon the Congress and the American people." The particular executive being questioned, Silas Lapham, asked Strong for permission to confer with his, Lapham's, legal counsel. Strong refused permission, whereupon Lapham refused to answer the question on the grounds that the subcommittee had no authority to ask the question. Strong replied that Lapham was trying to cover up the facts of this "monstrous conspiracy" and later recommended that the Senate cite Lapham for contempt. This the Senate did, and the District Court found Lapham guilty, holding that the discretion of the Congress itself must be relied upon to prevent any abuses in the exercise of its investigatory power. A year later the United States Supreme Court reversed the conviction on the ground that the questions asked of Lapham did not come within the terms of the resolution which authorized the Strong committee investigation.

At the end of the investigation Strong submitted a subcommittee report to the full committee, which in turn submitted it to the Senate. No subcommittee members took exception to the report since none except Strong had attended more than one fifth of the hearings and committee meetings. Strong stated in the report that there was now incontrovertible evidence (which, however, could not be made public without exposing private business secrets to the scrutiny of competitors and revealing national defense matters) that the conspiracy originally alleged existed in more virulent form than had ever been imagined. Strong urged immediate legislation in order to require (1) that foreign ownership of stock in American companies be made part of the public record, and (2) that Congress forbid any firm to engage in interstate commerce if that firm was once American-owned and is now more than 20 per cent owned by foreign stockholders.

On the same day Strong submitted his report, the major American firms producing organic chemicals were indicted and, subsequently were convicted of having participated in an international cartel, which included in its activities monopolistic control of the

American market. The evidence adduced at the trial, though directed toward a somewhat different objective, was generally consistent with the charges made by Senator Strong.

Review in your text and lecture notes material relating to congressional investigations.

The legislation recommended by Strong is to be debated on the floor of the Senate. On the basis of a careful consideration of the facts of the Strong investigation and of all the legitimate values involved in the situation:

1. Assume you are administrative assistant to a senator who has led the attack on Strong and is of the opposite party. Prepare a carefully reasoned speech *attacking* the *procedures* followed by Strong and rebutting those who would defend him.

2. Assume you are administrative assistant to Senator Strong. Prepare for the Senator a thorough and carefully reasoned speech *defending* the *procedures* Strong followed in his investigation and rebutting the attacks made upon him.

3. Assume you are administrative assistant to a senator who has taken no part pro or con Strong or the issues raised by his investigation but who feels compelled to say something about the question of procedures. Prepare a carefully reasoned speech analyzing and evaluating the procedures followed by Strong in the light of what you believe to be ALL the relevant factors that must be considered in reaching a balanced judgment of congressional investigations.

PART VIII

THE EXECUTIVE POWER

PROBLEM 28

The Institutionalization of the Presidency

You are an Englishman and a Professor of Government at Oxford University. You have recently finished the manuscript of a book on American government in which you emphasized that

"the leadership of a series of strong Presidents has made the man in the White House the most important man in the land. The President of the United States makes the biggest decisions of public policy all by himself and no one effectively can challenge him. Congress cannot, for he dominates Congress; the courts cannot, for they have largely withdrawn from the arena of policy disputes. The job of President, therefore, is one bearing fearsome responsibility and demanding enormous capacity, first to absorb the relevant data on the host of major problems confronting the country, and then to decide the issues of war and peace, inflation and recession, equality and rewards, not only for the United States but for much of the rest of the world as well. Such concentration of power in the hands of one man might present as serious a threat to the health of democracy as it does to the health of the President were it not for one continuing fact: the President of the United States must each four years present himself and his decisions to the people for their approval. The judgment rendered by the electorate insures that the President's power will not be abused."

Shortly after submitting your manuscript to the publisher, you are having dinner in Washington with two American governmental officials, Roger Cash, who is Assistant to the Director of the Bureau of the Budget, and James Mars, who is Executive Secretary to the National Security Council. They begin to talk shop with each other.

CASH: Well, the agencies have submitted their budget requests to us. Now we have to pare them down to the over-all figure the White House gave us. There will be plenty of howls when we begin to slice some of those programs.

MARS: Who will be hit hardest?

CASH: There is some sentiment to cut the farm programs, but most of them are set by legislation and there isn't much we can do to cut them. Military spending can't be cut much in these times. Veterans' programs are also required at about the present levels by existing legislation and there is no chance of repealing or modifying it. I guess public works and foreign aid will get most of the blow. Especially since the run-in between Savage (Director of the Budget Bureau) and those western senators, there will be little money for new dam construction when we get through preparing the budget.

MARS: I thought Congress already authorized those dams to be built.

CASH: They did, but they haven't appropriated much money for them yet, and in order for them to do it this year, they will either have to cut the military program or run into deficit spending. Those are not attractive alternatives, and Savage thinks that they will settle for much talk and little money this year.

YOU, THE OXFORD DON: I thought the President had promised to build those dams. How can Savage cut them out of the budget?

CASH: I doubt if the President is really enthusiastic about the dams. Anyway, Defense says they must have so much, State says the same thing, and the political advisors say that a balanced budget is an absolute necessity. So the White House sends down an over-all figure and Savage and the rest of us decide how to break it down among the various agencies. The President doesn't interfere with the details.

MARS: Don't you have any idea what the White House wants?

CASH: Not any very definite idea, except that we can't cut military spending much, and of course the programs required by legislation have to be kept up unless things like grants-in-aid for old age assistance and highways are repealed, and nobody is seriously suggesting that they should be. The President said in his press conference that we would have to make sacrifices in order to gain military security, but when Savage asked Herman Williams (Chief Assistant to the President) what this meant he didn't give us much help.

MARS: Who set the over-all spending limit?

CASH: Savage himself and Treasury provided the figures on requests and anticipated tax revenues, and Williams and Dick Almead (Chairman of the National Committee of the President's party) insisted on two things: a balanced budget and adequate funds for urban housing programs. The cities are where the party people hope to make their real gains in the next election. Add this to Savage's disapproval of federal power projects as a matter of principle and it spells little money for dam construction.

MARS: What is the scuttlebutt on foreign aid? I understand that the President wanted a big increase and was talked out of it.

CASH: Didn't you decide that in the National Security Council?

MARS: Not really. We talked about it, but the Treasury people weren't at the meeting, so the decision was postponed. I heard it was taken up at a Cabinet meeting.

CASH: My information is that Williams and the Treasury people told the President an increase was impossible and that ended it. The State Department wouldn't settle for less than last year's figure so that fixed the size of the request.

MARS: We did decide the size of the Defense Budget in the NSC.

CASH: That was done while the President was away at the NATO meeting, wasn't it?

MARS: Yes. He was in on the earlier discussions, but the main problem was getting some kind of compromise worked out between the various branches of the armed forces that would come within the over-all limits insisted on by the Treasury people and the Budget Bureau people. The President wanted to knock some heads together to get the research programs under one unified control, but nobody could agree on *who* should control, so the matter was left pretty much as it had been. The Secretary of Defense may get some additional authority over the services but—

CASH: I doubt that. That request from Defense needs legislation from Congress, and until the State Department is convinced that Defense is on the right track we can't clear the request.

YOU: What do you mean?

CASH: All requests for legislation emanating from executive agencies come to us before they are submitted to Congress and we clear them—get the views of other agencies, see how they square with the President's legislative program, and so on. Until they are cleared and the major agencies involved agree, they can't be submitted.

YOU: Wait a minute. You mean that if the President wants to ask Congress for legislation, he can't just go ahead and do it?

CASH: Legally, of course he can, but he won't as a rule. The agencies that have to carry out the program, or whose interests are affected by the program, must support the recommendations, or there would be an awful hassle. The President wouldn't risk that even if he wanted to, which he doesn't because he doesn't really know enough of the details to have an opinion. So clearance is our job.

MARS: Your man Savage and the Treasury boys are not so dominant in the Council as they were. Defense and State and the Joint Chiefs of Staff have been calling the shots for the last few weeks. I hear that Defense and State dominate the Cabinet too.

CASH: They're bound to with the international picture dominating everything the way it has lately. By the way, what do you think of Alsmann's column that the Cabinet is being revived as the truly deliberative body it was supposed to be?

MARS: I don't think it is, not yet anyway. *We* make the decisions on defense and a whole lot of other foreign policy, which in turn means two thirds of the budget. You people are the key agency for the rest of the budget and for the legislative program. The influential members of the Cabinet also attend NSC meetings, and exert their influence there. Between Budget and NSC the important decisions are taken care of. What is there left for the Cabinet to do as an institution? Ultimately it might become the agency that co-ordinates you with us and brings in the viewpoint of, say, Health, Education, and Welfare, but not now.

CASH: I agree. And since patronage is handled by Williams and Almead, there isn't any party work for them to do. The Council of Economic Advisers has been getting increasingly secure jurisdiction over economic policy questions. You know, I don't think that many people really understand what is involved in the way executive agencies are piling up and handling the planning and co-ordination of the policy-making side of things. Even the newspaper boys write very little about it, and precious few of the academics even suspect what is happening.

YOU: Look here, I'm an academic and an outsider as well. I've heard a little about the kind of thing you've been discussing, but I thought that it only applied to the present administration; that it was not a permanent part of the Presidency.

CASH: Much of this machinery was established under Roosevelt and Truman. The process grew steadily in importance under them. We both had our present jobs under previous administrations. The developments have been a little more dramatic recently, but this machinery will survive and continue to function, with increasing authority, if anything, long after the present administration is gone.

YOU: Well, where is the President? What is his role?

CASH: Well, of course he is around. He is the one exposed to the public spotlight and he performs a lot of ceremonial duties. He doesn't play much part in making policy, though. That is our job, Mars, me, and a lot of others like us.

Having listened carefully to this conversation, you go out and check, as thoroughly as you can, the validity of what Cash and Mars have said. You find that their specific statements of fact are accurate, and that these facts are a fair sample of what normally goes on within the executive branch. However, there are many who disagree, some rather violently, with Cash's final evaluation of the President's role. They insist that the President still must make, personally, the broad policy decisions and that the responsibility is still his in the last analysis. You also come across the following material, which you had not seen previously, relating to the same general subject:

Dealing with the [presidency], a recent writer remarks:

"We have routinized the President's responsibility to take the policy lead. And at the same time, we have institutionalized, in marked degree, the exercise of that responsibility. President and presidency are synonymous no longer; the office now comprises an officialdom twelve-hundred strong. For almost every phase of policy development there is now institutional machinery engaged in preparations on the President's behalf; for the financial and administrative workplan of the government, the Budget Bureau; for the Administration's legislative program, the White House counsel and the Budget's clearance organization; for programming in economic and social spheres, the Council of Economic Advisers (and to some degree the Cabinet, Eisenhower-style); in foreign and military fields, the National Security Council; in spheres of domestic preparedness, the Office of Defense Mobilization; these pieces of machinery among others, each built around a program-making task, all lumped together, formally, under the rubric "The Executive Office of the President," an institutional conception and a statutory entity less than two decades old.

"These are significant developments, this routinizing, institutionalizing, of the initiative. They give the presidency nowadays a different look than it has worn before. . . ."[1]

[I]t is in the Eisenhower regime that tendencies toward bureaucratization, exhibited during the incumbencies of Truman and F.D.R., have become controlling, thanks in part to Mr. Eisenhower's military experience with the Chief of Staff work concept, in part to his settled preference for consensus and security as against debate and adventuring, and in part to inter-

---

[1] Richard E. Neustadt, "The Presidency at Mid-Century," *Law and Contemporary Problems,* XXI (August, 1956), 611.

vals of bad health. In consequence of all these factors combined, the institutionalizing process has been carried beyond the Truman model in four respects: (1) in the employment of Sherman Adams as Chief of Staff; (2) in use of the Cabinet for collective consultation; (3) in more effective use of the Vice-President; and (4) in regular, planned consultation with congressional leaders on legislative policies.

Sherman Adams . . . is accorded the title and enjoys a power in the White House second only to that of the President himself. Indeed, in light of what is now known about the matter it would seem that Mr. Adams was for all practical purposes President during the early stages of Mr. Eisenhower's illness. . . .

[A] marked characteristic of the Eisenhower administration is the frequent detachment of the President from the conduct of his subordinates. On several occasions he appears to have accomplished what President Truman and many commentators have said was impossible, "passing the buck" to the Secretary of Agriculture, the Secretary of State, the Secretary of the Army, the Attorney General. Each of these gentlemen, according to the President, is an independent officeholder with his own views of appropriate policy, with which the President has no warrant to interfere.

The same detachment, the same attitude of reigning rather than ruling, when coupled with efficient staff work, had already been carried so far by the time of the President's critical illness in midterm [1955] that the "administration" went on notwithstanding the disaster with scarcely a tremor. The persons most seriously inconvenienced were those whose commissions had to be signed by the President in person. It is true that at one time the suggestion was advanced within the administration itself that the Attorney General should explore the possibility of delegating further presidential power, totally ignoring the Vice-President. The idea was quickly dropped, however, on receipt of the first encouraging medical bulletin; and, Donovan writes, there was a further reason:

"This was that no papers of any great consequence awaited the President's signature. A key to the whole problem was the fact that his illness struck at the lowest period of government activity. Congress had adjourned. The President had acted on all bills requiring his attention. The Big Four Foreign Ministers' meeting was still nearly a month away. Many high officials had just got off on vacation. Preparation of the major messages to be submitted by the President to Congress in January was in the earliest stages. Even if he had been in the best of health, it was a time when the President's participation in the routine business of government would have been at a minimum." [2]

Meanwhile, the American public, bemused by bulletins purveying medical detail, concentrated on the President's illness and left Sherman Adams a free hand. When the President had recovered sufficiently to work an hour at a time, nearly six weeks after the onset of his illness, the official biographer of his first term commented:

"Adams, as usual, was the channel through which work flowed to and from Eisenhower, and in this period the influence of the Assistant to the President upon the operations of the government was very considerable. Working in a plain office . . . Adams was on the phone to Washington from morning until night, giving instructions, arranging conferences, summoning officials to see the President and making innumerable administrative decisions. He would lay out areas of policy in which the President alone must make decisions and then see to it that decisions were reached on matters beyond these boundaries. In Denver, as in Washington, his authority was enhanced by his unique prerogative in speaking for the President—'It is the President's wish that . . .' or 'The President hopes you will . . .' and so forth." [3]

Possibly a slight understatement! Eisenhower himself laughingly suggested that "there might even have been a few hints that the Cabinet did better without him" and expressed surprise that anyone should be surprised that "the Cabinet worked harmoniously and successfully in following the administration's

---

[2] Robert J. Donovan, *Eisenhower, The Inside Story* (New York: Harper and Brothers, 1956), 370.
[3] *Ibid.*, 378.

familiar and practicable middle course between the extremes of too little and too much."

Just how durable is President Eisenhower's impact on the presidency apt to be? Certainly the time is long past when the conception of the President as a sort of "boss of the works" had convincing connection with reality.

Rather, I suggest, there is a long-term trend at work in the world that consolidates power in the executive departments of all governments, first in the person of one individual, then in an "administration." The era of Roosevelt, Churchill, Stalin, Hitler, Mussolini—each a cornerstone of the national "cult of personality"—has been followed by collegial rule, collective responsibility, and *ad hoc* policies flowing out of completed staff work. . . .[4]

Review the materials in your text and lecture notes relating to the presidency, and, more specifically, to the operations of the Bureau of the Budget, the National Security Council, and other major agencies in the Executive Office of the President.

On the basis of the new material, but also bearing in mind the data (from text and lectures) on which your original analysis was based, prepare as a written exercise or for class discussion the following:

1. To what extent, if any, does your original summary statement concerning the job of President of the United States need to be revised?

2. What particular changes would you make in your manuscript?

3. Is your conclusion concerning the democratic control of the President's action still valid? If not, explain why not and suggest the changes that might re-establish democratic control without upsetting the performance of functions by the executive branch. If you believe that your conclusion on this point is still valid, be sure to justify it in terms of the newly acquired data.

4. How can you explain why the developments, which you have learned of in your conversations with Cash and Mars and your reading of Corwin, have occurred? Be as specific as possible.

---

[4] Edward S. Corwin, *The President: Office and Powers,* 4th edition. (New York: New York University Press, 1957) 300–304.

PROBLEM 29

The Role of the President in Legislation

In 1968, the United States had enjoyed for some time a period of genuine peace, prosperity, and tranquility. A reasonably harmonious coexistence between this nation and the Soviet Union had been worked out, and the two great national powers were engaged in a peaceful, not unfriendly, competition in which each nation expected its way of life to prove most successful in promoting the happiness of its people. International control of nuclear weapons, ballistic missiles, earth satellites, and space platforms had at last been achieved, and American and Russian space men often rocketed to visit with one another on either nation's space platforms. Domestically, the economic uncertainties and maladjustments that had troubled the United States in the late 1950's and early 1960's had been brought into a relatively stable balance, and observers remarked that even the "farm problem" appeared to have been "solved."

The Republican candidate for president in 1968 was Josiah Cabot, who was described by a history-minded journalist as "a modern, more capable Coolidge with a great record as an effective administrator." During the campaign, the Republican and Democratic parties found few issues on which to disagree, save one. The incumbent president, a Democrat who was completing his second term, had followed a pattern of strong, insistent leadership in his relations with Congress reminiscent of Franklin D. Roosevelt, and had repeatedly played the role of "Chief Legislator" as well as of "Chief Executive." Cabot, in his campaign, commented on the "international peace" and "domestic tranquility" of the times, and said that he thought a president ought to avoid any action that might "rock the boat." In his election eve telecast to the nation, he declared, "I do not conceive of the president as properly the legislative leader of this nation. In our system of separation of powers and responsibilities, the people elect the *Congress* to make the laws of this fair land; they elect the *president* to assure the able administration of those laws." The Republican party platform for 1968 reiterated these views, and committed the party to a conception of the president as an administrator who should leave the matter of legislation entirely in the hands of Congress. In addition, the party's congressional leadership itself was strongly committed to this view. As the Republican leader in the House, Joseph Shortworth, put it, "The executive department of a government like ours should be subordinate to the legislative branch; in short, the president should enforce the laws, leaving to the people the task of correcting any errors or omissions Congress may commit; this, and only this, is our conception of the proper role of the presidency in relation to Congress." The stand taken by Cabot, the Republican party platform, and the party's congressional leaders seemed sound doctrine to most voters at the time. It was a major factor in Josiah Cabot's election by a majority of 55 per cent to 45 per cent for his opponent, and in the election of Republican majorities in both houses of Congress.

There was, however, one flaw in the national tranquility. The tempo and pressures of an increasingly complicated and perplexing life generated tensions that took toll of the nation's health. The rate of heart ailments had risen sharply through the 1960's. In May, 1969, four months after President Cabot had taken office, announcement was made of a new cortisone derivative, C2D, which when processed proved to be a positive preventive and cure for heart disease. The General Pharmaceutical Corporation had developed the new drug, as an application of basic research activities that had been going on for some time in the nation's medical schools and other centers of biological, biochemical, and chemical research. Before it announced the development of C2D, General Pharmaceutical had, through patents on its processes, obtained sole rights to its manufacture and distribution. The supply that General Pharmaceutical was able to provide was limited, and, taking into account the limited supply and the probability of a great demand, General Pharmaceutical fixed a very high price for C2D.

Following the announcement concerning the development and marketing of C2D, members of Congress were virtually flooded with clearly spontaneous mail. This mail reflected a widespread popular opinion that the federal government should take action to insure manufacture of C2D in quantity, fair and impartial distribution, and a lower price. Some important newspapers echoed these demands, as did a number of nationally organized interest groups, particularly the Council for the Nation's Health, the American Federation of Labor–Congress of Industrial Organizations, and the National Association for the Welfare of the Aged. Spokesmen for these groups compared the development of C2D to the development of the atomic bomb, arguing that the General Pharmaceutical Corporation had only made "a lucky break-through" in the application of basic research carried on by thousands of scientists and physicians over the years, and that C2D like the atomic bomb was really "a national discovery." Thus, they argued, the drug should be used "for the benefit of all, fairly and impartially, regardless of ability to pay," and they declared that federal government action was the only effective way to assure that this would be done. On the other hand, other newspapers opposed federal government action, and such groups as the National Physicians' Association, the American Pharmacists' Institute, and the Committee to Defend the States denounced national governmental intervention as "an abuse of the federal government's proper powers."

In June, 1969, Senator Daniel Deer Benton, Republican, of Winnemac, introduced a bill to "ensure fair standards for the manufacture, distribution, and pricing" of C2D. It would have provided for a special commission of physicians, government officials, and public members to operate the program. The bill was referred to the Committee on Labor and Public Welfare, and thence to a subcommittee headed by Senator Thomas Meadows Linn, Republican, of Sunshine, which had jurisdiction over such legislation. It soon became apparent that Senator Linn, a former druggist who acted frequently as a congressional spokesman for the National Physicians' Association and the American Pharmacists' Institute, intended to smother the bill in committee if he could, and furthermore that he was exerting all his considerable influence in the Senate and in the House to prevent any action on the C2D issue. In the House, confusion developed when party and committee spokesmen disagreed on the kind of legislative action that was in order. Most influential House leaders supported a proposal contained in a bill introduced by Joseph Shortworth, the Republican Majority Leader, which would have required General Pharmaceutical to license other drug firms to manufacture and sell C2D. On the other hand, many House members opposed any legislation. In addition, observers predicted that, if legislation was passed in the Senate or in the House, the Senate on the one hand and the House on the other would each insist on its own plan—that is, a federal commission in the Senate, or compulsory licensing in the House.

In this situation, President Cabot was informed by friends in Congress that Senator Linn's influence, the confused situation in the House, and the chance of a Senate-House deadlock might prevent *any* action on the issue, *unless* the President himself entered the controversy and took leadership in the fight for some sort of legislation. He was also advised by his Attorney General that existing statutes did not provide an adequate basis for purely executive or administrative action with reference to the manufacture, distribution, or pricing of C2D. As a man at once humane and astute, President Cabot was sensitive to the welfare aspects of the problem, and also to its political potentialities.

The problem was summed up in an editorial that appeared in the Washington *Intelligencer* in mid-June, 1969:

> The President has up to now not indicated whether he will or will not take a position on this question, and although his active support is not absolutely essential for some sort of action, the general opinion is that without it there is a good chance of stalemate within Congress. The discovery itself is of unquestionable benefit to mankind, but the real issue before the nation is whether in the light of its importance it should or should not be made a public trust, as was atomic power originally, through the Atomic Energy Commission.
>
> The President, if he decides to act, can recommend and support a bill for the creation of a federal government commission to manufacture and distribute the drug C2D. Or, instead, he

may decide that the real issue is not one of governmental control, but rather one of the monopoly on the drug obtained by one company. If this is the case, he may urge legislation to provide compulsory licensing of other firms to produce, distribute, and sell C2D. Thus, if the President is wary of governmental management through a special commission, even with representation from physicians and the public, he can push for solution of the problem in terms of licensing to bring about "old-fashioned" competition. In either case, however, new legislation will be required.

This, of course, is the big question, the real problem—whether President Cabot, in view of his and his party's past position on the proper role of the president, will elect to do anything at all. He may choose to do nothing and leave the problem squarely up to Congress. In any case the public will watch with deep interest for his decision, and his justification for acting or not acting.

Review in your text and in your class notes materials relating to the presidency, the role of the president and presidential leadership in legislation, different conceptions of the proper role of the presidency, and presidential-congressional relations.

Next, read the following discussion of different conceptions of the role of the president.

From the point of view of their actions in office, the presidents may be divided broadly into two classes. First, there have been the *innovators*, generally "strong" presidents who have sought to carry out new policies and new programs, and who have sometimes also worked to make significant changes in the operation of the presidency itself—men like Jefferson, John Quincy Adams, Jackson, Polk, Lincoln, Theodore Roosevelt, Wilson, Franklin Roosevelt. Second, there have been the *routineers*, generally "mild" or "passive" if not "weak" presidents who have been largely content to accept a conventional view of the office —men like Monroe, Fillmore, Pierce, Buchanan, Grant, Benjamin Harrison, McKinley, Taft, Harding, and Coolidge. Men of the first type have generally sought the frontiers of the potentialities of the presidency. Men of the second type have been willing to live within a more confined notion of the office. . . . It is useful . . . to think of *innovator* and *routineer* as two ideal-typical poles at the ends of a continuum. Most presidents in fact would fall not at the ends, but at various points along the continuum line.

Generally, though not invariably, times of relative calm have been associated with routineers in the White House, while times of crisis have been associated with innovators. This, apparently, is related to the differing expectations the nation or a majority of the population entertains toward the presidency in periods of calm or crisis. In times of trouble the nation or a majority of its population is likely to demand that "something be done," and look to the president to do it. The president in office may not always respond, but if he does not he is likely to be succeeded by a man who will—as Buchanan was succeeded by Lincoln, and Hoover by Roosevelt. Generally, also, crisis and innovation have in modern times meant steps toward "strong" . . . or "positive" government, and an enlarged scope of power for the president and the executive branch. This was not entirely the case under Jefferson and Jackson *before* the Civil War, but it has held true *since* that time in the administrations of Lincoln, Theodore Roosevelt, Wilson, and Franklin Roosevelt. Generally, also, innovators in the White House have meant an intensification of the conflict between the president and Congress.[1]

Assume now that you are a trusted assistant of Josiah Cabot. He says that he has been urged by some to intervene actively in the C2D conflict and lead a fight for effective legislation of some sort; and that he has been urged by others to abide by the conception of the president's role he, his party platform, and Republican leaders in Congress have expressed, and let Congress alone determine what action, if any, to take. He says that he does not object to either the federal commission or the licensing proposals as such; that his decision will not be determined by such catch phrases as "socialized medicine" or "sacredness of patent rights," which

---

[1] Stuart A. Queen, William N. Chambers, and Charles M. Winston, *The American Social System: Social Control, Personal Choice, and Public Decision* (Boston: Houghton Mifflin Company, 1956), 314.

may be misleading and immaterial in the present situation. He says that he looks upon both Senator Benton and Majority Leader Shortworth as vigorous, effective Congressional leaders, but he is not sure whether they can overcome the obstacles to getting legislation passed. He is undecided as to whether he, President Cabot, should try to be a legislative leader or leave the issue entirely to Congress. He knows that whatever decision he makes, he will have to justify it to the nation.

As his assistant, you are asked by President Cabot to prepare for him three different, well-informed, carefully thought-out documents:

Document 1. A draft of part of a message which he could send to Congress, *if* he decides to assume legislative leadership on the C2D issue; this part should justify President Cabot's undertaking such leadership in terms of alternative conceptions of the president's role with reference to legislation.

NOTE: Another assistant will prepare those parts of the draft message that will deal with the details of the legislative proposals the President may finally decide to recommend.

Document 2. A work paper, as detailed as possible, setting forth the most successful *strategy* and *tactics* you think President Cabot could employ in order to secure legislation, *if* he decides to take legislative leadership.

NOTE: This paper would have to deal with presidential-congressional relationships on legislation and the ways in which the president could marshal support for his proposals, directly with Congressmen, through his potential role as party leader, through appeals to public opinion as these might affect congressional action, and through any other means at his disposal.

Document 3. A draft of a press release which President Cabot could issue, *if* he decides to leave the C2D question entirely up to Congress; this release should justify as fully as possible, on general grounds, his refusal to assume legislative leadership on the issue, without being based on disapproval of either Benton's or Shortworth's bill.

As a written assignment, or for class discussion, work out in a careful, orderly fashion, and a minimum of mere rhetoric, the contents of the three documents indicated above.

PROBLEM 30

Independent Regulatory Commissions and Interest Groups

Consider carefully the following statements, which offer contrasting views of the independent regulatory commissions as a device for the control of business:

[T]he development of the policy of regulation by commission has grown out of the belief that lawmaking bodies, courts, and the ordinary executive officials are incompetent to deal with problems raised by unsatisfactory relations between public utilities and the public. The legislatures cannot deal with these problems intelligently and effectively, because to do so requires a body possessing expert knowledge and in practically continuous session. In both of these respects lawmaking bodies are deficient. The courts cannot satisfactorily deal with these problems because they lack expert knowledge and have many other kinds of business to transact, and because their slow, cumbrous, and formal process excludes classes of evidence which, while logically irrelevant to a lawsuit, are precisely the considerations that would influence a business man in deciding a business proposition. The ordinary executive or law-enforcing officials are incompetent to deal with the problems of regulation because they lack expert knowledge, because they have other and entirely different duties to perform, and because a regulating body should approach its work in a judicial spirit which is incompatible with the executive spirit by which the ordinary law-enforcing officials should be animated. . . .

The disqualifications of legislatures, courts, and ordinary executive officials for the regulation of business suggest some of the qualifications that ought to be possessed by the members of regulating commissions. Ability, expert knowledge, fairness in utterance and act, moral courage to resist public opinion when it is wrong, as well as to enforce their duty on refractory public utility managements when they are wrong—these are the prime essentials. . . .

The true theory of regulation seems to be this: The management of public utilities should be left in the hands of the owners or those that they choose to represent them. The regulating commissions should be strong enough in personnel and statutory power to exercise corrective authority over the managements when the acts of the managements are unreasonable and unjust to the public. And such commissions having been created should be left free to perform their duties without interference from the public or any public body except the courts, and then only when it can be shown that the commissions have exceeded their constitutional authority in a manner plainly unreasonable and unjust to the concerns over which their jurisdiction extends. The success of regulation will probably be in proportion to the consistency, fairness, and integrity with which we carry out these principles.[1]

[T]he commission tends to insulate itself from the government as a whole. It tends to deplore presidential support and interest even though its political survival and regulatory effectiveness are heavily dependent upon the president's leadership. The commission tends to rely upon the presumed expertness of its staff rather than political leadership and widespread popular support for effective regulation. The commission's activity does not have an educative effect upon the public, which scarcely comprehends the detail of regulatory administration. Nor is the public encouraged to maintain interest and concern in regulatory problems. The fear of control by the executive usually leaves a commission without the political strength and stamina needed to balance the advice and counsel of the regulated

---

[1] Samuel O. Dunn, "Regulation by Commission," *North American Review,* 199 (February, 1914), 205–6, 217.

groups. Insulation from sources of popular political strength is matched by close relations with the regulated groups.

A commission's capacity for securing clarification of its legislative mandate normally is severely limited. Periods of regulatory advance are those in which a strong president is able to command the support of a legislative majority in Congress and an aroused public demands regulatory reform. While commissions frequently recommend legislative amendments to the appropriate Congressional committees, they have had little success in obtaining progressive revision of their statutes. They have been unable to mobilize the necessary political support for the enactment of legislation in controversial areas of public policy. It has not been sufficient that a proposed amendment is firmly rooted in the regulatory experience of a commission and in the expert judgment of its staff. Congress is more apt to be impressed with popular clamor for action than with expert recommendations. . . .

[Commissions] have been singularly uninventive and unadaptable. The commission form tends to enthrone not adaptability and consistency of policy, but apathy and passiveness. It increases opportunities for the exercise of influence by regulated groups and minimizes the impact of the democratic political process upon regulation. Where continuity of attention and stability of policy have prevailed, they have tended to reflect inability to adapt to changing conditions. Commissions appear to have no unique qualities which enable their staffs to rise above the general level of competence in government agencies. While commissions exercise broad discretion in regulatory matters, the devices and institutions available for maintaining their political accountability are unsatisfactory. Consequently, their wide scope of discretion is not controlled by firm lines of responsibility.[2]

Review in your text and lecture notes the material relating to independent regulatory commissions.

Now assume the existence of the following situation:
For the past four years there has been expressed in the nation's

---

[2] Marver H. Bernstein, *Regulating Business by Independent Commission* (Princeton, N.J.: Princeton University Press, 1955), 291–296.

press and by a number of citizens' committees a growing concern over the practices of the gasoline industry. Time and again in the large cities of the country independent brands of gasoline have appeared at cut-rate prices, price wars have broken out between the independent brands and the established brands, retail dealers of both groups have suffered considerable loss of profits and many have gone into bankruptcy, and the patterns of retail gasoline distribution have been extremely unstable.

The retail gasoline dealers are independent businessmen who lease stations built by the oil refining companies, buy gasoline from the companies, and sell the gasoline to consumers. The dealers benefit from the advertising of the brand of gas which is done by the oil refining companies. Sometimes during a price war the refinery will assist the retailer by giving him lower prices on the gas he buys so that he, in turn, can cut his retail price and still maintain a margin of profit. Many refining companies, however, are quite willing to supply unbranded gasoline to the independents, who then compete with the branded retailers. The refinery is interested primarily in selling gasoline through whatever channels are available, and often the price wars are encouraged by the refineries in order to sell more gas.

The fact that many refineries encouraged the independent, cut-rate retailers, coupled with the great economic power of the refiners compared with the small retail station owner, has been the basis of conflict between these two groups for many years. The retail dealers have sought to have their relationships with the refineries subjected to governmental control in order to protect the retail profit margin. Until the recent prolonged price wars, however, there was little interest in this issue among other groups in the public. The issue now has become broader than the protection of the small businessmen represented by the retailer, since some of the refining companies have attempted to increase the sale of their gas even more by constructing a large number of new stations. This has presented the issue of waste and has resulted in an even greater threat to the solvency of the older retailers. The instability in the retail gasoline business has been accentuated by the wasteful station construction, and the instability, in turn, has upset the dependability of service to automobile owners.

Many members of Congress, most newspapers in the nation,

and a number of organizations representing automobile owners have joined the retail station owners in demanding some kind of governmental program to reform the practices in the industry. Both political parties supported reform in a general way in their most recent platforms, and so did the presidential candidates in the last election.

Now this general support has crystallized in behalf of legislation to accomplish three results: (1) cut down wasteful station construction by requiring a permit from the federal government and a demonstration of public demand before new stations could be built, (2) prevent wildly fluctuating gasoline prices by establishing governmental control over the retail price of gasoline, and (3) protect the profit margin of retail gasoline distributors by guaranteeing a stated margin above the price which the retail dealer pays for the gas to the refiner. There is little articulate opposition to this program except on the part of the oil refiners, and it seems clear that Congress will enact the program into law. The only real question remaining concerns the kind of administrative arrangements to establish in order to carry out the three parts of the program. The oil refiners, having decided that they cannot defeat the legislation, have concentrated on getting the most advantageous administrative machinery possible.

The alternatives are three: (1) establishing an independent commission composed of seven members appointed by the President for staggered, overlapping terms of seven years, (2) vesting the new regulatory powers in an existing office of the Department of Commerce that already is responsible for providing useful statistical information to oil refining companies, or (3) creating a new agency to be located within the Department of the Interior expressly and solely for the purpose of carrying out this program, to be headed by a bureau chief appointed by the Secretary of the Interior.

For written exercise or class discussion:

1. Assume you are a lobbyist for the retail gasoline dealers. Which of the alternative administrative arrangements would you advocate? Explain fully your reasons.
2. Assume you are the lobbyist for the oil refining companies.

Which of the alternative administrative arrangements would you advocate? Explain fully your reasons.

3. Assume you are a professor of political science. You are asked by the congressional committee considering the legislation to give your views concerning which of the alternative administrative arrangements would best preserve popular democratic control of the administrative process to be established. Which of the alternatives would you advocate? Explain fully your reasons.

PROBLEM 31

Quasi-Legislative and Quasi-Judicial Functions

The executive branch has the job of enforcing the laws made by the legislative branch. This duty usually compels the executive branch to perform certain law-making or "quasi-legislative" functions. The ordinary regulatory statute confers responsibility for enforcement on a designated executive agency, and says that that agency shall make "rules and regulations" necessary to carry out the law. For instance, the Fair Labor Standards Act of 1938 authorized the Wage and Hour Administrator to make such rules and regulations. The regulations that are made (and published in the *Federal Register*) are the law of the land, and to violate them is to act just as illegally as when one disobeys an Act of Congress. The Administrator, for example, issued a regulation requiring employers subject to the law to keep full records of the hours worked by employees and the wages paid to them, and to retain such records for four years after the performance of the particular work recorded. This was a reasonable requirement, needed if the law was to be properly enforced. But it was also a binding general rule of conduct, just as binding as the general rules laid down by the statute requiring the payment of a minimum wage. In this aspect it was legislation, or something very much like it. In issuing this type of regulation, then, the Administrator was acting in a "quasi-legislative" capacity.

The executive branch also frequently performs "quasi-legislative" functions of a different sort. Often the statute that must be enforced includes ambiguous language, which must be interpreted, and its first interpreter is the executive agency responsible for its enforcement. For instance, the Fair Labor Standards Act does not cover "executive and administrative employees." But what does this phrase mean? Shortly after World War II, a number of men who had lost their wartime jobs complained that their employers had unlawfully failed to pay them time-and-a-half compensation for overtime work, as required by the statute. These men had been employed as "expediters." Their job was to visit the firms supplying materials for their employers, and to try to obtain quick delivery from such suppliers. During the war, many big defense manufacturers were competing hotly for materials in short supply, and a successful "expediter" helped them to fulfill their government contracts on time. The typical "expediter" reported at the home office about every other day; for the rest of the time, he was "on the road," usually in his own car, visiting small factories, ascertaining the position of the needed materials in the suppliers' production schedules, and urging, cajoling, or otherwise persuading production managers to speed up their efforts.

Were these "expediters" administrative employees, or not? The first official answer to that question had to be given by the Wage and Hour Division of the U.S. Department of Labor. This was the executive agency responsible for the enforcement of the Fair Labor Standards Act. If the "expediters" were *not* administrative employees, then their employers had broken the law, and the Division must compel such employers to pay up. In fact, the Division could initiate civil or even criminal proceedings against them. But if the "expediters" *were* administrative employees, then their employers were not required to pay them time and a half for overtime and so had not violated the law.

Therefore, the Division had to *interpret* the words of the statute, "administrative employees." Formally, this was the responsibility of the head of the Division, the Wage and Hour Administrator; actually, he leaned heavily on the advice of the Division's lawyers.

This task of *interpretation,* then, is another of the *quasi-legislative* duties frequently performed by the executive branch. To be sure, in a case like this the ultimate power to interpret the statute rests with the courts. But this does not mean that the executive agency's interpretation is unimportant. Far from it. Take the question of the "expediters." For some big companies, the "expediters' " claims amounted to $50,000 or $75,000. If the Administrator should rule that the "expediters" were administrative employees, these companies could breathe easily. They would not be prosecuted with all the bad publicity and legal expense that a prosecution would entail. As for the "expediters," if they wanted a court decision they would have to seek it themselves, instead of relying on the enforcement activities of the executive agency. Private litigation is expensive, especially if there is an appeal to the Supreme Court. Few, if any, "expediters" were likely to bring suit. They knew that even if they won in the trial court, the big companies, with ample financial resources, would appeal, and the "expediters" would then be forced to spend large amounts of money or drop their case.

Conversely, should the Administrator rule that the "expediters" were covered by the Act, this would be a great boon to the "expediters." Even if a court should later interpret the Act otherwise, the "expediters" would not have borne any costs of litigation—and there would always be the chance, perhaps a very good chance, that the employers would not go to court, but would accept the Administrator's ruling and pay up.

This question of the "expediters" illustrates the general proposition that despite the ultimate right to judicial review, statutory interpretation by the executive branch, in many or most instances, is the effective and final interpretation of the law. We have called this function "quasi-legislative" for, in a sense, the executive agency is "making" the law. It might seem that we could call it "quasi-judicial," for in interpreting the statute the executive agency is doing what courts often do. However, the administrative ruling as to whether "expediters" are "administrative employees" is made without a formal adversary proceeding or hearing and because these are lacking, the agency's action is not strictly "quasi-judicial."

The *quasi-judicial* functioning of an executive agency is illustrated by instances where a board or commission acts rather like a court in *hearing and deciding disputes* brought before it. Typical is the National Labor Relations Board. When the government finds reasonable cause to believe that an unfair labor practice has been committed, an agent of the Board, acting somewhat like a trial judge, hears the complaining parties and the company (or union) charged, and writes a report that amounts to a tentative decision;

the whole Board then may review the case and hold a further hearing, acting rather like an appellate court. The Board then issues its decision. There can be judicial review of its action, although the Board's decision is not likely to be overturned unless its procedure has been highhanded or the court disagrees with its interpretation of the statute. In other words, ordinarily the Board's assessment of the evidence and its decision resulting therefrom are final; most of its decisions are not subjected to judicial review.

This is a "quasi-judicial" proceeding, rather than a judicial one, for two reasons. First, in form, the Board is not a court, not a part of the judicial branch established by Article III of the Constitution. Second, in substance, the Board is not bound by all the legal rules that govern judicial procedure: for instance, it can consider "secondary" and "hearsay" evidence that would be barred in court.

Now assume that Robert J. Dickswell has been elected President of the United States after a campaign in which he promised to "clean the government's house and drive the red rats out of Washington." Shortly after his inauguration, a bill is introduced in the Senate by Senator Whaley reading in part as follows:

"No person of Russian or Chinese descent, and no other person who holds opinions subversive of the government or best interests of the United States, shall be employed in any sensitive position in the government of the United States. Any such person holding any such position shall be subject to fine and imprisonment, as hereinafter provided, and likewise the head of any department, board, commission, or other agency employing any such person shall be subjected to such fine and imprisonment." The bill contains specific provisions as to the maximum fine and prison term to be imposed on any person found guilty by a jury in Federal Court of violating this law.

Representative McQuillan introduces in the House a bill similar to the Whaley bill, except that it includes an additional section. The McQuillan bill provides for the establishment of a Federal Loyalty Board of three persons to be appointed by the President with the advice and consent of the Senate. The bill directs this Board to designate those positions which are to be deemed "sensitive," and to issue rules and regulations governing the employment procedures to be followed in hiring employees for sensitive positions, including the type of questionnaires to be filled out by applicants.

Representative T. J. Freeman announces that he will propose an amendment to the McQuillan bill. He says: "I recognize the constitutional right of the government to set standards for employment, and the need to have loyal employees in sensitive positions. But I fear that gossip and slander will cause many innocent people to be arrested and hauled into court. They may be acquitted, but their reputations will have been badly damaged. I want the Loyalty Board to hold completely private hearings, whenever a serious charge is made. Then if—and only if—the Board finds that the law has been violated, the Board should certify the case to the Department of Justice for prosecution."

There is no doubt that some bill to control the employment of "subversives" will be enacted. The Attorney-General, out of loyalty to the President, has issued a mild statement indicating his "support of the general purposes" of both the Whaley bill and the McQuillan bill. The Attorney-General, a few years ago when he was a judge of the U.S. Court of Appeals, handed down several decisions upholding First Amendment liberties and insisting on fair procedure by courts and investigating committees.

It is generally assumed that if a Loyalty Board is established, Representative McQuillan will be appointed chairman of the Board. The population of his State having decreased, it is losing one seat in Congress and a gerrymander is in the offing that will make it difficult for Mr. McQuillan to win re-election. He therefore believes that this is his last term in the House and wants a good job. Mr. McQuillan has won wide notice in the past by his vigor and vehemence in investigating "Un-American activities" and his sweeping denunciations of "socialistic subversives."

The Whaley bill comes up for hearings first, before the Senate Committee on the Judiciary. It soon becomes clear that the committee will make one of three choices. It may (1) approve the Whaley bill as introduced, or with some verbal changes. It may (2) report a new version of the Whaley bill, adding to it the Loyalty Board provisions of the McQuillan bill; or (3) it may also include the provisions proposed by Representative Freeman.

Which of these three courses (or modification thereof) would you advocate, and why, if you were:

1. The registered lobbyist of the United States Veterans Legion, a patriotic organization which holds that "the security of the nation is paramount; individual rights must be sacrificed when necessary"?
2. The registered lobbyist of the National Individual Liberties Federation, a respectable group (although once called "subversive" by Representative McQuillan) which believes that to sacrifice individual freedom and civil rights would be to lose most of what makes America worth saving.
3. A member of the Judiciary Committee, a former professor of constitutional law, and now a senator from a small state where the people have shown little interest in the issue.

In planning your answers, give careful consideration to the nature of quasi-legislative and quasi-judicial functions: the need for them, the possible harm from expanding them, and the impact that they have on the constitutional theory of separation of powers. You may, if you choose, develop a new plan for the committee's consideration, designed to achieve the same basic end as the Whaley bill.

PART IX

THE JUDICIAL POWER

PROBLEM 32

The Task of the Judge

There are many conceptions and misconceptions of the task a judge performs in deciding cases. Some have suggested that the judge merely takes the facts presented to him and applies the law in question to those facts, and that his decision is the result of this process. However, there is an assumption underlying this notion of the judicial process to the effect that determining facts, applying the law, and putting the two together to reach a decision is a straightforward, unambiguous job which, to the trained judge, presents no serious problems or possibilities of error. At the other extreme some have suggested that the trappings of law and facts are mostly decoration; that the decisions are based on "what the judge ate for breakfast," or on whether the defendant reminds the judge of his father. Neither of these interpretations adequately describes the intellectual processes which the judge goes through in arriving at a decision: the things he thinks about, the questions he asks himself, the sources he consults for advice and information. Judging cases in a court of law, like reaching judgments that will affect the lives of others in any walk of life, is a terribly difficult and responsible task, and one which must therefore be undertaken with full deliberation and use of all the resources available to the judge.

Of course, no judge operating in the twentieth century acts alone. He lives in and responds to a social environment as do we all. He is the heir to centuries of judicial tradition. He makes his decisions surrounded by the learning and opinion of countless others. Nevertheless, the individual judge must reach his own conclusions, and consequently an understanding of the basic procedures he must follow is important to an appreciation of the nature of the judicial process.

Review in your text and lecture notes the material relating to judges and the judicial process.

Now consider the following case:

John Larsen is charged with using the mails with intent to defraud. He has been indicted by a federal grand jury and waived a jury trial. The facts of the case are developed as follows: Larsen inherited from his father a secret formula for making a "magic bag," somewhat similar to an asafoetida bag. This bag contained an extremely aromatic combination of rare herbs, and both Larsen and his father claimed that when worn around the neck the bag would ward off a large variety of diseases. Larsen himself always wore such a bag and insisted that his family do likewise. Larsen worked at a regular job and engaged in no large-scale effort to promote his secret. However, he did praise the bag's qualities to all the people he met. Over a period of time, a good many people persuaded Larsen to make bags for them. The ingredients were difficult to obtain and Larsen had to engage in correspondence to secure the necessary items and on two occasions wrote letters to prospective buyers of the bags. Larsen charged $250 apiece for the bags, which price resulted in a profit to Larsen of $100 on each bag sold. With only two exceptions the purchasers of the bags were as enthusiastic about them as Larsen was himself. Expert witnesses testified, however, that the bags offered no medical benefits of any significance and certainly could not prevent the diseases claimed.

The law under which Larsen was indicted and under which conviction is sought is as follows:

> Whoever, having devised or intending to devise any scheme or artifice to defraud, or for obtaining money or property by

means of false or fraudulent pretenses, representations, or promises, or to sell, dispose of, loan, exchange, alter, give away, distribute, supply, or furnish or procure for unlawful use any counterfeit or spurious coin, obligation, security, or other article, or anything represented to be or intimated or held out to be such counterfeit or spurious article, for the purpose of executing such scheme or artifice or attempting to do so, places in any post office or authorized depository for mail matter, any matter or thing whatever to be sent or delivered by the Post Office Department, or takes or receives therefrom, any such matter or thing, or knowingly causes to be delivered by mail according to the direction thereon, or at the place at which is directed to be delivered by the person to whom it is addressed, any such matter or thing, shall be fined not more than $1,000 or imprisoned not more than five years, or both.[1]

As a written exercise or for class discussion prepare the following:

You are a federal district judge before whom this case is being tried. DO NOT concern yourself with arriving at a decision on Larsen's guilt or innocence. DO, carefully and thoughtfully, indicate *what considerations you would take into account, what procedures you would go through, what operations you would perform* in order to answer the following questions:

1. Is the law valid?
2. Does it apply to the facts of this case?
3. Under this law is Larsen guilty?

Again, *do not try to answer the questions themselves.* Rather, tell what you would do in order to find out the answers.

Now, *justify* each *procedure* you have suggested. What reasons have you for doing these things rather than something else? Do these procedures offer the best possibility of arriving at a *just* conclusion?

---

[1] Adapted from 18 U.S. Code 338.

PROBLEM 33

The Supreme Court, the Senate, and Democracy

The "independence of the judiciary," designed to assure the impartiality of judges and to enable them to stand fast against the gusts of public passion, is a value recognized by many Americans. Thinking of the federal judiciary and especially the Supreme Court, they assume that the desired independence is achieved by the system of appointing judges for life, instead of electing them for specified terms. (They seem to overlook the fact that in the United States most judges of state and local courts are elected to office for a term of years—usually in a typical party contest.) Belief in the importance of the independence of the Supreme Court is, of course, likely to be expressed most eloquently when that independence is threatened, as it seemed to be in 1937. In that depression year, after several state and federal statutes regulating various aspects of the economy had been held unconstitutional by a sharply divided court, often a bare 5-to-4 majority of the Justices, President Roosevelt proposed that Congress should increase the size of the Court. This would have given him the opportunity to appoint several new Justices who would presumably vote in favor of the validity of the challenged legislation. Appearing before a Senate committee considering this proposal, one eloquent opposition witness was columnist Dorothy Thompson, who said in part:

> There are always hundred percenters for democracy, those who want pure democracy. They want to do away with every impediment and march at high speed toward what they call a real or modern democracy, or the democracy in harmony with the

244

times. But precisely in such revolutionary times—and we live in one—it is most necessary to have a point of reference, a warrant, an instrument which confidently assures the legitimacy of what is being done. For without such a point of reference, there ceases to be a spontaneous social cohesion and what you then get as sure as fate is social cohesion by coercion. . . .

I think the disciplines of law are particularly needed in democracies and are especially needed at any moment when a powerful majority is in temporary control of the current political situation almost to the exclusion of minority representation. We have such a situation in this country now. The men who designed the structure of this Republic realized this. They did not believe that the cure for the evils of democracy was more democracy. They believed that the prevention against a democracy running away with itself, the prevention against a powerful majority riding roughshod over the temporary minority and selling short the whole future of the country, the prevention against today's majority mortgaging tomorrow's majority, lay in a written constitution and an independent Supreme Court to interpret that constitution.

There is a reason why Supreme Court judges are appointed for life, and removable only by impeachment. That reason is obvious. It was certain that successive executives and successive Senates would seek to put upon the Supreme Court Bench men responsive to their own ideas. Everybody is human, but it was arranged that the Supreme Court, only by the merest chance, by a very remote mathematical chance, would ever coincide with the majority of the moment. It was so arranged that the Court should represent, not the momentary dominant majority, but the continuity and tradition in American life. . . .

It is true that the Supreme Court is conservative. I think it is conservative by its very nature. And that, gentlemen, is its function—to conserve. It represents, the opponents say, the past. Yes; perhaps it does. It represents continuity; it demands that today's laws shall be checked against the whole body of law and the principles governing the state, and thus it insures that new laws shall be designed in some conformity with certain long-established customs and ways of life. And just because it represents continuity, because it exerts a constant reminder on the people that they have a past, a past to which they have a duty; just because it reminds them that when they act, however radically, however drastically, they must keep an eye on long-established patterns of law and behavior—just for that reason I think it safeguards the future. . . .[1]

But there is another side to this controversy. When the Court struck down laws for minimum wages, for instance, as "arbitrary and unreasonable" even though they were the product of long consideration and debate in legislative halls, critics said that the judicial branch was usurping the functions of the legislative branch. And if, indeed, judges thus engage in law-making, is not the exercise of such power by men who are not responsible to the voters a defiance of the fundamental principles of democracy? Read and ponder following excerpts from a forthright advocate of democracy:

> Democracy is more than an ideal; it is also a method. . . . The method is government responsible to the people. Hence, the essential democratic institution is the ballot box and all that goes with it. All [of the great advocates of democracy] place electoral responsibility at the very center of the democratic system. . . .
>
> [Electoral responsibility] promotes self direction through participation in making public policy. The ballot and the system of political parties are the means and the assurance of that participation. They are the means because, however much the process of voting may be obscured, the basic decision on policy is always the choice of the policy-makers. They are the assurance because all the paraphernalia of participation (campaigning, petitioning, canvassing, propagandizing) is the one essential way to compel rulers to respond to pressure from the ruled. . . .
>
> Democracy is a form of government in which the rulers are fully responsible to the ruled. . . .
>
> If government is to be fully responsible, [elections and parties] ought to make [popular] majorities effective. If the rulers

---

[1] Hearings before the Committee on the Judiciary, United States Senate, 75th Congress, 1st Session on S. 1392 (Washington, D.C.: Government Printing Office, 1937) 861–862.

chosen by electoral majorities do not have the power to govern, then responsible government is as impossible as if there were no majority at all. The idea of [an electoral] sanction is simply praise and blame leading to rewards and punishments. Yet praise and blame cannot be rationally assigned unless rulers have in fact the power to carry out the majority will. If rulers have not the power to govern, how can they be fairly blamed for failure to enact electoral decisions? . . . Government truly responsible to the people . . . can thus be said to depend upon [popular] majorities. . . .

[According to Aristotle], "Another attribute of democracy is to dispense with all life offices—or at least to curtail the powers of any such offices, if they have been left surviving from some earlier epoch. . . ."

A latent obstructiveness lies deep in the [Supreme] Court's nature. Although most of the time it is rationally repressed, now and again it breaks loose and springs upward to direct judicial action. . . .

Of course, the danger would be insignificant were it not that the Court really has enough resources, even when besieged for a long time, to refuse to unite with the rest of government. Its granary is its irresponsibility, life tenure uncontrolled by popular sanction. Its armory is its share, small but crucial, of the power to govern. We do not need the goggle-eyed perceptiveness of a man from Mars to see the inconsistency in our constitutional myth. Dispassionate analysis, as well as the amazement of casual visitors from Europe and Asia, ought to point it out. We say that Sovereignty resides in elected officials, yet we regularly permit the Court, whose responsibility to the people is very indistinct, to exercise a sizable share of it. . . . Many people may prefer an only vaguely responsible Court to elected representatives; but they cannot possibly reconcile their preference with the democratic method. What is democracy, but government by public opinion determined in partisan elections? and what public opinion can there ever be but the public opinion of the most recent election or "hour"? If one does not wish to speak as bluntly as Hamilton of legislative oppression or popular incapacity, one can then . . . cast slurs on the democratic process itself, suggesting by the words "passionate party campaigns" or "mob passion" that Congressional legislation is first cousin to lynch law. The slander is insidious. It does not argue the case; it merely hints of some vague dire peril. Mob passion there may be in the United States, but judicial review has never been used against it. Rather the statutes the Court has nullified have been enacted after mature and lengthy deliberation. Consider the AAA, for example. During the late twenties, and early thirties, bills dealing with farm surpluses were, as Solicitor General Reed pointed out in his argument in the Butler case, reported out eight times by the House Committee on Agriculture, ten times by the Senate Committee. Of these the Senate passed five, the House four, and Presidents signed two. The slow and tortuous path of a bill through Congress . . . can hardly be called mob passion. And the proposal that finally matured as the AAA had been before Congress since 1923, so that it can hardly be called the product of a passionate party campaign. The mob passion, from which the proponents of judicial review say the Court saves us, was in this case a popular emotion stable and thoughtful enough to endure through five campaigns and a decade of argument. . . .

American democrats should not be misled by insinuations about mob passion or by the suggestion that life tenure works better in democracy than the electoral sanction can. They should understand the justification of life tenure for what it is: a distrust of democratic government and a preference for irresponsibility.

The Court is indispensable to the constitutional system. Without a highest court of appeal, differences in decision between equal courts would produce intolerable confusion. Even the basic outlines of law would be different in different jurisdictions. And without a supreme federal court, state courts could not be relied upon to enforce federal law. Hence democrats cannot simply abolish the Court. They might perhaps return to the medieval tradition, still partially continued in England, in which the legislature is the high court of appeal. So Senator La Follette suggested during his campaign for President in 1924: appeal to Congress when the Court has refused to enforce one of its acts. Theodore Roosevelt had earlier (during his 1912 campaign) suggested popular referendums on Court-nullified law. The disease, as Theodore Roosevelt rightly saw, is judicial pride.

[T]o expect that judges can always restrain themselves requires a faith in fallen human nature greater than democrats dare have. The propensity of pride pervades the black-robed judges no less than other man; and as democrats are well aware, neither humility nor responsibility endures unless enforced by formal sanctions. Should the Court again be about to thwart majority leadership, again about to harass us with the most unworkable of separated powers, we then ought to remember the advice of Jefferson:

"Before the canker is become inveterate, before its venom has reached so much of the body politic as to get beyond control, remedy should be applied. Let the future appointments of judges be for four or six years, and renewable by the President and Senate. This will bring their conduct, at regular periods, under revision and probation. . . . We have erred in this point, by copying England, where . . . it is a good thing to have the judges independent to the King. But we have omitted to copy their caution also, which makes a judge removeable on the address of both legislative Houses. That there should be public functionaries independent of the nation, whatever may be their demerit, is a solecism in a republic, of the first order of absurdity and inconsistency." [2]

Now it appears that in "pure" democratic theory there is something highly anachronistic about allowing major decisions to be made by either an unrepresentative group, such as the Court, or a minority of a representative body, such as the United States Senate. Yet even in the Senate it is true that a minority can sometimes force the Senate to make a major decision, namely, the decision not to pass a bill. True, like the Court's nullification of a law, such a decision is a negative one; the Court strikes down a statute, and the Senate minority prevents a statute from being made. Yet the nullification of a law and the defeat of a bill are examples of important governmental decision-making. They are decisions to put things back to where they were, or to leave them where they are.

---

[2] William H. Riker, *Democracy in the United States* (New York, N.Y.: The Macmillan Company, 1953).

The method by which a minority of senators can cause the Senate to make this kind of negative decision is the *filibuster*. A filibuster is a determined effort of a group of Senators to talk so long about a pending bill that the Senate, wishing or needing to get other business done, eventually agrees to withdraw the bill from consideration. The Senate rules make it possible to shut off a really determined filibuster, but only if at least 66 senators vote in favor of a motion to terminate debate.

It is true that if 66 or more senators are sufficiently determined to see a bill passed, they can stop a filibuster. Some senators, however, are reluctant to vote for any curtailment of unlimited debate; and many bills, of course, are supported by a majority of the Senate yet by fewer than 66 senators. Such bills can be killed by a persistent and long-winded minority. The right to filibuster in effect sometimes deprives the majority of its right to make laws. Nevertheless, the antimajoritarian principle of the filibuster has been earnestly defended:

> Although the question before the Senate is whether to amend the rules, [to make it easier for the Senate to close debate] the issue is not one of parliamentary procedure. It is whether there shall be a profound and far-reaching constitutional change in the character of the American government. . . . If the amendment is carried, the existing power of a minority of the states to stop legislation will have been abolished.

"Stripped of all mumbo-jumbo and flag waving," says *The New York Times*, the issue "is whether the country's highest legislative body will permit important measures to be kept from a vote through the activities of a few leather-throated, iron-legged members who don't want democratic decision." This is an unduly scornful and superficial way to dispose of a great constitutional problem. For the real issue is whether any majority, even a two-thirds majority, shall now assume the power to override the opposition of a large minority of the states.

In the American system of government, the right of "democratic decision" has never been identified with majority rule as such. The genius of the American system, unique I believe among the democracies of the world, is that it limits all power—including the power of the majority. Absolute power, whether in a king, a president, a legislative majority, a popular majority, is alien to the American idea of democratic decision.

The American idea of a democratic decision has always been that important minorities must not be coerced. When there is strong opposition, it is neither wise nor practical to force a decision. It is necessary and it is better to postpone the decision—to respect the opposition and then to accept the burden of trying to persuade it.

For a decision which has to be enforced against the determined opposition of large communities and regions of the country will, as Americans have long realized, almost never produce the results it is supposed to produce. The opposition and the resistance, having been overridden, will not disappear. They will merely find some other way of avoiding, evading, obstructing or nullifying the decision.

For that reason it is a cardinal principle of the American democracy that great decisions on issues that men regard as vital shall not be taken by the vote of the majority until the consent of the minority has been obtained. Where the consent of the minority has been lacking, as for example in the case of the prohibition amendment, the "democratic decision" has produced hypocrisy and lawlessness.

This is the issue in the Senate. It is not whether there shall be unlimited debates. The right of unlimited debates is merely a device, rather an awkward and tiresome device, to prevent large and determined communities from being coerced.

The issue is whether the fundamental principle of American democratic decision—that strong minorities must be persuaded and not coerced—shall be altered radically, not by constitutional amendment but by a subtle change in the rules of the Senate.

The issue has been raised in connection with the civil rights legislation. The question is whether the vindication of these civil rights requires the sacrifice of the American limitation on majority rule. The question is a painful one. But I believe the answer has to be that the rights of Negroes will in the end be made more secure, even if they are vindicated more slowly, if the cardinal principle—that minorities shall not be coerced by majorities—is conserved.

For if that principle is abandoned, then the great limitations on the absolutism and tyranny of transient majorities will be gone, and the path will be much more open than it now is to the demagogic dictator who, having aroused a mob, destroys the liberties of the people.[3]

Now, assume the existence of the following situation:

The Supreme Court, whose decision on the segregation issue aroused some vehement opposition in the South, later angers other large groups by holding the Communist Control Act of 1954 unconstitutional, and by overruling its earlier opinions and holding the Fair Labor Standards Act and the Agricultural Adjustment Act unconstitutional. After much criticism of the Court, a resolution is introduced in the Senate by Senator Ricker to *amend* Article III of the Constitution, to provide that while judges shall be appointed as heretofore, they shall not serve for life, *but for a term of six years.* A large majority of senators have stated publicly that they will favor it. While the resolution is still before the Senate Judiciary Committee, however, a group of 20 senators, calling themselves "The Defenders of the Faith," announce that they are prepared to filibuster "till hell freezes over," in order to prevent a vote ever being taken on the resolution. Thereupon Senator Ricker moves to amend the rules of the Senate, to provide that after every senator has had the opportunity to speak for one hour on any bill or resolution, debate may be terminated by a simple majority vote.

The first question before the Senate next week will be Senator Ricker's motion to amend the rules. After that, on the Senate's schedule, will be the Ricker resolution to amend the Constitution.

You are a senator. You have always leaned heavily for advice and counsel on an ancient friend who taught you political science in college long ago. From this friend comes a letter which says,

"Joe, for Heaven's sake, go slow. Remember Madison! Remember the separation of powers. Read Walter Lippmann. But far be it from me to tell you how to vote. Whatever you do, though, try to be true to yourself. Be *consistent,* Joe. You're going to have to make two difficult decisions. My advice is, be sure of what you believe about government, clarify your principles in your own mind, and vote in accordance with those principles."

---

[3] Walter Lippmann in the *New York Herald Tribune,* March 3, 1949. Copyright, 1949, New York Herald Tribune, Inc. By permission.

The Supreme Court, the Senate, and Democracy 253

From your 25-year-old son, a highly skilled airplane mechanic, comes another letter:

"Our mechanics' union wouldn't last a week if we didn't all abide by the principle of majority rule. And our union president might ruin the whole organization if he didn't have to stand for re-election every two years. You brought me up, Dad, to revere Abraham Lincoln. Lincoln said: 'government of the people, for the people, by the people.' You'll remember that, won't you, when you vote next week?"

Think carefully about all of the reading assigned in this problem exercise. *Then, as a written exercise or for class discussion, prepare thoughtful replies to both letters.* Indicate how you expect to vote on BOTH issues, and EXPLAIN your reasoning. In your replies, remember that you are to deal with the points raised by both your friend the professor and your son. Make it clear to them that you have pondered their advice. Remember also that your replies should emphasize your REASONS for the votes you intend to cast on both the issues before the Senate.

PROBLEM 34

The Judicial Power as a Check on the Executive

The Constitution vests "the executive Power" in the President, makes him Commander-in-Chief of the armed forces, and directs him to "take care that the laws be faithfully executed."

In *Marbury* v. *Madison* (1803) the Supreme Court considered an application by Marbury for a writ of mandamus to compel Madison, Secretary of State, to deliver to Marbury the latter's commission as Justice of the Peace. Among other things, the Court said:

> By the constitution of the United States, the President is invested with certain important political powers, in the exercise of which he is to use his own discretion, and is accountable only to his country in his political character, and to his own conscience. To aid him in the performance of these duties, he is authorized to appoint certain officers, who act by his authority and in conformity with his orders.
>
> In such cases, their acts are his acts; and whatever opinion may be entertained of the manner in which executive discretion may be used, still there exists, and can exist, no power to control that discretion. The subjects are political. . . .
>
> The conclusion from this reasoning is, that where the heads of departments are the political or confidential agents of the executive, merely to execute the will of the President, or rather to act in cases in which the executive possesses a constitutional or legal discretion, nothing can be more perfectly clear than that their acts are only politically examinable. But where a specific duty is assigned by law, and individual rights depend upon the per-

formance of that duty, it seems equally clear that the individual who considers himself injured has a right to resort to the laws of his country for a remedy. . . .

It is, then, the opinion of the Court,

1st. That by signing the commission of Mr. Marbury, the president of the United States appointed him a justice of peace for the county of Washington in the district of Columbia; and that the seal of the United States, affixed thereto by the secretary of state, is conclusive testimony of the verity of the signature, and of the completion of the appointment; and that the appointment conferred on him a legal right to the office for the space of five years.

2dly. That, having this legal title to the office, he has a consequent right to the commission; a refusal to deliver which, is a plain violation of that right, for which the laws of his country afford him a remedy.[1]

In *Mississippi* v. *Johnson* (1867) the State of Mississippi asked the Supreme Court to "enjoin" (prohibit) President Andrew Johnson from enforcing the Reconstruction Acts, which were laws duly passed by Congress. The Court's opinion included the following language:

> The Attorney-General objected to the leave asked for, upon the ground that no bill which makes a President a defendant, and seeks an injunction against him to restrain the performance of his duties as President, should be allowed to be filed in this court. . . .
>
> The single point which requires consideration is this: Can the President be restrained by injunction from carrying into effect an Act of Congress alleged to be unconstitutional?
>
> It is assumed by the counsel for the State of Mississippi, that the President, in the execution of the Reconstruction Acts, is required to perform a mere ministerial duty. In this assumption there is, we think, a confounding of the terms ministerial and executive, which are by no means equivalent in import.

---

[1] The opinion continued, however, to explain that his remedy could not be given him by the Supreme Court, as the Constitution did not authorize the Supreme Court to act as a trial court in his case. Presumably Marbury could have got what he wanted if he had brought suit in a lower court. (Ed.)

A ministerial duty, the performance of which may, in proper cases, be required of the head of a department, by judicial process, is one in respect to which nothing is left to discretion. It is a simple, definite duty, arising under conditions admitted or proved to exist, and imposed by law.

The case of *Marbury* v. *Madison* . . . furnishes an illustration. A citizen had been nominated, confirmed, and appointed a justice of the peace for the District of Columbia, and his commission had been made out, signed, and sealed. Nothing remained to be done except delivery, and the duty of delivery was imposed by law on the Secretary of State. It was held that the performance of this duty might be enforced by *mandamus* issuing from a court having jurisdiction. . . .

Very different is the duty of the President in the exercise of the power to see that the laws are faithfully executed, and among these laws the acts named in the bill. By the first of these acts he is required to assign generals to command in the several military districts, and to detail sufficient military force to enable such officers to discharge their duties under the law. By the supplementary act, other duties are imposed on the several commanding generals, and these duties must necessarily be performed under the supervision of the President as commander-in-chief. The duty thus imposed on the President is in no just sense ministerial. It is purely executive and political.

An attempt on the part of the judicial department of the government to enforce the performance of such duties by the President might be justly characterized, in the language of Chief Justice Marshall, as "an absurd and excessive extravagance."

It is true that in the instance before us the interposition of the court is not sought to enforce action by the Executive under constitutional legislation, but to restrain such action under legislation alleged to be unconstitutional. But we are unable to perceive that this circumstance takes the case out of the general principles which forbid judicial interference with the exercise of Executive discretion.

In *Youngstown Sheet & Tube Co.* v. *Sawyer* (1952), the question was whether, during the Korean War, President Truman had the constitutional power to direct his Secretary of Commerce (Sawyer) to seize and operate the steel mills, which were idle because of a prolonged strike. On this issue, the members of the court differed; but the majority held that the President's action had been unlawful and that the mills must be returned to their owners.

Several judges wrote opinions. For the majority, Mr. Justice Black said:

> The President's power, if any, to issue the order must stem either from an act of Congress or from the Constitution itself. There is no statute that expressly authorizes the President to take possession of property as he did here. Nor is there any act of Congress to which our attention has been directed from which such a power can fairly be implied. Indeed, we do not understand the Government to rely on statutory authorization for this seizure. . . .
>
> Moreover, the use of the seizure technique to solve labor disputes in order to prevent work stoppages was not only unauthorized by any congressional enactment; prior to this controversy, Congress has refused to adopt that method of settling disputes. When the Taft-Hartley Act was under consideration in 1947, Congress rejected an amendment which would have authorized such governmental seizures in cases of emergency. . . .
>
> It is clear that if the President had authority to issue the order he did, it must be found in some provision of the Constitution. And it is not claimed that express constitutional language grants this power to the President. The contention is that presidential power should be implied from the aggregate of his powers under the Constitution. Particular reliance is placed on provisions in Article II which says that "the executive Power shall be vested in a President . . ."; that "he shall take Care that the Laws be faithfully executed"; and that he "shall be Commander in Chief of the Army and Navy of the United States."
>
> The order cannot properly be sustained as an exercise of the President's military power as Commander in Chief of the Armed Forces. The Government attempts to do so by citing a number of cases upholding broad powers in military commanders engaged in day-to-day fighting in a theater of war. Such cases need not concern us here. Even though "theater of war" be an expanding concept, we cannot with faithfulness to our constitu-

tional system hold that the Commander in Chief of the Armed Forces has the ultimate power as such to take possession of private property in order to keep labor disputes from stopping production. This is a job for the Nation's lawmakers, not for its military authorities.

Nor can the seizure order be sustained because of the several constitutional provisions that grant executive power to the President. In the framework of our Constitution, the President's power to see that the laws are faithfully executed refutes the idea that he is to be a lawmaker. The Constitution limits his functions in the lawmaking process to the recommending of laws he thinks wise and the vetoing of laws he thinks bad. And the Constitution is neither silent nor equivocal about who shall make laws which the President is to execute. The first section of the first article says that "All legislative Powers herein granted shall be vested in a Congress of the United States. . . ." After granting many Powers to the Congress, Article I goes on to provide that Congress may "make all Laws which shall be necessary and proper for carrying into Execution the foregoing Powers and all other Powers vested by this Constitution in the Government of the United States, or in any Department or Officer thereof.". . .

It is said that other Presidents without congressional authority have taken possession of private business enterprises in order to settle labor disputes. But even if this be true, Congress has not thereby lost its exclusive constitutional authority to make laws necessary and proper to carry out the powers vested by the Constitution "in the Government of the United States, or any Department or Officer thereof."

The Founders of this Nation entrusted the law-making power to the Congress alone in both good and bad times. It would do no good to recall the historical events, the fears of power and the hopes for freedom that lay behind their choice. Such a review would but confirm our holding that this seizure order cannot stand.

Mr. Justice Frankfurter said:

A scheme of government like ours no doubt at times feels the lack of power to act with complete, all-embracing, swiftly moving authority. No doubt a government with distributed authority, subject to be challenged in the courts of law, at least long enough to consider and adjudicate the challenge, labors under restrictions from which other governments are free. It has not been our tradition to envy such governments. In any event our government was designed to have such restrictions. The price was deemed not too high in view of the safeguards which these restrictions afford.

And Mr. Justice Douglas said:

> The language of the Constitution is not ambiguous or qualified. It places not *some* legislative power in the Congress; Article 1, #1 says "All legislative Powers herein granted shall be vested in a Congress of the United States, which shall consist of a Senate and House of Representatives."
>
> The legislative nature of the action taken by the President seems to me to be clear. When the United States takes over an industrial plant to settle a labor controversy, it is condemning property. The seizure of the plant is a taking in the constitutional sense. . . . A permanent taking would amount to the nationalization of the industry. A temporary taking falls short of that goal. But though the seizure is only for a week or a month, the condemnation is complete and the United States must pay compensation for the temporary possession.

On the other hand, three justices dissented, including Chief Justice Vinson, who said:

> Admitting that the Government could seize the mills, plaintiffs claim that the implied power of eminent domain can be exercised only under an Act of Congress; under no circumstances, they say, can that power be exercised by the President unless he can point to an express provision in enabling legislation. This was the view adopted by the District Judge when he granted the preliminary injunction. Without an answer, without hearing evidence, he determined the issue on the basis of his "fixed conclusion . . . that defendant's acts are illegal" because the President's only course in the face of an emergency is to present the matter to Congress and await the final passage of legislation which will enable the Government to cope with threatened disaster.

Under this view, the President is left powerless at the very moment when the need for action may be most pressing and when no one, other than he, is immediately capable of action. Under this view, he is left powerless because a power not expressly given to Congress is nevertheless found to rest exclusively with Congress. . . .

In passing upon the grave constitutional question presented in this case, we must never forget, as Chief Justice Marshall admonished, that the Constitution is "intended to endure for ages to come, and, consequently, to be adapted to the various *crises* of human affairs," and that "[i]ts means are adequate to its ends." Cases do arise presenting questions which could not have been foreseen by the Framers. In such cases, the Constitution has been treated as a living document adaptable to new situations. But we are not called upon today to expand the Constitution to meet a new situation. For, in this case, we need only look to history and time-honored principles of constitutional law —principles that have been applied consistently by all branches of the Government throughout our history. It is those who assert the invalidity of the Executive Order who seek to amend the Constitution in this case. . . .

A review of executive action demonstrates that our Presidents have on many occasions exhibited the leadership contemplated by the Framers when they made the President Commander in Chief, and imposed upon him the trust to "take Care that the Laws be faithfully executed." With or without explicit statutory authorization, Presidents have at such times dealt with national emergencies by acting promptly and resolutely to enforce legislative programs, at least to save those programs until Congress could act. Congress and the Courts have responded to such executive initiative with consistent approval.

As the District Judge stated, this is no time for "timorous" judicial action. But neither is this a time for timorous executive action. Faced with the duty of executing the defense programs which Congress had enacted and the disastrous effects that any stoppage in steel production would have on those programs, the President acted to preserve those programs by seizing the steel mills. There is no question that the possession was other than temporary in character and subject to congressional direction—

either approving, disapproving or regulating the manner in which the mills were to be administered and returned to the owners. The President immediately informed Congress of his action and clearly stated his intention to abide by the legislative will. No basis for claims of arbitrary action, unlimited powers or dictatorial usurpation of congressional power appears from the facts of this case. On the contrary, judicial, legislative and executive precedents throughout our history demonstrate that in this case the President acted in full conformity with his duties under the Constitution. . . .

Assume that, in some future year, the following events take place:

1. Congress enacts a law authorizing and directing the President, when he finds that the public control of property or materials designated by him is essential to the national defense, to seize and dispose of such property or materials, paying just compensation therefor—*provided* that the owner of such property or materials has, prior to such seizure, been held by a United States Court to be in violation of the antitrust laws (Sherman Act).

2. The mineralogists of a small research company, Albaux, Inc., discover a mineral, urathorium, which could be of great use in manufacturing effective weapons.

3. The United States makes a contract with Strong Manufacturing Corporation, a leading weapons manufacturer, for the production of weapons containing urathorium.

4. Albaux quietly buys up all the urathorium deposits, and announces that it plans to build factories and make new weapons itself. In the meantime, Albaux says, it will not sell any urathorium to anyone. Admittedly, the new factories would not get into production for three years, while Strong could retool and start production in three months.

Now:

Assumption A. The United States brings suit against Albaux under the Sherman Act, and the U.S. District Court holds that Albaux is an illegal monopoly. Albaux appeals to the Court of Appeals. While the appeal is pending, the international situation grows tense. Senators and editors demand that the President seize Albaux's urathorium deposits. The President does nothing. Eventually Strong Manufacturing Corporation applies to the U.S. District Court for a writ of mandamus to compel the President to seize the deposits.

Assumption B (not in addition to Assumption A, but in contrast to it). No suit is brought against Albaux under the Sherman Act. The international situation grows tense. The President issues an order directing his Secretary of Defense to seize Albaux's urathorium deposits, paying just compensation therefor, and to make the urathorium available for the manufacture of weapons by selling it to the Strong Manufacturing Company. Albaux promptly applies to the U.S. District Court for an injunction against the seizure.

Reread and consider carefully the selections above. Then, for class discussion or as a written exercise, for both Assumption A and Assumption B:

(a) Analyze and explain the constitutional issues that confront the Court.

(b) Comment carefully on the following newspaper editorial paragraph pertaining to the situation: "When the safety of the nation is at stake, it is the President to whom we turn, not Congress or the courts. It is the President who must act to save the country. Stalemate spells disaster. Let the President know that all loyal Americans are in favor of strong and untrammeled presidential leadership in this desperate hour." Do you agree or disagree with this editorial? Why? In framing your answer, consider the durability of the Constitution under the pressures created by emergency, and give serious thought to the significance of the separation of powers and the role of each branch of government.

PART X

THE GOVERNMENTAL PROCESS: MAKING POLICY DECISIONS

PROBLEM 35

Democracy and the Making of Foreign Policy

In a public meeting in Bonn, West Germany, a rising star in West German politics named Hans Burger, a man with a considerable following throughout Western Europe, launches an attack on the United States. Burger's main argument is that the United States has lost any claim that it might have had to the support of Western Europeans in the struggle against totalitarian aggression because the United States has itself become undemocratic. Burger argues that since the United States is no longer a democracy West Germany and other free nations must turn elsewhere for leadership in the effort to defend the standards of freedom.

In support of his arguments Burger introduces seven statements taken from American publications. All these statements are authentic and come from responsible sources, and Burger asserts that they prove his contention that the United States is no longer a democracy.

1. It is not too much to say that since it was organized in 1947 the National Security Council has made the most basic decisions

in the field of international affairs. In fact, the decisions of the Council very probably will fix the course of the whole world for peace or war.

—Prominent Journalist

2. The decisions of the National Security Council are not fit subjects for public discussion.

—Member of the NSC

3. I will never reveal what goes on in the meetings of the NSC.
—President of the United States

4. Politics must stop at the water's edge. American foreign policy cannot be allowed to fall prey to the devious ins and outs of machine bosses and the unscrupulous efforts of men who seek political office without regard for the welfare of the nation. Issues of foreign policy should be decided without regard for the fortunes of a political party, and, once decided, they should receive the united support of all Americans.

—High-Ranking Member of the Senate Foreign Relations Committee

5. Too much information concerning the defense potential of the United States has been revealed to the public. Such information may well give aid and comfort to the enemy.

—Secretary of Defense

6. Surveys consistently show that 20 per cent to 25 per cent of the American public is not interested in even the most pressing problems of foreign affairs. Three years after the establishment of the United Nations, one fourth of the American public was not aware of its existence. One third of the public cannot answer such questions as "Where is Formosa?" and "Who is Marshall Tito?" A similar proportion is totally unaware of current international problems. Only 5 per cent can identify the Point Four Program, and in 1948, whereas 92 per cent were keenly interested in cost-of-living news, only 54 per cent were vitally concerned with United States relations with the Soviet Union.

—Public Opinion Analyst

7. The military establishment of the United States has grown tremendously in size and in influence in the making of foreign pol-

icy. Even though civilians occupy the top positions in the Defense Department, they speak for military values and objectives, and their voices are heard with great respect in the highest councils in the land. Military expenditures comprise two thirds of the national budget and are beyond any really effective control by Congress.
—American Political Scientist

Apparently there is considerable support for Burger's view in the audience, an audience which many newspaper correspondents believe accurately reflects the thinking of most Western Europeans today. A substantial number of people in the audience, however, are confused and uncertain. They are unsure of the advantages to be obtained from following the lead of the United States in world affairs and are therefore willing to be convinced by Burger that they should seek other leadership. However, they do not understand the connection between the statements Burger has read and the conclusion he has reached; namely, that the United States is undemocratic. Neither are they sure what difference it makes if the United States *is* undemocratic.

After Burger has spoken, a young German named Karl Klaus rises to challenge Burger's argument. Klaus has recently returned from the United States where he spent a year as an exchange student in music composition. He is not an expert in American politics and he does not have quotations from American publications to support his argument. Nevertheless, he says that during his stay in the United States he saw many examples of what he considered to be vigorous democracy with respect to foreign policy. He cites the many lively arguments he heard among students over foreign policy questions. He tells of the strong criticism leveled against the Democrats for their policy in the Far East, and against the Republicans for alleged failures in missile research and development. Klaus points out that members of Congress were constantly advocating changes in policy and threatening to withhold money from the President unless he shifted his stand. Foreign policy issues were frequently debated at length during election campaigns. Klaus remembers a study which showed that most Americans continued to receive much of their information and opinion about foreign policy issues from the leaders of the political party they normally supported. Various organizations devoted to the study and discussion of foreign policy problems could be found all over the country, and most interest groups, even though their primary concerns were domestic, had something to say about foreign policy. Klaus found that the American press was filled with information about all sorts of matters related to foreign affairs from guided missile research to the latest gossip about the Russian ambassador.

You are an American political scientist engaged in research on West German politics. During your researches you have become acquainted with several responsible and thoughtful West Germans who are widely respected in their country for their opinions about foreign affairs. These people are genuinely puzzled. They have been impressed by the warm regard which Klaus holds for the United States, and his argument has softened the force of Burger's charges considerably. Nevertheless, they are afraid that Klaus's rather fragmentary impressions do not give an accurate picture of the United States, and that, even if they do, the United States is still not really democratic in the way it makes foreign policy decisions. Your friends turn to you, with your expert knowledge in this field, and ask where the truth lies.

Review in your text and lecture notes the material relating to the making of foreign policy in the United States.

For written exercise or class discussion:

1. Explain to your friends as carefully and clearly as you can the way in which each statement quoted by Burger is related to his charge that the United States is undemocratic.

2. Explain to your friends the extent to which Klaus's impressions support the conclusion that the United States remains vigorously democratic.

3. Explain to your friends the other facts and arguments that you, on the basis of your broad knowledge and understanding of the American political system, believe should be included in arriving at a balanced judgment on this problem.

Remember, your job is not to defend the United States uncritically, nor should you uncritically condemn foreign policy-making procedures. Rather, you should provide a candid, balanced, and full statement of the significant facts and problems involved.

PROBLEM 36

President and Congress in Foreign Relations

The United States Constitution is remarkably vague in assigning the responsibility for conducting foreign relations. Certain specific powers are granted to Congress that are important to certain aspects of foreign policy, such as the requirement that two thirds of the senators present and voting must approve a treaty. Other more general legislative powers, such as the power to appropriate money, are also relevant to foreign policy. Though there is no explicit statement to this effect in the Constitution itself, it has not seriously been questioned that the chief authority and responsibility for making and carrying out foreign policy belongs to the President. Yet the language of the Constitution does not begin to solve the actual problems of making the necessary decisions, even though the division of authority between President and Congress assured that the two branches would have to work out some kind of harmonious relationship if positive foreign policy action was to be taken.

Congress has always played some part in the formation of United States foreign policy. Senate approval of treaties and of diplomatic appointments has always been required. Congressional authorization and appropriation of money has often been necessary in order to carry out a particular policy. And criticism from Congress has sometimes forced the Executive branch to follow new policy directions. In the period since World War II, however, the role played by Congress in the making of foreign policy has become vastly more significant. The greatly enlarged network of treaty alliances and other international agreements into which the United States has entered has given the Senate an unprecedented opportunity to influence policy. Furthermore, as foreign affairs have grown in importance, their impact has been felt as never before in American domestic politics. Congress, reflecting the interests of constituents, has become more and more concerned with various phases of foreign policy and in the consequences of that policy for domestic interests. Most important in contributing to this new role for Congress has been the greatly enlarged significance of money for American foreign policy. No longer is foreign policy composed mainly of declarations of intentions and diplomatic correspondence. Economic aid, military assistance, military preparedness, and even participation in the United Nations all require the appropriation of large sums of money by both houses of Congress. Very little of postwar U.S. policy could have been put into operation without the co-operation of majorities in Congress.

A number of consequences have resulted. The Executive branch has found it necessary to cultivate carefully as much congressional support as possible. Thus, whereas Wilson largely ignored the Senate in negotiating the Versailles Treaty and thereby helped to doom American participation in the League of Nations, Senate leaders of both parties were appointed as delegates to the San Francisco Conference to draft the United Nations Charter. Frequent briefings on foreign affairs are given Congressional leaders by the State Department and sometimes by the President to acquaint them with the thinking and planning of the Administration about present and future problems. Close co-operation between the committees of Congress responsible for foreign policy matters and administration officials has been the postwar rule. All difficulties between members of the two branches have not been eliminated, of course. But careful planning and long-term co-operation and consultation have certainly contributed to more harmonious relations between Congress and the Executive in making foreign policy.

The problems that Administration leaders face in trying to secure the necessary support from Congress to meet the problems of international relations are well illustrated by the following selection in which Dean Acheson, Secretary of State from 1949 to 1953, reflects on his experiences of those years:

When one speaks of the executive working with the Congress, one is using shorthand. The center and focus of legislative-executive relations lie in the congressional committees and in the method of their operation. Much as the President and his associates may influence the Congress through direct appeal to the people, the route from planning to action leads through the committees to legislation. For today nearly all programs require funds, authority, and men, which Congress may grant, skimp, or withhold. Legislation is more than the "oil of government"; it is the essential prerequisite of government. And it is in the committees, where Congress is least susceptible to party discipline, that it gives its legislative answer to the policies of the administration.

There is another fact, also, which must not escape us. While each one of these committees and subcommittees is a channel along which influence may flow from the Congress to the executive, it is quite possible for influence to flow in the other direction along the same channels. . . .

In the process of communication and mutual effort to influence between the committees and the executive a simple, prosaic, but deeply important fact stands out. The process takes a great deal of time and effort. It is obvious, too, that while there are many committees and subcommittees, there is only one Secretary in each department; and the committees, quite naturally, want to discuss important matters with the Secretary. On his part, the Secretary knows that he must do this, and do it effectively if the policies of the administration are to be carried out. . . .

On November 29, 1955, Secretary Dulles told us that he had met during his tenure of office "more than 100 times with bipartisan Congressional groups." This seems to me quite normal practice.

As nearly as I can reconstruct it from my appointment books, I met during four years as Secretary on 214 occasions with these groups. . . .

Congressional meetings before and after an international conference, useful as they are, have a disadvantage which is part of the great glare of publicity thrown on all preparations for these conferences as well as upon the conferences themselves. Flexibility even in minor matters is much more difficult when, before a meeting, all possibilities are analyzed in public and positions publicly taken. Agreement requires that some, perhaps all, modify their attitudes to meet changes by others. A position publicly proclaimed is more rigid by reason of its public nature. Furthermore, to announce all one's positions in advance of the negotiation is apt to make it merely a forum for reiterating final positions and not a true negotiation. But there are so many contributors to this situation that it would be unfair to attribute much of it to the liaison with Congress.

The occasions when the executive and the Congress are brought together in the origination or the development of policy are not found in these executive, and certainly not in the public, sessions of congressional committees. The latter have an important and useful place in the democratic governmental process. But it is in the public examination and criticism of proposed action. This both tests what is proposed, and, through press, radio, and television coverage, informs the electorate in regard to it. The creative process is both more individual and more elusive because more private. And being individual, it cannot be stated in a formula. It is secreted in the qualities of men. During his illness I had the rare opportunity of many talks with Senator Vandenberg on this subject, wholly divorced from any specific task. For many years I had observed him and worked with him. But these talks were contemplative. We reviewed our experience and tried to draw conclusions from it.

What then are the qualities in men and the posture of circumstances which make for this creative process, when policy is moved forward to a new phase? On the committee's side what is needed is a chairman or senior minority member who is widely respected and trusted in his own party. Such a man usually stands well with the opposition also. He must be able to think vigorously about new problems, though he need not have an original cast of mind. His great function is to bring suggestions within the realm of the possible, to use method as a means of molding a proposal to make it politically feasible. He will, of course, be a politician. He will protect the interests of his party, and perhaps of himself, so that what he becomes convinced is in the national interest is not done so as to injure his party or aggrandize its opponent. But he will not be tricky. What he requires as a condition of support will be frankly stated. He will keep in touch with his colleagues, particularly his own party colleagues, and have a pretty sound idea that what he agrees to back will have the needed support when the time for voting comes.

On the executive side what is needed is a man who can speak for the administration because he knows it and is trusted by it. He, too, must keep in touch, be frank and not tricky, and must pursue the main objective without being deflected by the nonessential. These two men must have confidence in one another.

An example of this sort of collaboration occurred in 1948 between Senator Vandenberg, then Chairman of the Foreign Relations Committee, and Mr. Robert Lovett, Under Secretary of State, which resulted in the Vandenberg Resolution, the precursor of the North Atlantic Treaty. Senator Vandenberg's position was unique. He was Chairman of the committee; by understanding with Senator Taft he was given the lead on the Republican side in foreign affairs while Senator Taft had it in domestic affairs. His influence in both parties was immense. He was a master of maneuver and a superb advocate. He and Mr. Lovett trusted and liked one another. Mr. Lovett could and did efface himself from the public eye. His ability matched the Senator's. He had at his finger tips the facts and needs of the situation, the desired policy. Their work together produced what neither could have accomplished separately.

Examples of similar work on a much broader base were the meetings which Mr. Hull held in 1944 with three separate groups from Congress in which were discussed drafts of the United Nations Charter prior to the Dumbarton Oaks Conference. Mr. Hull has described these fully.

The Secretary met first on four occasions with eight members of the Senate Foreign Relations Committee. That committee was then organized with a view to having on it leaders of senatorial opinion. That it had is seen by the composition of the group—Senators Connally, Barkley, George, Gillette, Vandenberg, La Follette, White, and Austin. But other Senators were interested in the Charter, too, and to draw them in without questioning the prerogative of the committee, the Secretary held a separate consultation with what was then known as the B2H2 group—Senators Ball, Burton, Hatch, and Hill. Since the House Committee on Foreign Affairs did not then normally include the party leaders in the House, the group invited to meet with the Secretary consisted of the Speaker and Majority Leader, Mr. Rayburn and Mr. McCormack, the Minority Leader, Mr. Martin, the Chairman and ranking minority member of the committee, Messrs. Bloom and Eaton, and Representatives Ramspeck and Arends. The Secretary also used his great influence, in the quiet way of which he was a master, to induce the national conventions of both parties to adopt planks favoring an international organization to keep the peace. This whole effort was outstandingly successful—a classic example of persuasion through participation by a man who thoroughly understood congressional processes.

If these occasions of real accomplishment in cooperation are rare, they would be even more rare were it not for the far larger number of meetings—which are also the "oil of government," preventing grievances from going unaired, preserving *amour propre*, giving [to Congress] a sense of participation and an opportunity to exercise authority over detail.

It is often said that the executive must "get along" with Congress and particularly with the Senate. If this means that concessions of policy must be made in the interest of outward affability, I do not agree. Personal relations will for the most part be courteous and friendly, as one would expect between gentlemen. But no one knows better than politicians and lawyers that men can battle most bitterly in the arena over important differences and yet maintain amicable personal relations and cooperate on other matters. The Eightieth Congress, with which President Truman had his fiercest battles, worked admirably in foreign affairs; and many of those who demanded the dismissal of the Secretary of State in 1950–52 joined in passing all the major legislation he laid before the Congress, including the Japanese and German treaties on the very eve of the campaign of 1952. Mutual respect is more important than affability.

We return always, I think, to a central truth. The relations between the executive and legislative branches of our government were not designed to be restful. We must not be disturbed and think that things have gone amiss when power striking against power, and being restrained, produces sparks.[1]

Consider carefully the following situation:

In 1965 one of the most pressing problems confronting the United States in the field of foreign relations is the uncertain relationship between this country and the nation of Atlantis. Atlantis is a relatively new nation, having for several centuries been under the colonial control of Great Britain. It is a country large in area and population but relatively poor in industrial development and per capita wealth. However, Atlantis possesses much potentially fertile farmland and sufficient mineral resources, particularly copper and iron ore, to provide the basis for industrialization if adequate sources of power could be obtained.

The matter that is of most concern to American military and diplomatic leaders is the geographical location of Atlantis in relation to (1) the Soviet Union, and (2) one of the most vital waterways in the world, the Straits of Atlantis. Military leaders in the United States are unanimous in their conviction that airplane and missile bases in Atlantis would strengthen immeasurably the military security of the West against the Soviet Union. At present, Atlantis constitutes the only gap in a ring of bases encircling the USSR, and the gap is a wide and potentially disastrous one. The Straits of Atlantis are also of great strategic significance, for through these Straits flow oil and other vital materials for the industries of Europe and the bulk of the military supplies to American bases in the Middle East. The Straits flow through one corner of Atlantis, and that country controls their use.

Atlantis is among the so-called "uncommitted" nations of the world, not firmly allied with either the Western nations or with the Soviet Union. It is governed by a hereditary monarch who retains considerable personal power to make decisions, and recently he has exhibited willingness to co-operate with the United States more fully than in the past. It is not expected that he can maintain his power, however, unless he can make rapid strides in raising the economic level of his people, and should he fail, the probable successor government would be more hostile to the West. The ruler of

[1] Dean Acheson, *A Citizen Looks at Congress* (New York: Harper and Brothers, 1956), 61–62, 64–65, 70–77.

Atlantis has proclaimed a Six-Year Plan which calls for a sharp increase in the production of the two basic crops of Atlantis, cotton and wheat. With the money earned from the export of these crops, the development of manufacturing of textiles, farm machinery, fertilizer, and machine tools is to be much expanded. The Plan has been notably successful in stimulating the expansion of agricultural exports, to the extent that markets formerly supplied by American cotton and wheat have substantially switched to Atlantis as their main source of supply. Not enough capital has been raised, however, to permit the construction of facilities necessary to enable the large-scale industrial development envisioned in the Six-Year Plan. The most pressing need is electric power, and to meet this need the Atlantis Government is planning the construction of a giant dam that will provide both water for irrigation and a huge amount of hydroelectric power. To construct this dam will require nearly two billion dollars in capital over the next ten years, and Atlantis can provide less than one fourth of this amount from its own resources.

For several years the USSR has been making overtures of friendship to Atlantis, and a significant number of Atlantis citizens, though not those presently in power, look with favor on the Soviet Union. Since the Six-Year Plan was inaugurated, Russia has offered to buy large quantities of cotton and wheat, to send technical assistance and machinery to aid in industrialization, and, most important, to lend to the Atlantis Government one billion dollars at very low interest to be used over a ten-year period to help build the dam. The USSR has not requested that military bases be made available to it, nor has it made any demands concerning the operation of the Straits of Atlantis. Nevertheless, Western diplomats are very much afraid that if Atlantis accepts the Soviet offer, it will mean not only that bases cannot be obtained for the West but that the traffic through the Straits will be subject to Russian control in time of crisis. Such a threat is regarded as very serious indeed.

The United States Government is considering four interrelated proposals designed to meet the situation in Atlantis:

A. The negotiation of an executive agreement with Atlantis to permit the establishment of American bases there.

B. A treaty between the United States, Atlantis, and all other interested nations to assure the free use by all nations of the Straits of

Atlantis, with the understanding that the American bases in Atlantis can be used to protect this freedom to use the Straits.

C. Provision to the Atlantis Government of substantial economic aid from the United States to assist in the construction of the dam. The exact amount to be recommended is still under consideration since no one, including the Atlantis Government, is sure how reliable the Soviet offer of aid may be. It is clear, however, that if Atlantis is to be persuaded to accept American bases, the aid figure over ten years will have to approximate the Russian offer.

D. An agreement with the Atlantis Government to lower the tariffs and import quota barriers that now restrict the importation of Atlantis products into the United States. Such an agreement is necessary to convince Atlantis of American reliability and good intentions. Such an agreement can be negotiated without any action by Congress, although Congress might later try to alter or reverse the agreement. At the present time the major exports of Atlantis would find no market in the United States, which has large surpluses of cotton and wheat already. In the fairly near future, however, if the Six-Year Plan succeeds, textiles and raw copper will be produced in Atlantis, and the American market for these products is very much desired by the Atlantis Government.

The problem faced by the U.S. administration is made more difficult by the presence of a number of interests which would suffer immediate loss from the agricultural and industrial expansion of Atlantis. Cotton and wheat producers in this country are already feeling the effects of enlarged sales abroad of Atlantis crops. Textile manufacturers, mainly in the South, are concerned that the possibility of Atlantis exports of textiles to the United States would seriously injure their position, which is already threatened by imports from other parts of the world. Copper-mining interests are in a state of economic depression that would be made more pronounced by the development of Atlantis mines. All these interests are strongly represented in the United States Congress by representatives and senators from the South, the Great Plains, and the Rocky Mountain states. Finally, there is a considerable number of journalists and academicians who argue that the Atlantis Six-Year Plan is doomed to failure, no matter what the United States does, and that any aid we might give will be wasted in the long run.

This view has some congressional adherents, but few supporters within the Administration.

You are a special assistant to the President of the Unites States. As a written exercise or for class discussion prepare for the President a report dealing with the following aspects of the Atlantis problem:

1. The extent to which the Administration will encounter congressional opposition to each of the four proposals, and the size and power of this opposition.

2. All the steps that the President and his advisers might take to minimize the potential congressional opposition to these proposals.

3. The probable ultimate success or failure in steering proposals B and C through Congress.

4. Your own recommendation, after considering every aspect of this problem, as to whether the Administration should make an all-out effort to push any or all of these four proposals to a successful conclusion. Give reasons to support your recommendation.

PROBLEM 37

Co-ordinating Action in an International Crisis

Thoroughly review your text and class notes concerning the presidency, the executive branch, the Senate, and foreign policy. Then for class discussion or as a written exercise, outline or prepare a careful, detailed paper on the subject indicated below. This paper should be one which, long after you cease being Assistant to the President, you can proudly show your grandchildren as an example of how a responsible public official acted promptly, wisely, and efficiently, within the narrow limits of his authority, at a time of crisis—and how, by his selection of issues and his knowledge of governmental organization, he contributed to important policy decisions.

Assume that on one Saturday afternoon in late November, the following events occur:

1. A small band, led by a Mexican general who is in revolt against his government, invades El Paso, Texas, shoots up the town, captures twenty leading citizens and, holding them as hostages, goes back across the border into the mountains of northern Mexico.

2. The press services report that vacationing U.S. Senator Roy Ladu, chairman of the Senate Foreign Relations Committee, arose at a bibulous banquet in Paris and, apparently humorously, urged that France extend its east border to the Rhine, saying: "Don't worry, mes amis, you can do it. We are with you. The Yanks are coming. Lafayette, we are here!" A cable from the U.S. Ambassador to West Germany states that the West German government is demanding a formal retraction and apology from the U.S. Government. The West German Ambassador to the United States happens to be home in Bonn, on vacation. A newly signed treaty of mutual assistance with West Germany will be referred to the Senate Foreign Relations Committee when Congress reconvenes in January.

3. An earthquake in India destroys two new dams and power plants, floods thousands of miles of farm lands, renders millions of people homeless, and smashes the chief water main and water purification plants of a large city.

4. An armed clash occurs between the troops of Pakistan and Afghanistan, on the border between the two countries. Each country denounces the other as the aggressor. One hour before the battle, Moscow radio announces that Afghanistan has been invaded and that the USSR is committed by treaty to defend Afghanistan.

You are Assistant to the President, who, that afternoon, is attending the Army-Navy football game at Philadelphia. Congress is not in session. You reach the President by telephone, between the halves, and tell him the news. He says he will return to Washington at once; and, with respect to these four matters, he instructs you to arrange a conference or series of conferences, to be held that evening at the White House, and to prepare for each conference an agenda—a carefully organized and detailed outline of topics to be discussed, issues to be raised, alternative choices to be explored. Whom would you invite to attend such conference(s), and in what order would you place matters on the agenda? Give reasons for your choices.

PROBLEM 38

Governmental Policies Concerning Labor

1. Congress enacted the National Labor Relations Act (Wagner Act) in 1935. This law applied to most of American industry. Among other things, it made it an "unfair labor practice" for an employer to discharge an employee or refuse to employ a person because of such person's union activity or membership. A National Labor Relations Board was established. Charges of unfair labor practices are heard and decided by the Board. Any proper order of the Board, forbidding a continuation of any such practice, is enforceable by the United States courts.

In 1947, the Wagner Act was modified by the Labor Management Relations Act (Taft-Hartley Act), but this basic protection against antiunion discrimination was retained. For the first time, however, Congress now made a special provision regarding "union shop" agreements. In a union shop agreement, an employer agrees that each of his employees, after a probationary period, must join the union as a condition of continuing employment. The Taft-Hartley Act allowed any state that wished to do so to prohibit union shop agreements in that State. Under Taft-Hartley, union shop agreements are valid except in those states that have outlawed them. State laws outlawing the union shop have been enacted in several states, despite labor's opposition; the supporters of such measures call them "right-to-work" laws.

2. Also in 1935, Congress enacted the Social Security Act. Parts of that statute were intended to stimulate the passage of state unemployment compensation laws. A tax was levied on employers, but with the provision that most of the tax would be forgiven if the employers were contributing to a state unemployment compensation fund. Furthermore, Congress authorized grants to the states to defray the reasonable administrative expenses (salaries, office rental, etc.) of carrying out the state laws. These two inducements were effective: every state in the Union soon enacted unemployment compensation laws. The federal Act, with some amendments, is still in effect.

Both the tax offset and the grant are conditioned on the state law meeting specified standards (such as the use of a merit system in the selection of personnel) and being administered efficiently and fairly. Each year, the responsible federal official (now the Secretary of Labor) certifies to the Secretary of the Treasury the names of those states where taxpayers are to be permitted the tax offset—in other words, those states which have satisfactory unemployment compensation laws and are administering those laws in accordance with the terms thereof. For employers in any state not certified, no tax offset is allowed. Likewise, grants to meet administrative costs are denied to a state where the law fails to satisfy the federal standards or where the responsible state administrators fail properly to carry out an approved law. For instance, grants are denied to a state where "there is a denial, in a substantial number of cases, of unemployment compensation to individuals entitled thereto under such (state) law," provided that the fact of each such individual's right to unemployment compensation has been established by a decision of the state's highest court. This means that a state will lose its grant if the state supreme court finds, in numerous cases, that the state agency has improperly rejected the claims of unemployed persons.

3. Now assume that the state of Winnemac in 1937 enacted an unemployment compensation law that is still in effect. In its provisions, it has met the federal standards. Winnemac taxpayers are forgiven most of the special federal payroll tax, and federal grants pay the operating expenses of the Winnemac Unemployment Compensation Commission. This state law provides that weekly unemployment benefits shall be paid, for a maximum of sixteen weeks, to any person who has become unemployed without fault on his part, and who remains unemployed although seeking to secure suitable employment within a twenty-mile radius of his home. It also provides that a person's unemployment caused by an employer's refusal to hire or employ him because of his union membership shall be deemed unemployment without fault on the part of such employee.

Assume, further, that in the last two years a series of major strikes has aroused some hostility between management and labor in Winnemac, and has sharply increased antilabor sentiment in the rural parts of the state. The Governor has much rural support; the man whom he has appointed to head the Unemployment Compensation Commission is the publisher of a farmers' weekly. A "right to work" bill is introduced in the state legislature, to outlaw the union shop. Strong antiunion feeling causes it to be expanded, so that as finally enacted the new state law not only prohibits union shop agreements, but also provides that union membership or union activity shall be deemed valid and proper reasons for discharge or refusal to hire in Winnemac. In this new statute, no reference is made to the unemployment compensation law.

Shortly after the enactment of this new labor law, the union representing the production workers of the big Solway Steel Corporation in Zenith announces that as its contract with the company has expired and the company seems unwilling to sign a "satisfactory" new contract, the union will call a strike one week hence. Immediately, without waiting for the week to pass, the company closes its doors and "locks out" the production workers. Two months later eighty-five workers, unable to find suitable employment in or near Zenith, and being denied unemployment compensation by the State Unemployment Compensation Commission, go to the company's employment office and offer to return to work. The company refuses to employ them, because they still belong to the union and won't resign from it.

Assume that you are the president of the union. You know that the series of recent strikes has depleted the union's own funds, so that "strike benefits" paid by the union to its members are getting very small. You fear that thousands of workers will be "starved right out of the union." You also despair of persuading the Winnemac legislature to repeal or amend the recently enacted statute.

Carefully analyze the situation and determine each point at which the interests of the union are threatened. (Remember that union membership may be adversely affected if the members feel that the union is not striving to help them.) Then prepare a plan of action designed to protect the union, outlining and justifying each step that you propose to take.

PROBLEM 39

Agriculture

Read carefully and thoughtfully the following excerpt from *Economic Policy for Agriculture,* a statement on national policy issued by the Committee for Economic Development (January, 1956):

American agriculture is *exceedingly diverse.* The twenty-two million Americans living on farms earn their incomes by producing a large variety of products under a large variety of conditions. About 30 per cent of these persons live on part-time or residential farms and do not generally have farming as the main source of family income. They have a quite different relation to farm problems than do most commercial farmers. About half of all farms are between 50 and 260 acres in size, but almost 10 per cent are under ten acres and about 6 per cent are over 500 acres. For some farmers export markets are of vital importance —as in the cases of cotton, wheat and tobacco—but many other farmers do not produce for export at all. Some farmers face a rising trend of domestic consumption; others face a decline.

Just as agriculture is diverse so are the problems of agriculture diverse. While the stocks of some farm commodities are very high, this is not true of all farm products. While some farm operators' incomes are persistently low, there are many families who usually receive satisfactory incomes. While prices received on all farms in the United States declined by about 8 per cent from the 1947–49 peak to 1954 . . . experience varied from a 15 per cent increase on North Carolina tobacco-cotton farms to a 23 per cent decrease on cattle ranches of the intermountain region.

The "parity" ratio, which attempts to measure the level of farm prices received relative to prices paid by farmers, is often cited as an indicator of agriculture's general health. [Parity is always based on some period in the past for which the parity ratio is said to be 100. Until recently the years 1910–1914 were used as the base period. In comparison with this base period,] during the late '30's the parity ratio averaged about 80; it rose to 105 in 1942 and hovered around 110 from 1943 until the end of the war. The ratio rose to an average of 115 in 1947, a level which was attained in only two other years since 1910, namely in 1917 and 1918.

By 1949 the ratio declined to 100 and then rose to 107 in 1951 as a result of the Korean conflict. Since then it has declined. It averaged about 85 for 1955, somewhat below the ratio that prevailed during the late '20's and somewhat above that of the late '30's. . . .

There are three underlying problems which seem to the Committee to be causing most of the troubles now afflicting agriculture. In this part we shall indicate what these problems are and why they have arisen.

Major Farm Problems

1. There is too much production of some farm products. . . .
2. Farmers' incomes are unstable. . . .
3. There are too many full-time farm families with very low incomes. . . .

TOO MUCH PRODUCTION OF SOME FARM PRODUCTS

Commodity surplus problems of agriculture involve two major types of adjustments:

1. The transition from war and the postwar foreign relief period to an approximate peacetime situation makes it desirable to reduce output of some products. We simply needed more of some commodities for war and relief than we do in peacetime—wheat, for example.

2. Long-run adjustments are forced by technological change,

by changing consumer wants, and by the fact that food consumptions grow only slowly as the real incomes of the population rise. . . .

WHEAT

Wheat poses the most acute of the supply adjustment problems. Wheat stocks now (1955) held in conjunction with price support activities are large—equal to a two-years' supply for food in the United States. This situation exists despite acreage restrictions in 1954 and 1955.

Farm output in general increased by more than 20 per cent between 1939 and 1946; the food grains, chiefly wheat, increased by 50 per cent. The increase in wheat was due in part to better weather, but also to a substantial increase in acreage planted. . . . The continued expansion of wheat output into the postwar period was caused by high prices due to export needs. . . .

It should be remembered that the output of wheat increased during the war and postwar periods in response to official actions. The greater volume made a substantial contribution to our war effort and to the recovery of western nations after the war. Legislation providing for postwar price and production adjustments was not put into effect. Thus the nation has a responsibility to help producers adjust to peace. Even if there were not this responsibility related to the war period, an economic adjustment involving the welfare of as many people as this one does deserves the sympathetic assistance of the community at large. But it should be realized that adjustments are now overdue, with the United States and Canada both having large surpluses of wheat production over demand in recent years, and prices should not be kept at the same high level as when demand was greater for extraordinary reasons during and just after the war.

The export demand for our wheat is not likely to increase significantly over the next few years, due to large stocks in other exporting countries, chiefly Canada. . . . The United States share of world exports has been declining while that of non-dollar countries—notably Australia, Argentina, and France—has been rising.

The United States has maintained a wheat export subsidy for the last six years. The wheat subsidy averaged about 60 cents a bushel during most of the period, and rose to 75 cents a bushel in 1954–55. Without this substantial subsidy, we would export almost no wheat at current price support levels. . . .

In every year except two since 1946 the U.S. wheat crop exceeded the sum of domestic uses plus exports, and the carry over (stock) of wheat increased. In 1950 and especially in 1951, large exports plus low crops combined to bring about some reduction in the accumulated stocks. The expected addition to the carry over in the current crop year, 1955–56, is expected to be small, chiefly because production has been drastically restricted by acreage controls.

In 1953 seventy-nine million acres of land were planted to wheat, and produced 1,169 million bushels. In 1954 the acreage was reduced to 63 million and the production of 977 million bushels. Acreage for 1955 is estimated at 57 million and production at 916 million bushels. The wheat needed for domestic consumption for food, seed, and feed uses—600 to 625 million bushels—can be produced in normal years on about 40 million acres. There are four uses that can be made of the remaining acreage:

1. It can raise wheat that goes into government storage. We have been doing this to a substantial degree and this is the cause of our present surpluses.

2. It can be retired from use entirely or turned into pasture.

3. It can be diverted into production of other crops—oats, barley, grain sorghums, etc.—which would be mainly used for livestock feed. We have been doing this on a large scale during the last two years. Acreage controls in 1954 and 1955 took about twenty million acres out of wheat production and most of this found its way into feed production.

4. It can continue to produce wheat that is exported or fed to livestock. For wheat to move freely into export or livestock feeding it is estimated that a drop of about one third in the price of average grade wheat would be required.

All of these uses—except storage—involve additions to the feed supply from land formerly planted to wheat. Turning the land into pasture would yield less feed than continued crop production. Allowing the price of average quality wheat to fall to a livestock feed level would result in a smaller addition to the feed supply than would diversion of the land to other crops, because more wheat would be exported at a lower price. The acreage not required for domestic food consumption would produce about 20 million tons of grains. At the lower wheat price about 8 million tons of this might be exported, leaving 12 million tons for livestock feed.

COTTON

The stock of cotton in CCC hands on August 1, 1955 (the beginning of a new crop year) was 8.1 million bales; this amounts to about a year's consumption by U.S. mills. By next August 1, CCC holdings are expected to be larger by some 3 million bales. If this expectation is borne out, CCC stocks at that time will be almost as large as the combined U.S. mill use and exports during the current crop year.

Stocks of cotton in the United States have increased by more than 5 million bales in the last two years. The further substantial increase expected this year is a warning that cotton is moving rapidly toward a surplus situation as acute as that in wheat.

Rising production on the one hand and declining exports on the other characterize the cotton problem. . . .

While American cotton producers are losing foreign markets, producers in other free world countries are steadily increasing output at prices that undersell U.S. cotton at support levels.

Some decline in the United States price of cotton would be required if the supply and demand were to be balanced in a free market. United States prices of cotton are now from 10 and 20 per cent above world prices, depending upon the variety. This gives some indication of the degree of price decline that might be needed to clear the market.

FEED GRAINS AND LIVESTOCK

The total supply of feed grains (*including corn*) under the control of the CCC is about 25 per cent of a year's utilization. Percentage-wise, the supply situation requires much less of an adjustment than either wheat or cotton. Stocks in private hands are not as large as usual, and the stocks held by CCC would be sharply reduced if we had a short crop like that of 1947.

Contrary to the cases of wheat and cotton, the long-run demand situation under conditions of high employment is relatively favorable for livestock, the final users of the feed grains. Not only will the growth of population add to the demand for the feed grains, but as incomes grow people will eat more livestock products per capita, if not in pounds certainly in value. Thus, if feed grain output were held in check over the next three or four years, by 1960 the increased demand should be enough to maintain prices at satisfactory levels.

TOO MUCH INSTABILITY

Even during periods of full employment and general price stability in the rest of the economy . . . many farmers are subject to wide fluctuations in prices and incomes. Large parts of agriculture are subject to erratic and unpredictable changes in weather. This is particularly true of the Great Plains. . . . Weather and other natural phenomena can result in significant unplanned variations in farm output. Because consumption increases very little in response to a fairly large decline in price, such fluctuations in output lead to large variations in prices of farm products.

In recent years farm price supports have achieved a considerable degree of price stability for some farm products, though the supports have failed in other instances. Wheat and cotton prices have been relatively stable for the past three years. However, the loan program for corn has not operated to keep market prices of corn at the loan rates, or to prevent the wide swing in hog prices in the recent past.

TOO MANY LOW-INCOME FARM FAMILIES

Despite a large migration of persons off farms in recent years, there remain many farm families with extremely low incomes. While most of these families are concentrated in the South, there are other, though much smaller, areas where low incomes have persisted. There are considerably fewer farm families with low incomes than there were in 1940, but there are still more than a million full-time farm operators of working age who produce little and as a consequence receive very meager incomes. The

Federal agricultural policies that have been followed have contributed little or nothing to the solution of the problems faced by these families. Such improvement as there has been is the result of expansion of the industrial economy, including the movement of industry into rural areas.

In the areas where farm incomes are lowest, farms are extremely small compared to the rest of the country. Increasing prices would not succeed in raising the level of incomes of these families to an acceptable level. They produce very little and many of them consume a large share of what they do produce.

The statement quoted above asserts that "American agriculture is exceedingly diverse." Some of this diversity is reflected in the large number of farm organizations in the United States. Many of these organizations are small and confined to a particular region or to growers of a particular crop. A few organizations, however, are sufficiently large and powerful to exercise considerable influence in shaping legislative policy in Congress; particularly, of course, legislation which affects agriculture. One of the most powerful organizations is the American Farm Bureau Federation. The Farm Bureau is generally the most "conservative" of the major farm organizations and is often allied with business groups on legislative policy. The Farm Bureau is composed primarily of two types of farmers: cotton growers, and raisers of corn and livestock. In recent years the corn-livestock elements have seemed to have the strongest voice in Farm Bureau affairs. Many of the Farm Bureau members are large and relatively prosperous farmers whose incomes are apt to be more stable than those of some other kinds of farmers.

A second major farm organization, different in many ways from the Farm Bureau, is the National Farmers Educational and Cooperative Union. The National Farmers Union is most strongly entrenched in the wheat-growing sections of the country. The NFU has allied itself since World War II with the more "liberal" labor organizations and has expressed considerable interest in expanding governmental aid to the small family farm.

In recent years three issues of agricultural policy have been among the many debated and voted upon in the Congress. Consider carefully the following brief descriptions of each issue:

1. Price supports. High fixed price supports at 90 per cent of parity would provide for basic crops (corn, cotton, wheat, etc.) the assurance of 90 per cent of parity as the minimum price farmers would receive. This is the program which under normal conditions, i.e., the absence of war, results in surpluses unless controls are placed on the number of acres that may be planted. Under this plan there is little incentive for farmers to shift production from a crop of which a surplus is on hand to crops in shorter supply. An alternative plan would provide flexible price supports ranging from 75 to 90 per cent of parity. Crops in oversupply would be given a lower support price, while crops for which there is a lower supply and/or a higher demand would get a higher support price. This program would encourage at least some readjustment from one crop to another. Readjustment would, in the short run, benefit those farmers who grow crops for which the demand is great and hurt farmers whose crops are in the greatest surplus.

2. Surplus Disposal Program. Under this program the United States Government uses various techniques to send abroad the major agricultural commodities of which there are surpluses in this country. The countries receiving surplus commodities use them to strengthen their own economies, and the program is thus related to other foreign aid activities. Surplus disposal agreements are not supposed to interfere with normal export trade channels, and therefore, they do not normally threaten the regular commercial export of farm products. The program has accounted for the disposition of a substantial portion of the surplus stocks held by the Commodity Credit Corporation.

3. The Farmers Home Administration. This agency is designed to assist small, poorer farmers who are unable to make an adequate living from the marketing of farm products. The program is designed to make these farmers more efficient by providing low cost credit and expert advice on the management and operation of their farms. From this assistance farmers are able to increase their production and thus their incomes.

You are a newspaper correspondent from Australia where agricultural politics is also of great importance. You are assigned to prepare for your paper an analysis of the battle over agricultural policy that will shortly take place in the United States Senate. The three problems outlined above will be debated and the issues will be voted on as follows:

(A) A proposal to continue "flexible" price supports in force with the support level ranging from 75 per cent to 90 per cent of parity. This will be opposed by those who desire "fixed" supports at 90 per cent of parity.

(B) A proposal to enlarge and expand the surplus disposal program.

(C) A proposal to double the appropriation and enlarge the program of the Farmers Home Administration.

Assume that members of Congress and organized interest groups will decide how they stand on the issues in accordance with the interests of the people they represent. The farmers involved, in turn, will interpret their interests on the basis of the data presented in the material you have read. Although the problems in real life may often be more complex than they are here, you should be able to reach generally valid conclusions with the material given.

Review in your text and lecture notes the materials relating to agricultural policy and also the materials relating generally to patterns of American politics, particularly to the geographical centers of strength of each of the major parties. Also consult some convenient geography text or encyclopedia to discover where the major production of wheat, cotton, and corn occurs in the United States.

As a written exercise or for class discussion:

1. Predict how each of the following senators will vote on each of the three issues mentioned. Ignore any complications which might be introduced by their party affiliations.

       (a) a senator from Iowa
       (b) a senator from Alabama
       (c) a senator from North Dakota

2. What stand will be taken on each issue by the American Farm Bureau Federation? The National Farmers Union?

Explain carefully and fully the reasons that led you to make each of your predictions.

PROBLEM 40

Natural Resources Policy

First, please read carefully and thoughtfully the following three selections:

A. Excerpts from Barrow Lyons, *Tomorrow's Birthright* (New York: Funk & Wagnalls Co., 1955), 176–181 (adapted):

Jefferson's doctrine of small farms to bona-fide settlers at low cost became a reality as the result of the Homestead Movement supported by Senator Thomas Hart Benton of Missouri. In 1828 the House Committee on Public Lands reported in favor of this policy, and President Andrew Jackson in his message of December 4, 1832 declared that "the public lands should cease as soon as practicable to be a source of revenue." But it was not until the Preemption Act of 1841 that the right was given to the head of a family, a man over 21 years of age or a widow, to claim 160 acres of western land upon which to homestead. The applicant for a preemption claim was required to swear that he had no more than 320 acres of other land.

This law firmly established the principle of acreage limitation in our policy of disposition of public lands. In 1860 both houses of Congress passed a more constructive homestead act, but it was vetoed by President Buchanan, despite the increasing clamor against land speculators in the West. But when a similar bill, The Homestead Act, was passed by Congress again in 1862, it was signed by President Lincoln. It permitted any single person over 21 years of age to acquire title to 160 acres of land after living on it for five years and completing certain requirements as to cultivation.

With this background, the Reclamation Act of 1902 placed a top limit of 160 acres in one ownership to which the federal government might deliver water in an irrigation project. Later this was interpreted to mean 320 acres to a farm owned jointly by farmer and wife, in those states where community property rights had been established. Both man and wife were considered as separate owners, each entitled to receive water on 160 acres. This is now the rule on all projects.

Then, when the Bureau of Reclamation undertakes to construct a project, under the law it can provide water to no more than 160 acres in one ownership, 320 of property owned in community by man and wife. To safeguard settlers on projects, the antispeculation clauses in Reclamation law make it necessary for those who receive water to sign contracts that they will not dispose of land in excess of 160 acres receiving water, at values increased by the water supply. . . .

B. Neil MacNeil and Harold W. Metz, *The Hoover Report* (New York: The Macmillan Co., 1956), 129–130, 131:

Because preference clauses have outlived their usefulness, the [second Hoover] Commission recommended that privately owned utilities should be permitted to purchase power generated at Federal projects.

All too often, to provide power for preference customers or for other reasons, the Federal Government has constructed transmission lines that duplicate and compete with those of private industry. To correct this practice, which hurts both the taxpayer and private industry, the Commission recommended that the Federal Government cease to build transmission lines where such service can be provided by non-Federal agencies.

The Federal Government's activities in the production and transmission of electrical energy constitute, the Commission said, the clearest case of unnecessary and undesirable Government competition with private enterprise that has been found. The Commission concluded: "Such competition by the Government with private enterprise in the power field is more extensive than in any other single governmental field and has taken on many aspects which are the negation of our fundamental economic system." And it went on to say that "where private enterprise is driven from the field in large areas, the Federal Government creates an element of monopoly in and must assume for all time the responsibility to furnish power to those areas."

But in attempting to find a solution for this undesirable competition it should be remembered, it adds, that as a consequence of the construction of necessary and desirable multipurpose dams the Federal Government is in the business of producing electrical energy. As a result, the Commission does "not entertain the idea of the sale of dams and their powerhouses." These structures perform important services for irrigation, navigation, and flood control, and the Federal Government has maintained control over them to discharge its responsibilities. The Commission found that "the problems involved cannot be solved by simple recommendations that such activities should cease and these projects be sold.". . .

[D]uring the past thirteen years private investment in power facilities has been over $13,000,000,000, while the total expenditure of the Government on power from the very beginning through 1953 amounts to only $2,300,000,000. Thus, the Commission concluded that "financially there is no present or prospective need for Federal financing of power activities."

At one time it might have been argued, the Commission said, that Government production of power was needed because privately owned electric utilities were not being regulated in the public interest. At present, it added, there is no basis for such a belief, because both Federal and State bodies are effectively regulating such enterprises as to rates, service, and sale of securities. Therefore, the Commission recommended two approaches to the problem of Federal power facilities, one to be applied to areas where the Government already has constructed large undertakings and another in areas where the Government has not previously been engaged in this function. . . .

The Commission recommended that private enterprise be offered the opportunity to provide the necessary capital for the electrical facilities, but that the structures when built should be under the control of the Federal Government. If such capital is not available, the power, prior to construction, should be offered to private utilities, States, and municipalities on such terms as will recover the cost of the Federal investment, with interest as well as operating and maintenance expenses. In all probability, if power cannot be disposed of in advance by either of these two methods, the project is not economically sound and should not be undertaken.

C. Speech by Senator Robert M. LaFollette, Jr. *Congressional Record,* Vol. 91, Pt. 4 (1945):

(The Senate was considering an amendment to the appropriation bill for the Interior Department, to provide funds for the Bureau of Reclamation to erect high-voltage transmission lines from the U.S.-built Shasta Dam to cities, towns, and REA districts in the Central Valley of California).

There is nothing extraordinary in attempting to provide cheaper power for the people. During the last 20 years, as every Senator well knows, the development of many sections of our country has been aided by cheap power; in fact, I believe it is generally conceded by everyone that without the great low-cost Federal power developments in the Tennessee and Columbia River Valleys, we would not have been able in so short a time to make anywhere near so great a production record in this war as our people have made. It has not only astounded ourselves, but the entire world as well. Cheap power, a better life on the farm, and the growth of industry all go hand in hand. . . .

The Senator from Ohio said that one purpose of the transmission lines would be to bring "cheap" power to the people. This is correct. . . . If the power is turned over near Shasta Dam to the corporation for resale, with the company building the lines, of course the consumers will have to pay more than they now pay. Their rates will reflect not only a proper charge on the capital investment, but also a handsome profit to the company. . . .

The Senator from Oklahoma [Mr. Thomas] indicated on Monday last that to have the Reclamation Bureau go into the business of power development would be something new. Actually, it is anything but new. The great dam at Grand Coulee is a Bureau of Reclamation dam. The power developed at Grand

Coulee will produce sufficient revenue to make it possible to develop the vast Columbia Basin irrigation project, which otherwise would be far too expensive for the farmers. Because Grand Coulee power, although selling at an extremely low rate, provides more than enough money to amortize the power investment, the water charges to farmers in the Columbia Basin project can be reduced to a point which makes the project feasible for the farmers, while the whole development is self-liquidating from the standpoint of the Government and the taxpayers. Grand Coulee is only one example. There are multiple-purpose reclamation projects in Montana, Wyoming, Idaho, and in the Southwest, all of which use power revenues to help make the irrigation features of the project feasible to supply water to the farmers at a price which they can afford to pay, and at the same time enable them to repay what they borrow from the Government. The Central Valley project is not a startling new departure. It is based on sound and tested policy. Indeed, I may remind the Senate that Congress first amended the Reclamation Act to permit power development as far back as 1906. . . .

You are a correspondent for an Australian newspaper. Because of Australian interest in water problems, you are sent to the United States to "cover" a controversy over the use of the water of the Minnetonka River in the State of Catawba on the Pacific Coast. After reading the above selections and interviewing many Catawbans, you proceed to Washington, D.C., and from there send the following factual dispatch to your newspaper:

Catawba is a large state, but the southern half of it is sparsely inhabited because lack of rainfall keeps the potentially fertile soil arid and unproductive. The Catawba Land Company has bought up a tract of 4,000,000 acres in this area at 50 cents per acre, but so far has not earned a penny on this $2,000,000 investment.

The Minnetonka River rises in the mountains in the state of Westmont, east of Catawba, and flows westward across Catawba to the sea. Near the eastern edge of Catawba it drops 500 feet very rapidly, then broadens out to a width of nearly half a mile. Halfway across the state it is joined by the Little Minnetonka, flowing down from the north.

Catawba Power and Light Company has a monopoly of the electric power business of the state. It generates power at steam plants and dams on the Little Minnetonka. C.P.&L., as it is commonly called, is by far the most powerful corporation in the state. Its longtime president, Stephen Ackerson, has been a friend and supporter of each of the last four governors of Catawba, and each of them has appointed to the State Utilities Commission men who are acceptable to Mr. Ackerson. As the Commission fixes the price of electricity in Catawba, having "acceptable" members on it is very convenient for C.P.&L. Nevertheless, C.P.&L.'s rates are only about average for the country, and if Catawba residents pay more for electricity than do residents of Tennessee or Oregon, they pay less than do residents of New Hampshire or Maine.

The officials of C.P.&L. have invested in the state's leading newspapers, and if citizens criticize C.P.&L., such criticisms are seldom reported. Your correspondent did find vocal critics of C.P.&L. in agricultural areas in the northern part of the state. These critics are farmers who lack electricity. They complain that C.P.&L. refuses to build transmission lines to their area because, C.P.&L. says, the market is not large enough to justify the cost of such construction.

Mr. Ackerson and four of his vice presidents are the organizers and sole stockholders of Catawba Land Company, mentioned above.

Recently the U.S. Defense Department released tentative plans for new installations in Catawba, to develop new weapons by a secret process that requires vast quantities of electric power. Senator Morrison of Westmont promptly introduced a bill in the U.S. Congress to authorize the U.S. Bureau of Reclamation to (1) build a high dam at Devil's Gulch on the Minnetonka, (2) build transmission lines, (3) sell electricity at prices fixed by itself, giving priority to public bodies (such as towns and cities) first, and farm co-operatives second, (4) build irrigation canals to southern Catawba and equally arid regions in southern Westmont, and (5) sell water for irrigation, in accordance with the Reclamation Act of 1902.

No sooner was this bill introduced than C.P.&L. applied to the Federal Power Commission to build a low dam at Devil's Gulch, stating that such a dam would generate all the power needed by the new defense installations.

Last week the Morrison bill was called up in the Senate, and debate has been raging for several days. So far, it has centered on two proposed amendments offered by the two Senators from Catawba—both of whom, incidentally, were Governors of that State in recent years. Senator Downton's amendment provides that irrigation water from the Minnetonka may be sold without regard to the acreage restrictions of the Reclamation Act. Senator Bruneau's amendment would eliminate the authority to build transmission lines, and strike out the provision that cities, towns, or other public bodies would be preferred customers for the Minnetonka Dam's power.

As the vote nears, interested groups have conducted vigorous publicity campaigns, some of them taking full-page advertisements in the Washington News-Post. Here are a few illustrations of these campaigns:

1. Full-page advertisement of the Associated Electric Companies of America: "Shall we remain the land of the free? Public ownership is socialism—socialism leads to tyranny. How do we stay free? By creating conditions where private enterprise can thrive—and by beating down every socialistic scheme. We speak not only for free enterprise—we utter what has always been in the hearts of the American people. We call upon the United States Senate to save freedom in America by defeating the communistic Morrison bill."

2. Public statement by the president of the American Farmers Union: "The acreage limitation is sacred. Shall a public resource be used for American type family farms or to bring fabulous riches to a few land sharks? We demand the defeat of the Downton amendment."

3. Editorial in the Baltimore Star: "We will always have an insoluble farm problem until we realize that in this day and age, the only economically satisfactory system of agriculture must be based on large holdings, worked by modern machinery. What seemed sensible in Teddy Roosevelt's day is harmful today. The development of small farms should not be encouraged, for few small farmers can ever succeed."

4. Open letter, to every Senator, from the Catawba chapter of the Daughters of American Democracy: "Our Federal Union

—it must be preserved! Not just a Union, but a Federal Union of Sovereign States! The Morrison Bill Destroys State's Rights and Puts the People of Catawba at the Mercy of the Washington Bureaucracy. State's Rights Forever! Defeat the Morrison Bill!"

5. Half-page advertisement in the Washington News-Post, signed by officers of an organization calling itself "Minnetonka Power Committee":

"A TVA for the Minnetonka will bring to Catawba and Westmont new hope, new opportunities, new prosperity, new industry, new freedom. We call upon the Senate to defeat the Bruneau amendment, just as similar attempts to cripple TVA have been defeated. We call upon the Senate to pass the Morrison bill (with or without the Downton amendment), and thus create a western TVA, a duplicate of America's greatest single achievement in intelligent self-government."

6. Excerpts of letter from Stephen Ackerson to the 210,000 stockholders of C.P.&L.:

"Your officers and directors have represented your interests in connection with certain legislation now pending in Washington. They feel that it would be to the national interest for the company to build its proposed dam at Devil's Gulch, thus saving $5,000,000 for the American taxpayer. However, they recognize that Congress has the constitutional right to authorize dams on navigable streams, such as the Minnetonka. They believe, however, that you will agree that it is unconstitutional, unAmerican, and uneconomic for the government to build transmission lines and sell electricity at retail. Accordingly your company's general counsel, Herman Dry, has registered under the Congressional Reorganization Act of 1946 to advocate the adoption of the amendments offered by Senators Bruneau and Downton of Catawba."

Your correspondent is in no position to predict the outcome.

Your editor in Australia cables you: "Don't try to predict outcome in Senate. Your story provides background but issues appear confused. Please clarify in your next dispatch, indicating exactly what the real issues are on both amendments and bill itself. Show how Catawba will be affected by passage of original bill, passage of bill with either amendment or both amendments, and defeat of bill."

After carefully reviewing your advance reading and your first dispatch, prepare this second dispatch as requested.